Nuggets Of Deliverance

Uncovering the Keys to Spiritual Freedom

Shena Martin

Copyright © 2025. Manna Inspirations

All rights reserved. No part of this publication may be reproduced, distributed, or transmitted in any form or by any means, including photocopying, recording, or other electronic or mechanical methods, without the prior written permission of the publisher, except in the case of brief quotations embodied in critical reviews and certain other non-commercial uses permitted by copyright law.

For permissions requests, write to the publisher at the email address below:

mim.info@mannainspirations.com OR
mannainspirations@gmail.com

This is a publication of Manna Inspirations
www.mannainspirations.com

Contents

Introduction iii
My Story 1
Theological Foundations of Deliverance 15
Understanding Spiritual Warfare 19
Identifying Different Types of Spirits 30
The Process of Deliverance 47
Common challenges to deliverance 69
Types of Deliverance 74
Keys to Spiritual Freedom 77
Living in Spiritual Freedom 84
Breaking Satanic Covenants 88
Providing Biblical Insights into Satanic Covenants 99
Scriptural Promises for Freedom 109
Understanding Prayer as Spiritual Warfare 113
Living in Freedom and Restoration 133
Sharing Testimonies 140
Introduction to the Prayer Points 147
The Courtroom of Heaven 336
About the Author 386
Also by Shena Martin 388

Introduction

Explanation of deliverance

Deliverance refers to the process of being set free from bondage, oppression, or spiritual strongholds by the power of God. It is a biblical concept that is rooted in the belief that there are spiritual forces of darkness at work in the world we live in, and that they seek to hinder and harm us. These forces can take many forms, including addiction, fear, anxiety, depression, anger, unforgiveness, and other negative emotions and behaviors.

Deliverance involves acknowledging the presence of these spiritual forces and seeking the help of God to be set free from them. This process typically involves repentance, prayer, and the power of the Holy Spirit working through the individual or a deliverance minister to break the bondage of the enemy. The ultimate goal of deliverance is to restore individuals to a place of spiritual health and wholeness, and to enable them to live fully in the freedom and power of Christ.

It's important to note that deliverance is not a one-time event but rather an ongoing process of growth and transformation. It requires a commitment to continually walk in obedience to God's Word and to resist the enemy's attempts to regain ground in our lives. Deliverance is a powerful tool for overcoming the spiritual battles that we all face, and it can lead to a deeper and more fulfilling relationship with God.

Importance of understanding principles of deliverance

Understanding the principles of deliverance is essential for Christians who desire to live a victorious and spiritually fulfilling life. Here are some reasons why:

- Freedom from spiritual bondage: Deliverance is about breaking free from the bondage of sin, strongholds, and other negative influences in our lives. When we understand the principles of deliverance, we can identify areas of our lives where we need to seek freedom and healing and take the necessary steps to experience God's transformative power.
- Deeper spiritual growth: Deliverance is not just about being set free from negative influences but also about growing in our relationship with God. As we experience deliverance, we learn to trust God more deeply and rely on His power to overcome the challenges that we face in life. This leads to a deeper and more meaningful spiritual life.
- Better understanding of spiritual warfare: The principles of deliverance provide us with a better understanding of the nature of spiritual warfare and the tactics of the enemy. This knowledge helps us to be better equipped to resist the enemy's attacks and to live in the victory that Christ has already won for us.
- Ability to help others: When we understand the principles of deliverance, we can help others who are struggling with spiritual bondage and provide them with the guidance and support they need to experience

freedom in Christ. This is a powerful ministry that can bring hope and healing to others.

Understanding the principles of deliverance is crucial for Christians who desire to experience the fullness of God's power and live in spiritual freedom. It helps us to identify areas of our lives that need healing, grow deeper in our relationship with God, better understand spiritual warfare, and help others who are struggling.

My Story

There was a time in my life when I battled deep depression, feeling like I was trapped in a darkness I couldn't escape. I wanted to be set free so badly, but I didn't know how to break free or even where to start. I remember thinking of all my options—counselling, seeing a doctor, maybe even starting on antidepressants. Yet, in my heart, I felt like something deeper was needed, something that went beyond what medication or counselling could provide.

I didn't know of any deliverance ministers I could reach out to, and, truthfully, I wasn't even sure if deliverance was something I could do on my own. Growing up, I had always heard that deliverance was something only those with a special "office" or ministry could help with, that freedom could only come from going to someone with that specific calling. I'm grateful for those who serve in that ministry, but for my journey, God was showing me that He alone could be my deliverer. I needed to look to Him.

As I sought God's guidance, I felt the Holy Spirit teaching me how to pray in ways I'd never known. I started learning about the power of self-deliverance and began to understand how the Word of God could truly set me free. The Bible isn't just words on a page; it's alive, powerful, and able to break strongholds in our lives. I learned to channel my prayers according to His

Word, and with each prayer, the chains that held me down started to break. Some deliverance cases took place in my dreams and visions and so I realized that those cases God himself had to do it and not by my efforts. So yes, you can go to your bed bound and wake up being delivered. I didn't realize at first that there were open doors in my life—small things I hadn't noticed or recognized—that were allowing darkness to come in.

Through repentance and renouncing things from my past, those doors began to close, one by one. I would pair these prayers with fasting, focusing on breaking any strongholds that kept me bound. And slowly, as God brought these things to light, through visions, dreams and his word, I felt my freedom come. It was a journey that took time, commitment, and trust in Him. But the beautiful part? I can now say with confidence, *I am free*. And freedom, oh, it is so sweet.

The Bible says, "Who the Son sets free is free indeed" (John 8:36). If God did this for me—someone who felt so lost and trapped—He can do it for you too. Your freedom is within reach, and God is more than willing to walk with you on your journey to complete deliverance.

My journey to freedom wasn't an easy one. I've faced darkness, battled deep depression, and experienced firsthand the bondage that many of us feel trapped in. I've also witnessed a lot of evil around me—moments where it felt like the enemy's grip was strong and unbreakable. Yet, despite the darkness, I have seen God's power move mightily in my life, breaking chains that I thought could never be broken. These experiences, both of despair and of deliverance, are what motivated me to write *Nuggets of Deliverance*.

Through my journey, God taught me that deliverance isn't something distant or impossible. Although there are different levels of deliverance, I do not write this book to claim that I know everything, but through experience and what the Lord has taught me, I am sharing these nuggets to help someone who is in despair. It's real, and it's available to anyone who seeks it. In my darkest hours, when I didn't know where to turn, I discovered that God was my Deliverer, my Redeemer, and my Salvation. As I grew in understanding, the Holy Spirit began teaching me how to pray and fight spiritual battles through self-deliverance. It was humbling and powerful to learn that, while others can support and guide us, God's deliverance is personal and available to each of us directly.

I'm still in the midst of some battles, but I know that God is faithful, that He fights for me, and that He will never leave me to face these challenges alone. Being a child of God doesn't mean we're immune to battles; in fact, it's often the opposite. We will face resistance, we will face attacks, but the Lord fights for His children. He gives us the tools, strength, and wisdom we need to claim victory.

Nuggets of Deliverance is a testimony of this journey—of the power of God's deliverance and of the truth that *who the Son sets free is free indeed*. I wrote this book to share the freedom I found in Christ, to encourage those who feel trapped, and to equip believers with the knowledge that they, too, can break free from spiritual bondage. My prayer is that it serves as a guide, an encouragement, and a source of hope for anyone seeking true deliverance.

The Patterns I Couldn't Ignore

There comes a point in your journey where you stop chalking things up to coincidence. You realize that what you're dealing with is not just a bad season or a string of unfortunate events—it's a cycle. That's exactly what I began to see in my own life. Certain doors would open just enough for me to hope, but never fully swing wide. Promises I had believed God for—particularly in the areas of relationships, finances, ministry, and destiny—remained unfulfilled far longer than they should have.

I wasn't lazy. I wasn't living in rebellion. I was seeking God, fasting, praying, serving, sowing, and believing. But over time, I noticed a painful pattern: everything took longer than it should. Opportunities slipped away without reason. Relationships would begin with potential but end prematurely. Financial breakthroughs came with delay or were devoured by unexpected crises. Ministry assignments would birth but then stall or be met with heavy resistance.

At first, I questioned myself. Was I doing something wrong? Did I lack faith? But the more I prayed, the more the Holy Spirit began to unveil that I was not just experiencing hardship—I was contending with spiritual resistance. There were ancient altars and demonic systems in operation behind the scenes, attempting to block the flow of God's promises in my life.

This was more than just "life happening." This was warfare. This was spiritual contention. And I had to learn how to fight differently. The enemy had legal grounds, and until I dealt with those root issues, I would continue to see the same cycles manifest in different seasons. I came across Ephesians 6:12, and it struck me deeply:

> *"For we wrestle not against flesh and blood, but against principalities, against powers, against the rulers of the darkness of this world, against spiritual wickedness in high places."*

This Scripture revealed that my battle wasn't natural—it was spiritual. I wasn't just facing bad luck or bad timing; I was wrestling with unseen powers that didn't want me to walk in purpose. Once I recognized that truth, everything shifted. I stopped fighting with people and started warring in the Spirit. I began to dismantle strongholds in prayer. I renounced every agreement—spoken or unspoken—that tied me to delay, sabotage, and frustration.

I won't pretend it was easy. But what I can say is this: the moment I recognized the pattern was the moment I reclaimed my power. God never called us to tolerate demonic interference. He called us to overcome it.

Waking Up to the Warfare

It's one thing to feel frustrated by what's happening in your life. It's another thing entirely to recognize the source behind it. For years, I dealt with cycles of delay, resistance, and missed moments—until one day, I had to confront a hard truth: this battle wasn't natural—it was spiritual.

I grew up in a Christian home. I knew the power of prayer, the importance of faith, and the value of obedience. But even with all that foundation, I found myself in recurring struggles that didn't match my lifestyle of surrender to God. That's when the Holy Spirit began to pull back the veil. What I was facing wasn't just life being "hard" or the enemy throwing random darts. I was dealing with deep-rooted spiritual strongholds, some of which were ancestral in nature.

Through prayer, fasting, and intentional seeking, I discovered that my family line had patterns—cycles that repeated across generations: late marriages, broken covenants, financial instability, and unfulfilled destinies. These patterns were not mere coincidence; they were the evidence of hidden altars and generational agreements still speaking.

As I began to press into deeper deliverance prayers, I would cry out to God for clarity, and the Holy Spirit responded with revelation. He started to expose the strongmen operating in the background—demonic gatekeepers assigned to maintain bondage in my bloodline. Some of these strongmen were attached to generational curses, idolatry, and disobedience in my bloodline—things I had never personally participated in but inherited spiritually.

It was a sobering awakening. I realized that while salvation is instant, deliverance is often a process. Jesus had given me authority, but I needed to apply that authority intentionally through prayer, repentance, renunciation, and spiritual warfare. I had to uproot evil covenants, break soul ties, and tear down altars that had been empowered over decades—if not centuries.

This wasn't a battle I could win with shallow prayers. It demanded consistency, spiritual discernment, and divine strategy. And most of all, it demanded my full partnership with the Holy Spirit. Once I embraced that, my deliverance journey truly began—not just for me, but for the generations after me.

Prayer Became My Weapon

Once I realized the nature of the warfare I was in, I couldn't afford to remain passive. I had to move from just praying *about* things to praying *through* them. I wasn't just having quiet time anymore—I was stepping onto the battlefield. Prayer became my weapon.

The Lord began to wake me up at midnight—the hour when demonic activity is often heightened—and waging war in the spirit. I didn't just whisper prayers; I cried out, travailed, declared, decreed, and dismantled. I renounced every evil covenant, both known and unknown. I spoke against altars built by my ancestors and cut ties with spiritual influences that were never part of God's plan for my life.

I saturated my space with Scripture, using the Word as my sword. When I felt weak, I quoted Psalm 18:34:

> *"He trains my hands for war, so that my arms can bend a bow of bronze."*

I didn't always see immediate results. There were days I wondered if I was really making progress. There were moments when the warfare intensified after a breakthrough—reminding me that the enemy never lets go easily. Sometimes I felt alone, misunderstood, and even spiritually exhausted. But I refused to stop. Every time I showed up in prayer, something shifted—even if it was invisible at first.

Through those battles, God was sharpening my discernment. I began to see and sense things in the spirit more clearly. I learned to recognize patterns, identify demonic interference, and move in prophetic accuracy. I wasn't just praying to survive—I was being trained to lead, to intercede, and to war for others too.

Prayer didn't just break chains in my life—it forged my spiritual identity. It taught me to hear God's voice above the noise. It made me bold. It made me unshakable. And most of all, it reminded me that I don't fight for victory—I fight from victory, in Christ.

Healing in Every Battle

Deliverance wasn't just about breaking chains—it was also about receiving healing in places I didn't even realize were broken. Every time I fought a battle in the spirit and pushed through, I saw the healing power of God show up in undeniable ways.

I remember moments in prayer when I could literally feel the weight of oppression lift—times when persistent depression would dissolve in the middle of worship. There were nights I cried myself to sleep, asking God for rest, and I'd wake up the next morning refreshed—*not just physically, but emotionally restored*. God was healing me in layers. Not all at once, but faithfully and consistently.

There were wounds in my soul—rejection, disappointment, grief, betrayal—that I had buried under busyness, ministry, and even faith. But the Holy Spirit, in His gentleness, brought those things to the surface not to shame me, but to heal me. In moments of worship, I would weep, and it wasn't from sadness—it was release. I was letting go of years of silent suffering, and Jehovah Rapha was making me whole.

I began to understand that true deliverance always comes with healing. When God breaks a stronghold, He doesn't leave a void—He fills it with His presence, His peace, and His power. And every time I broke through a spiritual barrier, healing followed like a river.

The more I went through, the more I stood on the Word. I would declare verses like:

> *"He sent His word and healed them, and delivered them from their destructions." – Psalm 107:20*
>
> *"But He was wounded for our transgressions... and by His stripes we are healed." – Isaiah 53:5*

I had to believe that healing wasn't just for others—it was for me. And I had to learn to trust God as my Healer, not just in theory, but in lived experience.

Now, when I look back, I see that every battle was birthing something in me—strength, resilience, compassion, and the authority to minister healing to others. What the enemy meant to break me, God used to build me.

When the Enemy Tried to Steal My Voice

There was a season where I felt completely muted—spiritually, emotionally, and creatively. I wasn't just quiet; I was silenced. Not by God, but by shame, fear, and internal warfare. The enemy had launched a targeted attack on my identity, and the bullseye was my voice.

It started subtly. I began second-guessing myself, shrinking back, feeling inadequate even when I knew I was called. I would start things and stop. Ideas for books, songs, messages, and projects would come—and I'd convince myself no one needed to hear them. I was battling silence rooted in spiritual sabotage. The kind of silence that keeps you from declaring truth, from praying with power, from taking your place in purpose.

But one day in prayer, the Holy Spirit interrupted my pity lets me know that my voice carried impact. That was the turning point.

I realized then that my voice wasn't just a gift—it was a weapon. And the enemy was terrified of what would happen if I started using it again. My prayers had weight. My songs had oil. My words had the power to break chains in others. The warfare around my voice wasn't random—it was strategic.

So I made a decision: I would not stay silent.

I started praying out loud, declaring Scripture boldly, rebuking fear, and taking my authority back. I began hosting podcasts, writing devotionals, and pouring my story into the very pages of this book. I sang again—not just to perform, but to release healing through sound. The very area the enemy tried to cripple was the area where God wanted to release breakthrough—not just for me, but through me.

There is power in your voice when it's yielded to God. And once I embraced that truth, I began walking in a deeper level of freedom and boldness.

> *"Death and life are in the power of the tongue..."* – Proverbs 18:21
>
> *"I believed, therefore I spoke..."* – 2 Corinthians 4:13

If you've ever felt silenced—by trauma, shame, insecurity, or spiritual attack—I want you to know this: your voice is dangerous to the enemy. That's why he fights it. But when you rise up and use your voice under the anointing of the Holy Spirit, hell trembles.

I am no longer silent. I am speaking, singing, praying, and writing—because freedom flows where truth is released.

From Nursing to Nations: Embracing My Call

Even though I began my professional journey in healthcare, serving as a nurse and caring for the physical needs of others, deep down I knew there was more. I loved helping people heal—but the healing I longed to see went beyond bandages and blood pressure monitors. It reached into the soul and spirit, the places where many suffer silently. God was calling me higher—to birth healing and deliverance on a much broader scale.

At first, I didn't fully understand it. All I knew was that there was a stirring inside me that nursing alone couldn't satisfy. I wanted to speak life into people. I wanted to write, to worship, to teach, to mentor. I wanted to *midwife destinies*, not just manage symptoms.

And that's exactly what God called me to do. One assignment after the next, He led me from one expression of purpose to another:

- Manna Inspirations was born—a platform to release encouragement, truth, and revelation through writing.

- Nurse as Midwife came alive—a podcast to mentor others in discovering and walking in their God-given purpose.
- Then came the music—the songs that flowed out of my secret place and carried messages of hope and deliverance.
- And now, mentoring and coaching—helping others not just dream, but deliver.

I look back and realize: I'm not just a nurse—I'm a midwife in the Spirit. I am not saying what I think I am, I saying what God called me to be; a spiritual midwife. I help people birth their purpose, their healing, their breakthroughs through the tools God gave me. I guide others through the labor pains of transition. I encourage them to push through the warfare, because on the other side is life, promise, and destiny.

Every battle I've endured—every delay, heartbreak, disappointment, and breakthrough—wasn't wasted. It became oil for the assignment. The pain was the press. The press was preparation. And the preparation birthed power.

Now, whether I'm writing a devotional, praying for someone at midnight, or speaking into someone's life, I know I'm walking in my call—not because it was easy, but because I fought for it. God didn't just call me to care for bodies. He called me to carry deliverance to the nations through empowerment.

The Purpose Behind My Pain

If there's one thing I've learned on this journey, it's this: deliverance is not a one-time event—it's a lifestyle. Freedom in Christ isn't just about casting out demons or breaking curses; it's about walking daily in the truth of who God says you are, refusing to go back to the chains that once held you.

I've lived through the kind of pain that doesn't always show on the outside. The kind that makes you smile in public and cry in secret. I know what it's like to be in a room full of people and still feel invisible. I've suffered in silence, afraid to speak, afraid to admit that I was in need of healing. But through it all, I also discovered this: there is purpose in the pain.

Every time I surrendered my wounds to God, He turned them into weapons. Every scar became a testimony. Every battle became oil.

One of the key moments in my journey came when the Holy Spirit led me to begin taking Holy Communion at home. At first, it felt simple—just bread and juice. But in the Spirit, it was much more than that. It was a divine exchange. Each time I took the bread, I was reminded of Christ's body broken for my healing. Each time I drank the cup, I reaffirmed the covenant of His blood that speaks better things over my life. Communion became a point of contact for deliverance. I would pray, declare the Word, and take it with expectation. Chains began to break. My mind became clearer. I felt spiritual layers of heaviness lifting. It wasn't a ritual—it was warfare. It was healing. It was intimacy with Jesus in a way I had never known before. I didn't just come out—I came out with power, with perspective, and with a mantle to help others break free too.

That's why I wrote this book. Not because I have all the answers, but because I've walked the road of deliverance, and I want you to know: you're not alone, and you don't have to stay bound.

I want you to fight for your freedom like I fought for mine. I want you to confront the patterns. Tear down the altars. Break the silence. Reclaim your voice. Walk in healing. And rise in purpose. Because on the other side of your pain is power. On the other side of your battle is authority. And on the other side of your deliverance is a destiny that hell cannot stop.

My story is still being written. But today, I walk in more clarity, boldness, and victory because I chose to fight—and by the grace of God, I won. And now, I'm here to help you win too.

Theological Foundations of Deliverance

The biblical basis of deliverance

Deliverance is a term that refers to the act of being rescued or liberated from oppression, captivity, or some other form of bondage. In the Christian context, deliverance refers to the process of being set free from the influence of evil spirits or demonic forces.

The biblical foundations of deliverance can be traced back to the Bible, which provides a clear and detailed account of the reality of demonic oppression and the need for deliverance. In fact, the Bible contains numerous references to deliverance and spiritual warfare, from the Old Testament to the New Testament.

In the Old Testament, we see examples of individuals who were delivered from demonic oppression. For instance, in 1 Samuel 16:14-23, we read about how King Saul was tormented by an evil spirit, and how David was called upon to play the harp to bring relief to Saul. This account provides a clear example of how the power of God can bring deliverance to those who are oppressed by demonic forces.

Similarly, in the New Testament, we see numerous accounts of Jesus and his disciples casting out demons and delivering people from various forms of bondage. For example, in Mark 5:1-20, we read about how Jesus delivered a man from a legion of demons that had possessed him, and how this man was then set free and able to testify to the power of Jesus.

Moreover, in the epistles of the New Testament, we find clear instruction and teaching regarding the reality of spiritual warfare and the need for believers to put on the full armor of God to withstand the attacks of the enemy. In Ephesians 6:10-18, for instance, we read about the spiritual armor of God and the need for believers to stand firm in the face of spiritual opposition.

The nature of spiritual warfare

The nature of spiritual warfare is a critical theological foundation for understanding deliverance. The Bible clearly states that there is a spiritual realm in addition to the physical world we can see and touch. Ephesians 6:12 says, "For we do not wrestle against flesh and blood, but against the rulers, against the authorities, against the enormous powers over this present darkness, against the spiritual forces of evil in the heavenly places."

This verse highlights the reality of spiritual warfare, where there are unseen forces at work seeking to harm us and hinder our spiritual growth. The enemy seeks to deceive and discourage us, but we have hope in the victory that Jesus has already won for us through His death and resurrection.

As believers, we are called to be aware of the spiritual battle we face and to actively engage in it. This includes using the spiritual weapons that God has given us, such as prayer, fasting, and the Word of God. We also have the power of the Holy Spirit within us, which helps us to discern truth from lies and to resist the schemes of the enemy.

Understanding the nature of spiritual warfare is crucial in recognizing the need for deliverance and seeking the help of God and other agents of deliverance in overcoming the spiritual strongholds in our lives. Through prayer, faith, and the power of the Holy Spirit, we can overcome the spiritual forces of darkness and live in the freedom that God has promised us.

The work of the Holy Spirit in deliverance

The work of the Holy Spirit is crucial in the process of deliverance. The Holy Spirit is the third person of the Godhead and is the source of power and authority for believers. He is the one who convicts us of sin and empowers us to overcome it.

In the context of deliverance, the Holy Spirit plays several important roles. Firstly, He helps us to identify and recognize the presence of demonic oppression and possession. He also gives us the discernment to distinguish between demonic activity and other issues such as physical or psychological problems.

Secondly, the Holy Spirit empowers us to resist the devil and his works. The Bible tells us that we are not fighting against flesh and blood, but against spiritual forces of evil in the heavenly realms (Ephesians 6:12). We need the power of the Holy Spirit to overcome these forces.

Finally, the Holy Spirit guides us in the process of deliverance. He shows us the root causes of our bondage and helps us to address them. He also gives us the words to speak in prayer and the wisdom to know how to proceed in each situation.

As agents of deliverance, it is important to rely on the Holy Spirit in all aspects of the ministry. We must seek His guidance and empowerment in order to be effective in setting people free from bondage and oppression.

Understanding Spiritual Warfare

Definition of spiritual warfare

Spiritual warfare refers to the ongoing battle between the forces of good and evil in the spiritual realm. It is a biblical concept that recognizes the existence of spiritual entities and forces that are at work in the world and seek to hinder and harm us. The apostle Paul wrote in Ephesians 6:12, "For our struggle is not against flesh and blood, but against the rulers, against the authorities, against the powers of this dark world and against the spiritual forces of evil in the heavenly realms."

Spiritual warfare involves a battle for our hearts, minds, and souls. The enemy seeks to deceive, discourage, and destroy us, while God desires to lead us into truth, freedom, and abundant life. This battle can take many forms, including temptation, doubt, fear, anxiety, oppression, depression, and other negative emotions and behaviors.

Christians are called to be active participants in spiritual warfare, standing firm in their faith, resisting the enemy's attacks, and putting on the full armor of God (Ephesians 6:13-17). This involves praying, reading and meditating on God's Word, confessing sin, seeking deliverance from strongholds and bondages, and relying on the power of the Holy Spirit.

Spiritual warfare is a reality that Christians must acknowledge and engage in if they desire to live victorious and spiritually fulfilling lives. By recognizing the tactics of the enemy and relying on God's power, Christians can experience freedom, joy, and peace amidst the battles of life.

The enemy and his tactics

The enemy, also known as Satan or the devil, is a spiritual being who is opposed to God and seeks to undermine His plans and purposes. The Bible describes Satan as a deceiver, a liar, and a thief who comes to steal, kill, and destroy (John 10:10). His primary tactics include:

1. Deception: The enemy seeks to deceive and mislead people into believing lies and false teachings. He often disguises himself as an angel of light and can even appear to be a source of wisdom and truth (2 Corinthians 11:14-15).
2. Temptation: The enemy uses temptation to entice people into sin and rebellion against God. He appeals to our desires and weaknesses, offering false promises of pleasure, and power (Matthew 4:1-11).
3. Accusation: The enemy accuses and condemns people, seeking to make them feel guilty, ashamed, and unworthy of God's love and forgiveness. He uses our past mistakes and failures to keep us in bondage and hinder our spiritual growth (Revelation 12:10).
4. Fear and intimidation: The enemy uses fear and intimidation to control and manipulate people. He seeks to create doubt, anxiety, and worry, and can even use

physical threats and violence to instill fear (1 Peter 5:8-9).

5. Division and discord: The enemy seeks to sow division and discord among people, causing conflict, strife, and disunity. He uses gossip, slander, and other forms of communication to spread lies and create misunderstandings (Ephesians 6:12).

Understanding the tactics of the enemy is essential for Christians who desire to resist his attacks and stand firm in their faith. By relying on God's power and putting on the full armor of God, we as 21hristians can overcome the enemy's tactics and live in spiritual victory (Ephesians 6:10-18).

The Armor of God

The armor of God is a spiritual description of the spiritual resources and protections that God has given to us as 21hristians to help us stand firm in our faith and resist the attacks of the enemy. The apostle Paul wrote about the armor of God in Ephesians 6:10-18, and the pieces of the armor are as follows:

1. Belt of truth: This represents the importance of being truthful and honest in our speech and actions and holding fast to the truth of God's Word.
2. Breastplate of righteousness: This represents the righteousness that comes from faith in Christ, which protects our hearts from the accusations and condemnation of the enemy.

3. Shoes of the gospel of peace: These represent the readiness and willingness to share the good news of Jesus Christ with others, and to be peacemakers in the world.
4. Shield of faith: This represents the trust and confidence we have in God's promises and protection, which enables us to extinguish the fiery darts of the enemy.
5. Helmet of salvation: This represents the assurance and security we have in our salvation through Christ, which protects our minds from doubt, fear, and confusion.
6. Sword of the Spirit: This represents the power and authority of God's Word, which is our weapon against the lies and deceptions of the enemy.
7. Prayer: This represents the vital communication and connection we have with God, which enables us to access His power, guidance, and protection in all situations.

The armor of God is not a physical armor, but a spiritual one that is activated by faith and prayer. By putting on the armor of God and relying on His power, we as Christians can overcome the tactics of the enemy and live in victory and freedom.

The Biblical Foundation of Spiritual Warfare

Spiritual warfare is deeply rooted in biblical teachings and encompasses the struggle between the forces of good and evil. This chapter explores key scriptures that establish the biblical foundation of spiritual warfare, focusing on Jesus's authority over demonic spirits and the role of the Holy Spirit in deliverance.

Key Scriptures on Spiritual Warfare

The Bible offers powerful insights into the reality of spiritual warfare, showing both the nature of this conflict and the resources available to believers in the battle. In Ephesians 6:10-18, Paul lays out what is known as the "armor of God," urging us to remember that our struggle is not against "flesh and blood" but against "spiritual forces of evil." He details the spiritual armor God has provided for us—truth, righteousness, the gospel of peace, faith, salvation, and the Word of God. This armor serves as our defense and offense, with prayer as a constant necessity, grounding us and fortifying our stand in spiritual battles.

In 2 Corinthians 10:3-5, Paul speaks to the power of spiritual weapons to break down strongholds. He emphasizes that, in this battle, we are called to take every thought captive and make it obedient to Christ, a reminder that the battle often takes place in our minds and hearts. Similarly, in James 4:7-8, believers are encouraged to "submit yourselves to God" and "resist the devil," with the promise that the devil will flee when we stand firm in alignment with God.

Peter, too, warns us of the nature of this conflict in 1 Peter 5:8-9, describing how "your enemy the devil prowls around like a roaring lion, looking for someone to devour." He urges us to be vigilant, to resist the devil, and to stand firm in faith. This call to alertness underlines the constant vigilance required in our daily spiritual lives. Together, these scriptures lay a foundation for understanding spiritual warfare and remind us of the strength and authority we have in Christ to stand against the forces of darkness.

Jesus's Authority Over Demonic Spirits

The New Testament reveals Jesus's authority over demonic spirits, underscoring His power to conquer darkness and evil. One striking example of this authority occurs during Jesus's temptation in the wilderness, as described in Matthew 4:1-11. Here, Jesus confronts Satan's temptations head-on, using the Word of God to counter each of Satan's deceitful offers. This encounter not only shows Jesus's ability to resist but also demonstrates the profound power of scripture in overcoming spiritual attacks.

Another compelling example is seen when Jesus casts out a legion of demons from a man in the region of the Gerasenes, recorded in both Mark 5:1-20 and Luke 8:26-39. The demons recognize Jesus's supreme authority, submitting to His command without resistance, showing that even the most powerful demonic forces are powerless in His presence. This episode illustrates the unmatched dominance of Christ over spiritual forces and the way His presence brings freedom to those oppressed.

Finally, in the Great Commission (Matthew 28:18-20), Jesus declares, "All authority in heaven and on earth has been given to me." With this, He empowers His disciples to go forth, make disciples, baptize, and teach His commands. This declaration not only reflects Jesus's ultimate authority but also extends that authority to His followers, equipping them to carry on His mission and engage in spiritual warfare with confidence, knowing they act under His name and power.

The Power of the Holy Spirit in Deliverance

The Holy Spirit plays a central role in spiritual warfare and deliverance, offering believers essential tools for navigating and overcoming spiritual challenges. One of the most crucial ways the Holy Spirit aids in this process is by granting the gift of spiritual discernment, as described in 1 Corinthians 12:10. This gift allows believers to distinguish between spirits, helping them to recognize and address demonic influences. Such discernment is invaluable for identifying spiritual oppression and is a key step toward deliverance.

Beyond discernment, the Holy Spirit also empowers believers for spiritual warfare. In Acts 1:8, Jesus promises that the Holy Spirit will come upon believers, providing them with power for their mission and for overcoming spiritual opposition. This divine empowerment not only strengthens believers for battle but also enables them to carry out the Great Commission with authority and conviction. The Holy Spirit is also our Guide and Comforter in times of spiritual conflict, as Jesus describes in John 14:16-17. Known as the Helper or Advocate, the Holy Spirit leads believers into all truth and brings comfort when faced with spiritual struggles. His guidance provides a steady light in the complexities of spiritual warfare, helping believers remain grounded and resilient.

Through the authority of Jesus over demonic spirits, the power of the Holy Spirit, and the wisdom found in scripture, believers are equipped to engage in spiritual warfare with faith and confidence. This understanding of spiritual warfare provides a foundation for recognizing and overcoming the various spirits that may seek to operate in our lives, preparing believers for the journey of deliverance.

The Reality of Spiritual Conflict

Spiritual conflict is a central theme in the Christian faith, describing the ongoing battle between the forces of good and evil. While much of this conflict occurs in the unseen realm, its effects are often felt in the physical world. This chapter explores the reality of spiritual conflict, delving into the unseen realm, understanding the enemy's strategies, and emphasizing the importance of spiritual discernment.

The Unseen Realm and Its Influence on the Physical World

The unseen realm is the stage for much of the spiritual conflict that affects our world. Although hidden from human sight, its influence on the physical realm is profound. The Bible makes clear the existence of spiritual beings, including angels, demons, and other celestial entities. In Ephesians 6:12, Paul writes that our struggle is against "spiritual forces of evil in the heavenly realms," underscoring that spiritual conflict is real and constant.

These spiritual battles often have tangible impacts, manifesting as struggles within individuals, families, communities, and even entire nations. Issues like personal turmoil, relational conflicts, and societal upheaval can sometimes reveal patterns of spiritual conflict originating in the unseen realm, spilling over to affect our daily lives in significant ways.

Scripture offers vivid examples of this dynamic. In Daniel 10, the prophet Daniel encounters an angel who describes a battle with a "prince of Persia," illustrating that spiritual warfare happens in the unseen realm yet can shape the course of our lives. These glimpses into spiritual reality provide us with a deeper understanding of the unseen forces at work and remind us of the ongoing nature of spiritual warfare.

Understanding the Enemy's Strategies

To engage effectively in spiritual warfare, it is essential to understand the strategies of the enemy. The Bible sheds light on how Satan and his demonic forces operate, revealing common tactics that they employ. A key strategy of the enemy is deception, as Satan is described as the "father of lies" in John 8:44. By using lies, he leads people away from truth, sowing confusion, doubt, and mistrust that can result in spiritual bondage.

Temptation is another tool, where Satan draws individuals away from God through worldly desires. This tactic is evident in the temptation of Jesus in the wilderness, as recounted in Matthew 4, where the enemy's enticements aim to shake a person's faith and commitment. Fear and intimidation also feature prominently in the enemy's approach, often paralyzing people and keeping them from God's purpose. The Bible's frequent reminders to "fear not" highlight how fear can be a powerful tool wielded against believers.

The enemy also seeks to create division, thriving on discord within families, churches, and communities. Through this tactic, Satan disrupts relationships, undermining unity and purpose. Spiritual oppression is another method, where the enemy places individuals in bondage, often seen through addictions, compulsive behaviors, or other destructive patterns. By recognizing these strategies, believers are better equipped to stand firm and engage in spiritual warfare with wisdom and faith.

The Importance of Spiritual Discernment

Spiritual discernment is essential for recognizing and responding to spiritual conflict. The ability to discern spiritual influences allows believers to identify the enemy's tactics and counter them effectively. Here's why spiritual discernment is crucial in this context:

- Discerning Truth from Lies: Discernment helps distinguish truth from deception. By staying grounded in God's word, believers can recognize false teachings and resist the enemy's lies.
- Identifying Spiritual Oppression: Spiritual discernment allows believers to identify signs of spiritual oppression, enabling them to address the underlying causes and seek deliverance through prayer and spiritual warfare.
- Guided by the Holy Spirit: Spiritual discernment is a gift of the Holy Spirit (1 Corinthians 12:10). By relying on

the Holy Spirit's guidance, believers can navigate spiritual conflict with wisdom and clarity.
- Recognizing Spiritual Influences: Discernment helps believers understand the spiritual influences at play in various situations. This understanding is critical for effective prayer and spiritual warfare.

The reality of spiritual conflict requires believers to be vigilant and prepared. The unseen realm exerts a significant influence on the physical world, and understanding the enemy's strategies is essential for effective spiritual warfare. Spiritual discernment plays a crucial role in identifying and addressing these conflicts, enabling believers to stand firm against the forces of darkness. This chapter sets the stage for deeper exploration into the different types of spirits that can operate in people's lives and the methods for defeating them through prayer and spiritual warfare.

Identifying Different Types of Spirits

Spirits of Deception and Lies

One of the primary strategies employed by Satan and his demonic forces is deception. Spirits of deception and lies can lead people away from the truth, causing confusion, error, and spiritual bondage. This chapter explores the characteristics of deceptive spirits, common manifestations in people's behavior and beliefs, and biblical examples of deception along with ways to combat it.

Characteristics of Deceptive Spirits

Deceptive spirits operate by distorting the truth, promoting falsehoods, and leading individuals into confusion. Here are some of the key characteristics of these spirits:

- Twisting the Truth: Deceptive spirits often mix truth with falsehood, making it difficult to discern their true intentions. They can manipulate words and concepts to create confusion.
- Promoting False Doctrines: These spirits encourage false teachings and heresies that contradict biblical truths. They can infiltrate religious communities, social institutions, social norms, and promote doctrines that lead people astray. So you may find yourself having learnt certain narratives that you grew up on, and you found out they were not the truth after educating yourself in the word of God as an adult. For example,

I've always heard the saying that "What you don't know won't hurt you" and Ignorance is bliss" but the bible says that "my people are destroyed for lack of knowledge. " (Hosea 4:6).

- Encouraging Relativism: Deceptive spirits often promote the idea that truth is relative or subjective, undermining the concept of absolute truth as found in the Bible.
- Sowing Doubt and Confusion: Deceptive spirits work to create doubt about God's word, His promises, and His nature. This doubt can lead to spiritual instability and a loss of faith.
- Offering Counterfeit Spiritual Experiences: Deceptive spirits may offer counterfeit experiences, such as false visions or revelations, designed to lure individuals away from genuine spiritual truth.

Common Manifestations in People's Behavior and Beliefs

Deceptive spirits can manifest in various ways, affecting people's behavior and beliefs. Here are common signs that indicate the presence of these spirits:

- Acceptance of False Teachings: When individuals readily accept teachings or doctrines that contradict biblical truths, it may be a sign of deceptive spirits at work.
- Resistance to Biblical Truth: People influenced by deceptive spirits may resist biblical teachings or reject foundational Christian beliefs, favoring alternative spiritual paths.

- Spreading Gossip and False Information: Deceptive spirits often encourage gossip, slander, and the spreading of false information, creating discord and division within communities.
- Engaging in Occult Practices: Involvement in occult or New Age practices can indicate the influence of deceptive spirits, leading individuals away from the truth of the gospel.
- Embracing Relativism and Moral Ambiguity: Deceptive spirits may lead individuals to embrace moral ambiguity, denying the existence of absolute truth and ethical standards.

Biblical Examples of Deception and How to Combat It

The Bible provides several examples of deception and outlines ways to combat it through prayer and spiritual warfare. Here are some notable examples and the lessons they offer:

- The Fall of Adam and Eve (Genesis 3): Satan, in the form of a serpent, deceives Eve by questioning God's command and suggesting that disobedience would lead to enlightenment. This story illustrates how deception can lead to sin and separation from God. Combatting this type of deception requires adherence to God's word and discernment to recognize lies.
- Jesus's Temptation in the Wilderness (Matthew 4:1-11): Satan attempts to deceive Jesus by misusing scripture and offering worldly temptations. Jesus combats these deceptive tactics by accurately quoting scripture and refusing to bow to temptation. This example underscores

the importance of knowing God's word and using it to refute lies.
- Ananias and Sapphira (Acts 5:1-11): This couple's deception about their offering to the early church demonstrates the consequences of lying and deceit. The swift judgment they face serves as a warning about the seriousness of deception and the need for honesty and integrity in the Christian community.
- Combating Deception with Truth (Ephesians 6:14; John 8:32): The "belt of truth" is part of the armor of God, emphasizing that truth is a key weapon against deception. Jesus's declaration that "the truth will set you free" (John 8:32) reinforces the idea that embracing and living by God's truth is the most effective way to combat deceptive spirits.

Spirits of deception and lies can be insidious, leading individuals away from the truth and into spiritual bondage. Understanding their characteristics and common manifestations is essential for recognizing and addressing their influence. Biblical examples provide valuable insights into the strategies of deceptive spirits and offer guidance on how to combat them. By grounding themselves in God's word, embracing the truth, and using prayer and spiritual warfare, believers can effectively overcome the influence of deceptive spirits and walk in spiritual freedom and integrity.

Spirits of Oppression and Bondage

Spirits of oppression and bondage are powerful forces that can severely impact individuals' lives, creating fear, anxiety, and spiritual chains that seem impossible to break. This chapter explores the nature of these spirits, their impact on mental health and relationships, and the strategies for breaking free through prayer and spiritual warfare.

Identifying Spirits that Cause Oppression, Fear, and Bondage

Spirits of oppression and bondage exert a heavy influence on individuals, often manifesting as overwhelming fear, anxiety, or destructive patterns that keep them trapped in a cycle of bondage. Here are some common characteristics of these spirits:

- Spirit of Fear: This spirit induces a pervasive sense of fear, often irrational, that hinders people from moving forward in life. It can lead to chronic anxiety, panic attacks, or a general sense of dread.
- Spirit of Depression: This spirit can cause deep feelings of hopelessness, sadness, and despair. It can lead to clinical depression, causing individuals to lose interest in life and isolate themselves.
- Spirit of Control: This spirit seeks to control and manipulate, often through intimidation or coercion. It can create bondage by exerting undue influence over a person's choices and behaviors.
- Spirit of Bondage: This spirit binds individuals to destructive patterns, whether it's addiction, harmful

relationships, or recurring sin. It keeps them from experiencing spiritual freedom.
- Spirit of Rejection: This spirit causes individuals to feel rejected and unworthy, leading to low self-esteem and a constant need for approval.

The Effects of These Spirits on Mental Health and Relationships

Spirits of oppression and bondage can have devastating effects on mental health and relationships. Here are some of the common outcomes of their influence:

- Mental Health Impact: These spirits can lead to a variety of mental health issues, including chronic anxiety, depression, panic disorders, and even suicidal thoughts. The constant oppression can be debilitating and affect every aspect of life.
- Relationship Strain: Oppression and bondage often create strain in relationships, causing conflict, mistrust, and isolation. The spirit of control, for example, can lead to manipulative behavior that damages relationships.
- Addictive Behaviors: The spirit of bondage often leads to addictive behaviors, such as substance abuse, compulsive gambling, or other forms of addiction. These behaviors can further exacerbate relationship issues and mental health problems.
- Spiritual Despair: Individuals affected by these spirits may experience spiritual despair, feeling distant from God and disconnected from the faith community. This

sense of spiritual isolation can make it challenging to find the support needed for deliverance.

Strategies for Breaking Free Through Prayer

Breaking free from spirits of oppression and bondage requires focused prayer and spiritual warfare. Here are strategies to help individuals gain freedom:

- Confession and Repentance: Begin by confessing any sins or behaviors that may have opened doors to these spirits. Repentance is a crucial step toward breaking free from spiritual bondage and reclaiming spiritual freedom.
- Prayers of Renunciation: Renounce any ties to spirits of oppression and bondage. Declare that these spirits have no power over you in the name of Jesus. This verbal renunciation is a powerful way to break spiritual chains.
- Invoking the Name of Jesus: The name of Jesus carries authority over all spiritual forces. Use His name in prayer to rebuke and cast out oppressive spirits. Declare the power of Jesus to break every chain of bondage.
- Prayers for Spiritual Protection: Seek God's protection and covering, asking Him to shield you from further spiritual attacks. This step is essential for preventing a return of oppressive spirits.
- Engaging in Spiritual Warfare: Equip yourself with the armor of God (Ephesians 6:10-18) and engage in spiritual warfare through prayer and scripture. This includes wielding the "sword of the Spirit" (the word of God) to counter the lies and intimidation of oppressive spirits.

- Seeking Community Support: Don't fight this battle alone. Seek support from a faith community, church leaders, or spiritual mentors. This community can provide encouragement, accountability, and additional prayer support.

Spirits of oppression and bondage can create significant fear, anxiety, and spiritual captivity. Identifying these spirits and understanding their effects on mental health and relationships is the first step toward breaking free. Through focused prayer, spiritual warfare, and the support of a faith community, individuals can overcome the influence of these spirits and experience the freedom that Jesus offers. By embracing the strategies outlined in this chapter, you can break the chains of spiritual bondage and step into a life of spiritual freedom and restoration.

Spirits of Addiction and Compulsion

Addiction and compulsion are significant issues that can trap individuals in harmful cycles, affecting their health, relationships, and spiritual well-being. This chapter explores how spirits can fuel addictive behaviors, identifies the spiritual roots of addiction, and provides guidance on deliverance through prayer and accountability.

How Spirits Can Fuel Addictive Behaviors

Addiction involves compulsive engagement in behaviors or substance use despite adverse consequences. While addiction can have various physical, psychological, and environmental factors, the spiritual dimension should not be overlooked. Here's how spirits can fuel addictive behaviors:

- Spiritual Bondage: Spirits of addiction and compulsion create spiritual bondage, keeping individuals trapped in cycles of addictive behavior. This bondage can be powerful, making it challenging to break free.
- Manipulating Desires: These spirits manipulate desires, leading individuals to seek satisfaction in substances or behaviors that ultimately harm them. This manipulation can create a stronghold that seems impossible to overcome.
- Deception and Denial: Spirits of addiction often foster deception, causing individuals to deny the severity of their addiction or rationalize their behaviors. This deception keeps them from seeking help or acknowledging their need for change.
- Cycle of Despair and Relief: Addictive behaviors can create a cycle where individuals experience despair, seek temporary relief through addiction, then feel guilt and shame, leading them back to despair. This cycle is often driven by spirits of addiction.

Recognizing the Spiritual Roots of Addiction

To address addiction from a spiritual perspective, it's essential to recognize its roots. Here's how to identify the spiritual factors contributing to addiction:

- Generational Patterns: Addiction can have generational roots, where patterns of addictive behavior are passed down through families. This generational influence can be a sign of spiritual bondage requiring deliverance.
- Emotional Wounds: Unhealed emotional wounds, such as trauma, rejection, or abandonment, can provide a foothold for spirits of addiction. Addressing these wounds is key to breaking free.
- Spiritual Void: A lack of spiritual connection or a sense of emptiness can lead individuals to seek help through addictive behaviors. Recognizing this spiritual void helps direct individuals toward true spiritual satisfaction.
- Influence of Deceptive Spirits: As discussed in the previous chapter, deceptive spirits can encourage addictive behaviors by promoting falsehoods, such as the idea that addiction provides comfort or relief. Recognizing these deceptions is crucial for breaking the cycle of addiction.

Spirits of Rebellion and Disobedience

Rebellion and disobedience are among the earliest manifestations of spiritual defiance against God's authority. The spirit of rebellion seeks to undermine divine order, leading individuals to reject God's guidance and pursue their own path.

This chapter explores the nature of the spirit of rebellion, its impact on individuals and communities, examines biblical stories of rebellion and their consequences, and provides a guide for praying for a spirit of obedience and submission to God.

Understanding the Spirit of Rebellion and Its Impact

The spirit of rebellion leads individuals to reject authority and pursue a path contrary to God's will. It is characterized by defiance, resistance to correction, and a desire to act independently of divine guidance. Here's a deeper look into this spirit and its impact:

Characteristics of the Spirit of Rebellion:
- Defiance: A persistent attitude of resistance against authority, rules, or guidance, especially those that align with God's word.
- Disregard for Consequences: A tendency to ignore the potential negative outcomes of one's actions, focusing instead on personal desires and impulses.
- Opposition to Spiritual Authority: Resistance to spiritual leaders, mentors, or biblical teaching, often accompanied by a rejection of godly counsel.
- Pride and Self-Reliance: A mindset that places personal autonomy above obedience to God, often rooted in pride and self-centeredness.

The Impact of Rebellion:
- Spiritual Separation: Rebellion creates a spiritual distance from God, leading to a breakdown in the relationship and a lack of spiritual growth.
- Conflict and Division: The spirit of rebellion often causes discord within families, churches, and communities, as it fosters resistance and defiance.
- Cycle of Disobedience: Rebellion can lead to a cycle of disobedience, where individuals find it increasingly difficult to align with God's will and spiritual authority.

Biblical Stories of Rebellion and Their Consequences

The Bible contains several stories that illustrate the consequences of rebellion and the importance of obedience to God. Here are some notable examples:

- The Fall of Lucifer (Isaiah 14:12-15; Ezekiel 28:12-17): Lucifer's rebellion against God led to his fall from heaven, becoming Satan. This story underscores the destructive consequences of rebellion and pride, leading to eternal separation from God.
- The Rebellion of Adam and Eve (Genesis 3:1-24): The disobedience of Adam and Eve in the Garden of Eden led to the fall of humanity, illustrating how rebellion against God's command has far-reaching consequences. This story emphasizes the importance of obedience and the consequences of defiance.
- The Israelites' Rebellion in the Wilderness (Numbers 14:1-45): The Israelites' rebellion against God's

instructions led to a generation wandering in the wilderness, unable to enter the Promised Land. This example highlights the impact of rebellion on God's plans and the resulting consequences.
- The Prodigal Son (Luke 15:11-32): The story of the Prodigal Son demonstrates the journey of rebellion and eventual repentance. Despite his initial rebellion, the son returns home to a loving father, illustrating the possibility of restoration when there is repentance and humility.

Praying for a Spirit of Obedience and Submission to God

Deliverance from the spirit of rebellion involves a change of heart and a commitment to obedience and submission to God. Here's how to pray for this transformation:

- Confession and Repentance:
  Begin by confessing any acts of rebellion or disobedience. Repentance is crucial in breaking the spirit of rebellion and restoring a right relationship with God.
- Prayers of Submission:
  Pray for a heart of submission to God's will. This involves yielding personal desires and plans to God and embracing His guidance.
- Prayers for a Spirit of Obedience:
  Seek God's help in cultivating a spirit of obedience. Ask for the Holy Spirit to guide and empower you to live according to God's commands.

- Praying Against the Spirit of Rebellion:
  Renounce the spirit of rebellion and disobedience, declaring in the name of Jesus that it has no power over you. Invite God's presence to fill you with a spirit of obedience and alignment with His will.
- Seeking Accountability and Spiritual Mentorship:
  Pray for spiritual mentors or accountability partners who can help guide and support you on the path of obedience. This support is crucial for staying on track and avoiding future rebellion.

Spirits of rebellion and disobedience can create significant barriers between individuals and God's plan for their lives. Understanding the nature and impact of these spirits, along with the biblical stories that illustrate their consequences, is key to breaking free from their influence. By engaging in focused prayer and embracing a spirit of obedience and submission to God, believers can overcome the spirit of rebellion and experience a restored relationship with God and others. This chapter provides the guidance and encouragement needed to turn from rebellion and walk in the path of obedience and spiritual freedom.

Spirits of Anger and Violence

Anger and violence can cause significant destruction, both within individuals and across societies. When these behaviors are driven by spiritual influences, they become even more dangerous and insidious. This chapter explores the destructive nature of anger and violent spirits, helps identify their sources in individuals and societies, and provides guidance on praying for peace and inner transformation.

The Destructive Nature of Anger and Violent Spirits

Anger, in its uncontrolled form, can lead to violence, division, and deep-seated bitterness. When fueled by spiritual forces, it becomes a potent weapon of destruction. Here's how these spirits manifest and the damage they can cause:

Characteristics of Anger and Violent Spirits:

- Uncontrollable Rage: A spirit of anger can lead to uncontrollable rage, often resulting in destructive outbursts, physical violence, or verbal abuse.
- Bitterness and Resentment: These spirits foster bitterness and resentment, causing individuals to hold onto grudges and seek revenge.
- Hatred and Malice: Anger and violent spirits often breed hatred, leading to harmful intentions and a desire to harm others.
- Destructive Violence: These spirits can manifest in extreme violence, affecting relationships, communities, and even entire societies.

The Impact of Anger and Violent Spirits:
- Broken Relationships: Uncontrolled anger and violence can lead to broken relationships, family strife, and a breakdown of trust and communication.
- Legal Consequences: Acts of violence driven by these spirits often result in legal repercussions, leading to arrests, imprisonment, and lifelong consequences.
- Societal Division: These spirits can cause societal unrest, contributing to division, conflict, and even widespread violence.
- Spiritual Damage: Anger and violent spirits can create spiritual barriers, preventing individuals from experiencing the peace and love that come from God.

Identifying Sources of These Spirits in Individuals and Societies

Identifying the sources of spirits of anger and violence is key to addressing their impact. Here are common sources of these spirits and how they manifest:

- Unresolved Trauma and Pain: Unresolved emotional trauma or deep-seated pain can be a breeding ground for spirits of anger and violence. Individuals who have experienced abuse, rejection, or significant loss may struggle with these spirits.
- Generational Patterns: Just as with other spirits, patterns of anger and violence can be passed down through generations, creating a cycle of destructive behavior.

- Cultural Influences: Societal and cultural factors can contribute to the spread of these spirits. Media that glorifies violence, social systems that perpetuate injustice, and environments that promote aggression can all fuel anger and violence.
- Spiritual Deception: Deceptive spirits can encourage anger and violence by promoting false narratives, encouraging hatred, or justifying violent behavior.

The Process of Deliverance

Preparation for deliverance

Preparation for deliverance is an essential part of the process of seeking freedom from spiritual bondage. The following are some important steps to take before entering into a deliverance session:

1. Repentance: The first step in preparation for deliverance is to confess and repent of any known sins, including sins of the ancestors, that may have given the enemy a legal right to oppress you. This may involve making amends with people you have wronged, forgiving those who have wronged you, and renouncing any involvement with occult or New Age practices.
2. Prayer and Fasting: Fasting and prayer can help to break strongholds and prepare your heart for deliverance. You may consider seeking the guidance of a pastor or prayer partner for support during this time.
3. Confession: Confessing your struggles and weaknesses to a trusted pastor, friend, or deliverance minister can be helpful in preparing for deliverance. It can also help to identify any underlying issues that may be contributing to your spiritual bondage.
4. Identify Triggers: Identifying triggers that can lead to temptation or spiritual attacks can help you to prepare for deliverance. This may include avoiding certain people, places, or activities that have led to sin or bondage in the past.

5. Surround Yourself with Support: Surrounding yourself with a supportive community of believers, such as a church small group or prayer group, can provide the encouragement and accountability needed to overcome spiritual bondage.
6. Submit to God: Submitting your will and surrendering to God's plan for your life is crucial in preparing for deliverance. This involves acknowledging that God's ways are higher than our ways and trusting that He has a plan to bring healing and freedom to our lives.

Preparing for deliverance is not a one-time event but an ongoing process of surrendering to God and seeking His guidance. By taking these steps, you can prepare your heart and mind for the freedom that God desires for you. Here are some Scripture references that support the process of preparation for deliverance:

- Repentance: "Repent, then, and turn to God, so that your sins may be wiped out, that times of refreshing may come from the Lord." (Acts 3:19)
- Confession: "Therefore, confess your sins to one another and pray for one another, that you may be healed. The prayer of a righteous person has great power as it is working." (James 5:16)
- Forgiveness: "And whenever you stand praying, forgive, if you have anything against anyone, so that your Father also who is in heaven may forgive you your trespasses." (Mark 11:25)
- Submission to God: "Submit yourselves therefore to God. Resist the devil, and he will flee from you." (James 4:7)

- Renewing the mind: "Do not conform to the pattern of this world but be transformed by the renewing of your mind. Then you will be able to test and approve what God's will is—his good, pleasing and perfect will." (Romans 12:2)
- Seeking God's presence: "But seek first his kingdom and his righteousness, and all these things will be given to you as well." (Matthew 6:33)
- Trusting in God: "Trust in the Lord with all your heart and lean not on your own understanding; in all your ways submit to him, and he will make your paths straight." (Proverbs 3:5-6)

These verses highlight the importance of repentance, confession, forgiveness, submission to God, renewing the mind, seeking God's presence, and trusting in Him as crucial aspects of the process of preparation for deliverance.

The role of prayer and fasting

Prayer and fasting play a significant role in the process of deliverance. Fasting is the act of abstaining from food or certain types of food for a period of time in order to focus on prayer and spiritual matters. Here are some ways that prayer and fasting are essential to the process of deliverance:

- Breaking strongholds: Prayer and fasting help to break strongholds and spiritual bondage that may be holding a person captive. This is because fasting and prayer help to shift the focus from physical needs to spiritual needs, creating a space for God to work in a person's life.

- Seeking God's guidance: During a time of prayer and fasting, a person can seek God's guidance on the specific issues that need to be addressed in deliverance. This can include identifying any underlying issues that may be contributing to the bondage and seeking God's wisdom on how to address them.
- Humbling oneself: Fasting and prayer can help a person to humble themselves before God and acknowledge their dependence on Him. This posture of humility is essential in the process of deliverance because it allows God to work in a person's life and empowers them to resist the enemy.
- Spiritual warfare: Fasting and prayer are powerful weapons in spiritual warfare because they help to increase a person's spiritual sensitivity and discernment. This can help a person to identify and resist the enemy's attacks and strategies.
- Strengthening faith: Fasting and prayer can help to strengthen a person's faith in God and His ability to deliver them from bondage. This is important because deliverance often requires a person to take bold steps of faith and trust in God's promises.

Prayer and fasting are essential components of the process of deliverance. They help to break strongholds, seek God's guidance, humble oneself, engage in spiritual warfare, and strengthen faith. By incorporating prayer and fasting into the deliverance process, a person can position themselves for the freedom and victory that God desires for them.

Here are some Scripture references that support the role of prayer and fasting in the process of deliverance:

- Breaking strongholds: "But this kind does not go out except by prayer and fasting." (Matthew 17:21)
- Seeking God's guidance: "And when you fast, do not look gloomy like the hypocrites, for they disfigure their faces that their fasting may be seen by others. Truly, I say to you, they have received their reward. But when you fast, anoint your head and wash your face, that your fasting may not be seen by others but by your Father who is in secret. And your Father who sees in secret will reward you." (Matthew 6:16-18)
- Spiritual warfare: "For though we walk in the flesh, we are not waging war according to the flesh. For the weapons of our warfare are not of the flesh but have divine power to destroy strongholds. We destroy arguments and every lofty opinion raised against the knowledge of God and take every thought captive to obey Christ." (2 Corinthians 10:3-5)
- Strengthening faith: "And Jesus said to him, 'If you can! All things are possible for one who believes.' Immediately the father of the child cried out and said, 'I believe; help my unbelief!'" (Mark 9:23-24

The importance of repentance

The process of deliverance is a spiritual journey that involves identifying and breaking free from bondages and strongholds in our lives. One of the most important aspects of this process is repentance. Repentance is a vital step towards experiencing freedom and deliverance from the grip of sin and bondage.

Repentance involves acknowledging our sins and shortcomings, confessing them to God, and turning away from them. It is not a one-time event but an ongoing process of turning away from sin and turning towards God. It involves a deep sense of remorse and a desire to change our ways and follow God's will.

In the Bible, repentance is often associated with confession. Confessing our sins to God and to one another can be a powerful tool in breaking free from the chains of sin and experiencing the freedom and peace that comes from a restored relationship with God. Most people may not be comfortable confessing to someone as it may be hard to confide in people these days. However, repentance and confession to God is important and if you find it hard to do it alone, get help from someone who is spiritually mature to guide you. Through repentance and confession, we can experience the transformative power of God's grace in our lives.

Repentance is also closely linked to the concept of forgiveness. As we repent and seek forgiveness, we are able to experience the incredible depth of God's mercy and grace. This forgiveness is not something that we can earn or deserve but is freely given to us through the sacrifice of Jesus Christ on the cross. In the process of deliverance, repentance is an essential step towards experiencing true freedom and healing. It involves a willingness to be honest with ourselves and with God about our struggles and shortcomings. Through repentance, we can open ourselves up to God's healing and transformative power and experience the freedom that comes from a restored relationship with Him.

Here are some Scripture references that highlight the importance of repentance:

- "Repent, then, and turn to God, so that your sins may be wiped out, that times of refreshing may come from the Lord." (Acts 3:19)
- "From that time on Jesus began to preach, 'Repent, for the kingdom of heaven has come near.'" (Matthew 4:17)
- "Or do you show contempt for the riches of his kindness, forbearance and patience, not realizing that God's kindness is intended to lead you to repentance?" (Romans 2:4)
- "I have not come to call the righteous, but sinners to repentance." (Luke 5:32)
- "The Lord is not slow in keeping his promise, as some understand slowness. Instead, he is patient with you, not wanting anyone to perish, but everyone to come to repentance." (2 Peter 3:9)

These verses show that repentance is not just a one-time event, but an ongoing process of turning away from sin and turning towards God. Repentance involves acknowledging and confessing our sins, seeking forgiveness, and making a conscious effort to change our behavior. Through repentance, we can receive God's forgiveness and experience true freedom from the bondage of sin.

The importance of Confession

Confession is an important part of the deliverance process. It involves acknowledging and confessing one's sins and weaknesses to God and to others. Confession is not just admitting wrongdoing, but renouncing your connections to the occult, ungodly practices, and any habitual behavior that is against the will of God and also seeking forgiveness and committing to turning away from the sinful behavior. Confession is important for several reasons:

1. It breaks down pride: Confession requires humility and honesty, which breaks down the pride that can prevent people from receiving deliverance.
2. It brings healing: Confession can bring healing to the wounds and hurts that have led to sinful behaviors. By confessing these things, people can receive healing and freedom from the pain that has been holding them back.
3. It opens the door to God's grace: Confession opens the door for God's grace to flow into a person's life. By confessing sins and weaknesses, people acknowledge their need for God's forgiveness and help, and God is able to work in their lives in a powerful way.
4. It brings accountability: Confessing to others can bring accountability, which can help people stay on track in their journey towards deliverance and spiritual freedom.

In the deliverance process, confession may take place in a variety of ways, including through private prayer, group confession, and individual prayer. It is important for agents/ministers of deliverance to create a safe and non-judgmental environment for people to confess their sins and weaknesses. This can help people feel comfortable enough to be honest and vulnerable, which is necessary for true confession to take place.

Scripture references that emphasize the importance of confession include James 5:16, which says, "Therefore, confess your sins to one another and pray for one another, that you may be healed. The prayer of a righteous person has great power as it is working." Another example is 1 John 1:9, which says, "If we confess our sins, he is faithful and just to forgive us our sins and to cleanse us from all unrighteousness."

The role of Inner healing and forgiveness

Inner healing and forgiveness play a crucial role in the process of deliverance. Deliverance is not just about casting out demons; it involves addressing the root causes of bondage and working towards healing and wholeness in all areas of a person's life. Inner healing involves addressing past wounds, trauma, and emotional pain that may have given the enemy a foothold in a person's life.

Forgiveness is also a crucial component of the deliverance process. Unforgiveness can be a major blockage to freedom and can even lead to demonic oppression. Forgiveness is not always easy, but it is necessary for healing and deliverance. It involves releasing any bitterness, resentment, and anger towards those who have hurt us and choosing to extend grace and mercy towards them.

The Bible teaches us that 55orgivenesss is not optional but is essential for our own spiritual growth and freedom. In Matthew 6:14-15, Jesus said, "For if you forgive other people when they sin against you, your heavenly Father will also forgive you. But if you do not forgive others their sins, your Father will not forgive your sins."

Inner healing and forgiveness can be facilitated through prayer, counselling, and other forms of support. It is important to seek out professional help when dealing with deep-seated emotional wounds and trauma. Inner healing and forgiveness are vital components of the deliverance process. Through addressing past hurts and choosing to forgive, we can experience freedom and wholeness in all areas of our lives.

The Foundation of True Deliverance

If you are not a Christian; meaning you have not yet accepted Jesus Christ as Lord and Savior, this is for you. Deliverance is not simply about being set free from demonic oppression, spiritual bondage, or generational curses—it's about entering into a new life under the Lordship of Jesus Christ. Many people seek deliverance because they are desperate for relief, but true and lasting freedom only comes when you fully surrender your life to Jesus.

Deliverance Without Jesus Leads to Greater Bondage

One of the most sobering warnings Jesus gives is found in Matthew 12:43–45:

"When an evil spirit leaves a person, it goes into the desert, seeking rest but finding none. Then it says, 'I will return to the person I came from.' So it returns and finds its former home

empty, swept, and in order. Then the spirit finds seven other spirits more evil than itself, and they all enter the person and live there. And so that person is worse off than before."

This scripture is a serious caution: if your spiritual "house" is swept clean through deliverance but not filled with the presence of Jesus and the Holy Spirit, you remain vulnerable. The enemy will look for a way to return—and the condition of your life can end up more tormented than before.

Salvation Is the Gateway to Protection and Transformation

Jesus is not just a Savior—He is Deliverer, Healer, and Protector. When you accept Jesus into your heart, you receive a new identity, and the authority to stand against the enemy.

John 1:12:

"But as many as received Him, to them He gave the right to become children of God, to those who believe in His name."

2 Corinthians 5:17:

"Therefore, if anyone is in Christ, he is a new creation; old things have passed away; behold, all things have become new."

Salvation is not a religious ritual—it is a divine exchange. Your sins are forgiven. Your past is washed clean. You are repositioned spiritually under the covering of Christ.

You Need the Holy Spirit to Sustain Your Freedom

After salvation, you must ask for the infilling of the Holy Spirit. The Holy Spirit is the one who empowers you to live holy, discern truth, resist temptation, and grow spiritually.

Romans 8:13–14:

"For if you live according to the flesh, you will die; but if by the Spirit you put to death the misdeeds of the body, you will live. For those who are led by the Spirit of God are the children of God."

Acts 1:8:

"But you shall receive power when the Holy Spirit has come upon you; and you shall be witnesses to Me..."

The power you need to walk in deliverance, victory, and transformation doesn't come from willpower—it comes from the Holy Spirit.

If You Are Not a Christian but Want to Be Free...

You may be seeking deliverance because of tormenting dreams, addiction, emotional pain, fear, or spiritual oppression. But the only lasting way to freedom is to give your life to Jesus.

Romans 10:9–10:

"If you openly declare that Jesus is Lord and believe in your heart that God raised him from the dead, you will be saved. For it is by believing in your heart that you are made right with God..."

Salvation is a gift. Jesus already paid the price. All you need to do is receive it.

The use of spiritual gifts in deliverance

The use of spiritual gifts in deliverance is an important aspect of the process. Spiritual gifts are given by the Holy Spirit to believers for the edification of the church and the furtherance of the gospel. Some of the gifts, such as discernment, prophecy, and words of knowledge, can be particularly helpful in the deliverance process.

Discernment is the ability to distinguish between the truth and deception. In the context of deliverance, this gift can help the deliverance minister identify the source of the spiritual oppression or possession and discern the appropriate course of action.

Prophecy and words of knowledge can also play a role in the deliverance process. These gifts involve receiving a message from God, which can be used to encourage and strengthen the person being delivered. The message may provide insight into the root causes of the spiritual bondage or offer hope and direction for the future.

Other spiritual gifts, such as healing and miracles, may also be used in the deliverance process. The power of the Holy Spirit can bring healing and restoration to areas of brokenness and pain, freeing the person from the grip of the enemy.

However, it is important to note that the use of spiritual gifts should always be grounded in biblical truth and used with wisdom and discernment. The focus should always be on glorifying God and bringing freedom and healing to the person being delivered.

The use of spiritual gifts in deliverance can be a powerful tool in breaking the chains of spiritual bondage and bringing freedom and healing to those in need.

Deliverance through the power of the Holy Spirit

The process of deliverance is not just a matter of changing our behavior or breaking free from negative patterns in our lives. It is ultimately a spiritual battle, and one that requires the power and guidance of the Holy Spirit. Throughout the Bible, we see numerous examples of individuals who were delivered from various forms of bondage through the power of the Holy Spirit. Jesus Himself performed countless miracles of deliverance, freeing people from demonic oppression, physical illness, and other forms of spiritual bondage.

In the process of deliverance, the Holy Spirit plays a vital role in guiding us, comforting us, and empowering us to break free from the chains of sin and bondage. Through prayer and fasting, we can invite the Holy Spirit into our lives and allow Him to lead us on the path to freedom and healing.

One of the key ways in which the Holy Spirit works in the process of deliverance is by helping us to identify the root causes of our struggles and bondages. Through prayer and reflection, the Holy Spirit can reveal to us the underlying spiritual strongholds that are keeping us in bondage and guide us in the process of breaking free from them.

Additionally, the Holy Spirit can give us the strength and courage we need to face our fears and overcome the obstacles that stand in our way. He can fill us with a deep sense of peace and comfort, even in the midst of difficult circumstances, and empower us to persevere in our journey towards freedom and healing.

In the process of deliverance, it is important to remember that we do not fight alone. The Holy Spirit is with us every step of the way, guiding us, comforting us, and empowering us to break free from the chains of sin and bondage. Through the power of the Holy Spirit, we can experience true freedom, healing, and transformation in our lives. Here are some Scripture references that highlight the role of the Holy Spirit in the process of deliverance:

- John 14:26 – "But the Helper, the Holy Spirit, whom the Father will send in my name, he will teach you all things and bring to your remembrance all that I have said to you."
- Romans 8:26 – "Likewise the Spirit helps us in our weakness. For we do not know what to pray for as we ought, but the Spirit himself intercedes for us with groanings too deep for words."
- Acts 1:8 – "But you will receive power when the Holy Spirit has come upon you, and you will be my witnesses in Jerusalem and in all Judea and Samaria, and to the end of the earth."
- Galatians 5:16-17 – "But I say, walk by the Spirit, and you will not gratify the desires of the flesh. For the desires of the flesh are against the Spirit, and the desires of the Spirit are against the flesh, for these are opposed

to each other, to keep you from doing the things you want to do."
- Ephesians 3:16 – "That according to the riches of his glory he may grant you to be strengthened with power through his Spirit in your inner being."
- 2 Timothy 1:7 – "For God gave us a spirit not of fear but of power and love and self-control."
- Luke 4:18 – "The Spirit of the Lord is upon me, because he has anointed me to proclaim good news to the poor. He has sent me to proclaim liberty to the captives and recovering of sight to the blind, to set at liberty those who are oppressed.

The role of the deliverance minister

In the process of deliverance, the role of the deliverance minister is crucial. Deliverance ministers are individuals who have been called and equipped by God to help others break free from spiritual bondage and find freedom in Christ.

The deliverance minister serves as a spiritual guide and mentor, offering support, encouragement, and guidance to those who are struggling with various forms of spiritual bondage. They are trained to recognize the signs of spiritual oppression and to help individuals identify the underlying spiritual strongholds that are keeping them in bondage.

The deliverance minister also plays a key role in leading individuals through the process of repentance, prayer, and spiritual warfare. They help individuals to identify and renounce any sins or negative patterns in their lives that are contributing to their bondage and guide them in the process of seeking God's forgiveness and healing.

Additionally, the deliverance minister serves as a vessel for the power of the Holy Spirit, inviting His presence and guidance into the deliverance process. They may pray for individuals, lay hands on them, and speak words of encouragement and healing as they lead them through the process of deliverance.

It is important to note that deliverance ministers do not have the power to deliver individuals on their own. Rather, they rely on the power and guidance of the Holy Spirit to lead individuals towards freedom and healing. The role of the deliverance minister is to serve as a facilitator, guiding individuals through the process of deliverance and providing spiritual support and guidance along the way.

The role of the deliverance minister Is crucial in the process of deliverance. They serve as a guide and mentor, helping individuals to identify and break free from spiritual bondage through repentance, prayer, and spiritual warfare. They rely on the power and guidance of the Holy Spirit to lead individuals towards freedom and healing and play an important role in helping individuals experience true transformation in their lives.

As deliverance ministers are agents of deliverance to facilitate the process of deliverance for individuals who are seeking freedom from spiritual oppression, bondage, and generational curses. Agents of deliverance can include pastors, intercessors, prayer warriors, and other individuals who have been equipped and called to engage in deliverance ministry.

Some of the specific roles that agents of deliverance may play include:

1. Providing spiritual guidance and support: Agents of deliverance may help individuals identify areas of spiritual oppression and provide guidance and support throughout the process of seeking deliverance.
2. Discernment: Agents of deliverance are called to exercise discernment in identifying the root causes of spiritual bondage and oppression in individuals seeking deliverance.
3. Intercession: Agents of deliverance may engage in intercessory prayer on behalf of individuals seeking deliverance.
4. Facilitation of deliverance: Agents of deliverance may facilitate the process of deliverance, which may involve the use of spiritual gifts such as prophetic insight, healing, and discernment.
5. Follow-up and aftercare: Agents of deliverance may provide ongoing support and follow-up care for individuals who have experienced deliverance, helping them to maintain their freedom and grow in their relationship with God.

The role of agents of deliverance is to help individuals experience spiritual freedom and healing through the power of the Holy Spirit. This involves a deep commitment to prayer, discernment, and sensitivity to the leading of the Holy Spirit, as well as ongoing growth and training in the area of deliverance ministry.

The Qualities of effective agents of deliverance

Effective agents of deliverance possess certain qualities that are essential to their ministry. These qualities include:

1. **Prayerfulness:** Effective agents of deliverance are people of prayer who rely on the power of God to bring about deliverance in the lives of those they minister to.
2. **Humility:** They recognize that they are not the source of deliverance but rather God is, and therefore they approach their ministry with humility.
3. **Knowledge of the Word of God:** Effective agents of deliverance are familiar with the Word of God and use it to bring about healing and deliverance in people's lives.
4. **Sensitivity to the Holy Spirit:** They are led by the Holy Spirit in their ministry and are sensitive to His leading.
5. **Compassion:** Effective agents of deliverance have a heart for people and are genuinely concerned about their well-being.
6. **Discernment:** They have the ability to discern between the work of the Holy Spirit and the work of the enemy.
7. **Boldness:** Effective agents of deliverance are not afraid to confront the enemy and stand against his schemes.
8. **Patience:** They understand that deliverance is a process and are patient with those they minister to.

By possessing these qualities, agents of deliverance are able to effectively minister to those who are in need of deliverance and bring about healing and freedom in their lives.

Personal Spiritual Preparation

Personal spiritual preparation is crucial for anyone who desires to be an effective agent of deliverance. It involves cultivating a close relationship with God through prayer, fasting, Bible study, and worship.

Spiritual preparation helps agents of deliverance to develop the sensitivity and discernment needed to recognize and confront demonic activity. It also helps them to maintain spiritual purity and integrity, which are essential for effective ministry.

Agents of deliverance should strive to live a holy and righteous life, walking in obedience to God's word and relying on the power of the Holy Spirit to overcome the enemy. They should also be willing to humble themselves and seek accountability from other mature believers, but most importantly accountability to God.

In addition, agents of deliverance should be well-versed in the principles and practices of deliverance ministry. They should have a deep understanding of the Bible and its teachings on spiritual warfare and be equipped with the knowledge and skills necessary to effectively minister to those in need of deliverance. Please note there are instances where a deliverance minister is unable to help someone due to the technicality and spiritual depths of the issues for some people. With that said, a deliverance minister has to be given the permission and the grace to address a certain situation.

Overall, personal spiritual preparation is essential for agents of deliverance, as it enables them to be effective vessels of God's power and instruments of His healing and deliverance.

The role of self-deliverance

While the role of the deliverance minister is important in the process of deliverance, it is also possible for individuals to practice self-deliverance. Self-deliverance involves taking personal responsibility for one's spiritual well-being and actively seeking freedom from any forms of spiritual bondage. The truth is, not everyone will have a deliverance minister come to pray over them. Nevertheless, it does not mean that you do not have the tools to deliver yourself. God has equipped every child of God with spiritual resources for deliverance, and you can do it!

Here are some steps that individuals can take to practice self-deliverance:

- Identify any areas of bondage: The first step in self-deliverance is to identify any areas of bondage in one's life. This could include addiction, negative thought patterns, or generational curses. It is important to be honest with oneself and ask God to reveal any areas of bondage that need to be addressed.
- Repent and renounce: Once the areas of bondage have been identified, it is important to repent of any sins or negative behaviors that may have contributed to these strongholds. This involves confessing any sins to God and asking for His forgiveness. It may also involve renouncing any negative thought patterns, beliefs, or behaviors that have kept one in bondage.
- Pray for deliverance: After repenting and renouncing, it is important to pray for deliverance. This involves asking God to break any chains of bondage and to fill one's life with His Holy Spirit. It may also involve

speaking aloud declarations of freedom and victory over one's life.

- Seek accountability: It can be helpful to seek accountability from a trusted friend or mentor who can offer support and encouragement in the process of self-deliverance. This could involve sharing one's struggles and progress and asking for prayer and support as needed.
- Practice spiritual disciplines: Finally, it is important to practice spiritual disciplines such as prayer, reading the Bible, worship, and fasting. These disciplines help to strengthen one's relationship with God and create a space for His healing and transformative power to work in one's life.

Common challenges to deliverance

Dealing with resistance and unbelief

Deliverance ministry is not always an easy task, and deliverance ministers often encounter various challenges along the way. One of the most common challenges is dealing with resistance and unbelief, both from the person seeking deliverance and sometimes even from other members of their family or community.

Resistance to deliverance can come from a variety of sources. Some people may be skeptical of the existence of demonic forces, while others may be fearful or ashamed to confront their own issues. Still, others may have a deep-seated attachment to the behavior or thought patterns that are causing their spiritual oppression.

As deliverance ministers, it is important to approach resistance with compassion and understanding. Rather than pushing the person to immediately accept deliverance, we should take the time to listen to their concerns and address any underlying fears or doubts they may have. We can also pray for God to soften their heart and give them the courage to confront the issues that are holding them back.

Another common challenge in deliverance is dealing with unbelief, either in ourselves or in the person seeking deliverance. It can be difficult to fully trust in God's power to bring about complete healing and deliverance, especially if we have not seen it happen before.

However, it is important to remember that Jesus himself encountered unbelief during his ministry, and he responded with love, patience, and unwavering faith in God's power. As deliverance ministers, we should follow his example and seek to cultivate a deeper trust in God's ability to bring about spiritual freedom.

Dealing with resistance and unbelief is an inevitable part of the deliverance process. However, by approaching these challenges with compassion, understanding, and unwavering faith in God's power, we can help facilitate a path to spiritual freedom and healing for those in need.

Dealing With unconfessed sins

Dealing with unconfessed sins is one of the common challenges that can hinder deliverance. Unconfessed sins can act as a barrier between an individual and God, blocking the flow of God's power and presence in their lives. This can make it difficult for the person to receive deliverance.

One of the first steps in dealing with unconfessed sins is to acknowledge their presence and take responsibility for them. This involves being honest with oneself and with God about the sins that have been committed. Confession is the act of acknowledging one's sins before God and asking for forgiveness. This is a crucial step in the process of deliverance, as it opens the way for God's power to work in a person's life.

Another important aspect of dealing with unconfessed sins is to seek out accountability and support from other believers. This may involve confessing one's sins to a trusted friend or seeking guidance from a pastor or spiritual mentor. Through accountability and support, a person can gain the strength and encouragement they need to overcome unconfessed sins and move forward in their journey towards deliverance.

Ultimately, dealing with unconfessed sins requires a willingness to humble oneself before God and others. It requires a recognition of one's own limitations and a willingness to seek help from others. By taking these steps, a person can begin to break free from the chains of unconfessed sins and experience the freedom and deliverance that God has promised to all who seek him with a repentant heart.

Avoiding Legalism and Superstition

One of the challenges in the area of deliverance is the temptation to fall into legalism and superstition. Legalism refers to the belief that following a set of rules or regulations will make us more righteous or holy, while superstition refers to the belief that certain objects or practices have power in themselves.

While it is important to have a biblical framework for deliverance and to follow principles based on scripture, we must guard against the idea that there is a formula or specific set of steps that will always result in deliverance. Many times, deliverance comes with different strategical approach and these strategies come from the Holy Spirit. The Holy Spirit helps you to get your target, so you don't shoot aimlessly. God is sovereign and works in unique ways in everyone's life.

Additionally, we must avoid superstition by recognizing that objects do not have any power in themselves. Our focus should be on the power of Jesus Christ and the work of the Holy Spirit, rather than relying on external symbols or rituals.

Ultimately, our faith should be grounded in a personal relationship with Jesus Christ, and our trust should be in His power to set us free from spiritual bondage. As we seek deliverance, we must maintain a humble and dependent attitude, trusting in God's sovereignty and grace rather than relying on our own efforts or methods.

Addressing Ethical Considerations

Addressing ethical concerns in deliverance is crucial for maintaining integrity and promoting safety in the process. Some ethical concerns that may arise include:

1. Consent: It is important to obtain informed consent from the person seeking deliverance. This includes explaining the process, potential risks, and benefits, and ensuring that the person understands and agrees to participate.
2. Confidentiality: Confidentiality should be maintained throughout the deliverance process. The deliverance minister should not share personal information or experiences of the person seeking deliverance without their permission.
3. Boundaries: Clear boundaries should be established and respected during the deliverance process. The deliverance minister should not engage in any inappropriate behavior or touch the person seeking deliverance in a way that makes them uncomfortable.

4. Referral: If the person seeking deliverance requires additional professional help, such as mental health consultation, the deliverance minister should refer them to appropriate resources.
5. Accountability: Deliverance ministers should have accountability and oversight to ensure that they are operating within ethical and biblical guidelines.
6. Protecting dignity: Protecting the dignity of the person being delivered is important. E.g., some people through deliverance may fall on the ground during the process. It is the responsibility of the minister to ensure their safety to prevent injury and cover them with a linen to prevent exposure.

It is important for deliverance ministers to approach their work with humility, sensitivity, and a deep respect for the dignity and autonomy of the person seeking deliverance.

Types of Deliverance

Deliverance from demonic oppression and possession

Deliverance from demonic oppression and possession is one of the most common types of deliverance sought after by people. Demonic oppression occurs when demonic forces exert their power and influence over an individual, causing them to experience negative physical, emotional, and spiritual effects. Demonic possession, on the other hand, occurs when a demonic spirit takes control of an individual's body, mind, and will, leading to a complete loss of control over their actions and behavior.

Deliverance from demonic oppression and possession involves recognizing the presence of demonic forces and exercising the authority of Jesus Christ to command them to leave. It requires a deep understanding of the power and authority of Jesus Christ and the importance of prayer and spiritual warfare in confronting and defeating demonic forces.

The process of deliverance from demonic oppression and possession can vary depending on the severity of the situation. It often involves identifying the specific demons that are present, renouncing any involvement with the occult or any other sinful behavior that may have opened the door for demonic influence, and seeking the help of an experienced and trained deliverance minister.

Scriptural references such as Mark 1:23-26, Mark 9:14-29, and Luke 8:26-39 describe instances of Jesus casting out demons and providing a model for deliverance ministry. It is important to remember that deliverance from demonic oppression and possession is not a one-time event, but a continual process of seeking God's protection, spiritual counseling, walking in obedience, and resisting the enemy's attacks.

Deliverance from generational curses

Deliverance from generational curses is another type of deliverance. A generational curse is a curse that is believed to be passed down from one generation to another. This curse can manifest in different forms such as financial difficulties, chronic illnesses, addictions, and dysfunctional relationships. The idea of generational curses is based on biblical teachings that suggest that the sins of one generation can affect the succeeding generations.

Deliverance from generational curses involves recognizing and renouncing the specific sins or patterns of behavior that have been passed down from one generation to another. This can be done through prayer, confession, and seeking forgiveness. It also involves breaking the power of the curse through the blood of Jesus and speaking blessings over oneself and one's family.

It is important to note that not all challenges or difficulties in life are the result of generational curses. However, it is important to seek deliverance from generational curses when there are patterns of destructive behavior or negative consequences that seem to be recurring in one's family. Through deliverance, individuals can break free from the cycle of negative patterns and experience the freedom that comes from living in the fullness of God's grace.

Deliverance from soul ties and unhealthy attachments

Deliverance from soul ties and unhealthy attachments is another type of deliverance that individuals may need. Soul ties can form when there is a strong emotional or spiritual bond between two individuals. These ties can be healthy, such as in a marriage relationship, but they can also be unhealthy and lead to negative consequences. Unhealthy attachments can include co-dependency, unhealthy friendships, and addictions.

Deliverance from soul ties and unhealthy attachments involves breaking the emotional and spiritual bonds that have formed and renouncing any negative influence they may have had on an individual's life. This can involve repentance, forgiveness, and prayer, as well as seeking the support of a trusted friend or deliverance minister.

Scriptural basis for deliverance from soul ties and unhealthy attachments can be found in 2 Corinthians 6:14, which says, "Do not be yoked together with unbelievers. For what do righteousness and wickedness have in common? Or what fellowship can light have with darkness?" Additionally, in 2 Corinthians 10:5, Paul instructs us to take every thought captive to Christ, indicating the importance of breaking negative thought patterns and attachments.

Keys to Spiritual Freedom

Renewing the mind

Renewing the mind is a key aspect of experiencing spiritual freedom. The Bible teaches that the mind is the battlefield of spiritual warfare and that the way we think can either lead us towards life or towards death. Therefore, it is important to renew our minds with the truth of God's Word in order to experience true spiritual freedom.

Here are some principles related to renewing the mind:

1. Acknowledge the need for transformation: Romans 12:2 states, "Do not conform to the pattern of this world, but be transformed by the renewing of your mind. Then you will be able to test and approve what God's will is—his good, pleasing and perfect will." This verse emphasizes that transformation starts with a conscious decision to break free from the patterns of the world and to allow God to renew our minds.
2. Fill the mind with the Word of God: Psalm 119:11 says, "I have hidden your word in my heart that I might not sin against you." Meditating on and memorizing Scripture can help us to replace negative thought patterns and beliefs with God's truth.
3. Guard against negative influences: Proverbs 4:23 warns us to guard our hearts above all else, for everything we do flows from it. This includes guarding against negative influences such as ungodly media, relationships, and thought patterns.

4. Practice gratitude and positive thinking: Philippians 4:8 encourages us to think about whatever is true, noble, right, pure, lovely, admirable, excellent, or praiseworthy. Focusing on these things can help us to cultivate a positive mindset and attitude of gratitude.
5. Embrace the power of forgiveness: Forgiveness is a crucial component of spiritual freedom. Unforgiveness can lead to bitterness, resentment, and emotional bondage. Ephesians 4:31-32 reminds us to "get rid of all bitterness, rage and anger, brawling and slander, along with every form of malice. Be kind and compassionate to one another, forgiving each other, just as in Christ God forgave you."

By renewing our minds with God's truth, we can break free from negative thought patterns, beliefs, and behaviors that have kept us in bondage. Through the power of the Holy Spirit, we can experience true spiritual freedom and live the abundant life that God has planned for us.

Breaking soul ties

I have mentioned soul ties before, but breaking it is one of the keys to spiritual freedom. Soul ties refer to the emotional and spiritual connections we have with other people, whether positive or negative. These connections can have a significant impact on our lives and can even lead to spiritual bondage if they are unhealthy or ungodly. Breaking soul ties is an important step towards experiencing spiritual freedom and wholeness.

Here are some principles related to breaking soul ties:

1. Identify unhealthy soul ties: Unhealthy soul ties can include relationships marked by co-dependency, emotional manipulation, and even sexual sin. It is important to identify and acknowledge these connections in order to break free from their negative effects.
2. Confess and repent: Confessing and repenting of any sinful actions or attitudes related to these relationships is an important step in breaking soul ties. This includes asking God for forgiveness and taking steps to make things right with any individuals involved.
3. Cut off contact: In some cases, it may be necessary to cut off contact with individuals who have been involved in unhealthy soul ties. This can be a difficult but necessary step towards freedom and healing.
4. Seek healing and restoration: Healing and restoration are possible through the power of the Holy Spirit. This can include seeking counsel from a trusted pastor or spiritual mentor, prayer and fasting, and surrendering our emotions and relationships to God.
5. Embrace healthy relationships: Embracing healthy relationships based on love, respect, and godly principles can help to break negative soul ties and promote spiritual freedom. This includes building strong relationships with family, friends, and members of our faith community.

By breaking unhealthy soul ties and embracing healthy relationships, we can experience spiritual freedom and wholeness. Through the power of the Holy Spirit and the truth of God's Word, we can break free from the negative effects of unhealthy relationships and live the abundant life that God has planned for us.

Forgiveness and healing

Forgiveness and healing are essential keys to experiencing spiritual freedom. Unforgiveness and emotional wounds can lead to spiritual bondage and hinder our growth in Christ. Here are some principles related to forgiveness and healing:

1. Recognize the need for forgiveness: Forgiveness is not always easy, but it is necessary for spiritual and emotional health. It is important to recognize the need for forgiveness in our own lives and to extend forgiveness to others who have hurt us.
2. Surrender to God: Forgiveness and healing are processes that require surrender to God. We need to surrender our pain, anger, and bitterness to Him and trust in His ability to heal us and those who have hurt us.
3. Confess and repent: Confessing our own sins and repenting of them is important for spiritual and emotional healing. We also need to be willing to forgive those who have sinned against us and release them from any debt we may feel they owe us.
4. Seek healing: Healing is a process that requires intentionality and effort. This may involve seeking counsel from a trusted pastor, friend or attending support groups, or engaging in spiritual practices such as prayer and fasting.
5. Embrace grace: Forgiveness and healing are possible through the grace of God. It is important to remember that we are not expected to achieve these things on our

own, but that we can rely on God's, grace and strength to guide us through the process.

By embracing forgiveness and healing, we can experience spiritual freedom and live the abundant life that God has planned for us. Through the power of the Holy Spirit and the truth of God's Word, we can break free from the bondage of unforgiveness and emotional wounds and live a life of joy, peace, and wholeness. Be encouraged by these verses:

1. Recognize the need for forgiveness: "For if you forgive other people when they sin against you, your heavenly Father will also forgive you." – Matthew 6:14
2. Surrender to God: "Cast all your anxiety on him because he cares for you." – 1 Peter 5:7
3. Confess and repent: "Therefore confess your sins to each other and pray for each other so that you may be healed. The prayer of a righteous person is powerful and effective." – James 5:16
4. Seek healing: "He heals the broken-hearted and binds up their wounds." – Psalm 147:3

Walking in the Spirit

Walking in the Spirit is a key to experiencing spiritual freedom. When we walk in the Spirit, we are led by the Holy Spirit and empowered to live a life that is pleasing to God. Here are some principles related to walking in the Spirit:

1. Seek God's will: Walking in the Spirit begins with seeking God's will. This requires spending time in prayer

and studying His Word to gain a better understanding of His character and desires for our lives.
2. Surrender to the Holy Spirit: Surrendering to the Holy Spirit means yielding to His guidance and allowing Him to lead us in all areas of our lives. This requires humility and a willingness to submit to His authority.
3. Live by faith: Walking in the Spirit requires living by faith rather than by our own understanding or abilities. We need to trust in God's promises and rely on His strength to guide us through life's challenges.
4. Develop spiritual disciplines: Developing spiritual disciplines such as prayer, worship, and fasting help us to stay connected to God and grow in our relationship with Him. These disciplines also help us to hear the Holy Spirit's guidance more clearly.
5. Avoid sin and temptation: Walking in the Spirit means avoiding sin and temptation that can lead us away from God. We need to be intentional about setting boundaries and avoiding situations that may lead us into sin.

By walking in the Spirit, we can experience spiritual freedom and live a life that honors God. Through the power of the Holy Spirit, we can overcome the bondage of sin and live a life that is characterized by love, joy, peace, patience, kindness, goodness, faithfulness, gentleness, and self-control (Galatians 5:22-23). Here are some scripture to meditate on:

1. Seek God's will: "Trust in the Lord with all your heart and lean not on your own understanding; in all your ways submit to him, and he will make your paths straight." – Proverbs 3:5-6

2. Surrender to the Holy Spirit: "But if you are led by the Spirit, you are not under the law." – Galatians 5:18
3. Live by faith: "And without faith it is impossible to please God, because anyone who comes to him must believe that he exists and that he rewards those who earnestly seek him." – Hebrews 11:6
4. Develop spiritual disciplines: "But grow in the grace and knowledge of our Lord and Savior Jesus Christ. To him be glory both now and forever! Amen." – 2 Peter 3:18
5. Avoid sin and temptation: "Submit yourselves, then, to God. Resist the devil, and he will flee from you." – James 4:7

"And do not give the devil a foothold." – Ephesians 4:27

"For though we live in the world, we do not wage war as the world does. The weapons we fight with are not the weapons of the world. On the contrary, they have divine power to demolish strongholds." – 2 Corinthians 10:3-4

Living in Spiritual Freedom

Maintaining deliverance

Deliverance is not the be all end all, once deliverance has taken place, there comes the responsibility to maintain that status, but the reward is that freedom is sweet. Therefore, if you desire to stay in that bliss of freedom, you have to play your part. Living in spiritual freedom involves maintaining the deliverance that has been received. It requires a continuous effort to keep one's mind, body, and spirit free from the influences of the enemy. Here are some key principles for maintaining deliverance:

1. Guard your heart: "Above all else, guard your heart, for everything you do flows from it." – Proverbs 4:23
2. Walk in the Spirit: "So I say, walk by the Spirit, and you will not gratify the desires of the flesh." – Galatians 5:16
3. Stay rooted in the Word of God: "I have hidden your word in my heart that I might not sin against you." – Psalm 119:11
4. Remain in fellowship with other believers: "And let us consider how we may spur one another on toward love and good deeds, not giving up meeting together, as some are in the habit of doing, but encouraging one another." – Hebrews 10:24-25
5. Continue to repent and forgive: "If we confess our sins, he is faithful and just and will forgive us our sins and purify us from all unrighteousness." – 1 John 1:9
6. Stay alert and be vigilant: "Be alert and of sober mind. Your enemy the devil prowls around like a roaring lion

looking for someone to devour. Resist him, standing firm in the faith, because you know that the family of believers throughout the world is undergoing the same kind of sufferings." – 1 Peter 5:8-9

By following these principles and seeking the Lord daily, one can maintain the freedom that has been received through deliverance and live a life pleasing to God

Growing in Christlikeness

Living in spiritual freedom involves growing in Christlikeness. When we surrender our lives to Jesus Christ, we become new creations in Him, and the Holy Spirit begins to transform us from the inside out. Here are some key principles for growing in Christlikeness:

1. Seek to know Christ: "I want to know Christ—yes, to know the power of his resurrection and participation in his sufferings, becoming like him in his death" – Philippians 3:10
2. Cultivate a personal relationship with God through prayer and the study of His Word: "Draw near to God, and he will draw near to you." – James 4:8
3. Allow the Holy Spirit to work in your life: "But the fruit of the Spirit is love, joy, peace, forbearance, kindness, goodness, faithfulness, gentleness and self-control." – Galatians 5:22-23
4. Serve others: "For even the Son of Man did not come to be served, but to serve, and to give his life as a ransom for many." – Mark 10:45

5. Practice humility: "Do nothing out of selfish ambition or vain conceit. Rather, in humility value others above yourselves" – Philippians 2:3
6. Pursue holiness: "But just as he who called you is holy, so be holy in all you do" – 1 Peter 1:15

By following these principles and seeking the Lord daily, we can grow in Christlikeness and become more like Him. As we live in spiritual freedom and grow in our relationship with Christ, we will experience the abundant life that He promised us.

Helping others find deliverance

Living in spiritual freedom also involves helping others find deliverance. As Christians, we are called to share the gospel and help others come to a saving knowledge of Jesus Christ. Here are some key principles for helping others find deliverance:

1. Pray for the person: "And pray in the Spirit on all occasions with all kinds of prayers and requests. With this in mind, be alert and always keep on praying for all the Lord's people." – Ephesians 6:18
2. Share the gospel: "Therefore go and make disciples of all nations, baptizing them in the name of the Father and of the Son and of the Holy Spirit" – Matthew 28:19
3. Minister deliverance in love: "Above all, love each other deeply, because love covers over a multitude of sins." – 1 Peter 4:8

4. Encourage the person to seek God and walk in obedience: "If you love me, keep my commands." – John 14:15
5. Provide support and discipleship: "Therefore encourage one another and build each other up, just as in fact you are doing." – 1 Thessalonians 5:11
6. Refer the person to experienced deliverance ministers or pastors, if needed: "Do not neglect the gift that is in you, which was given to you through prophecy when the body of elders laid their hands on you." – 1 Timothy 4:14

By following these principles, we can help others find deliverance and grow in their relationship with Christ. As we share the love of Christ with others, we can bring hope and healing to those who are struggling with bondage and oppression.

Breaking Satanic Covenants

The primary purpose of this chapter is to shed light on the dark and complex topic of satanic covenants while offering hope and solutions through biblical teachings and the power of prayer. This chapter aims to equip you with the knowledge, faith, and practical tools needed to break free from these covenants and experience spiritual deliverance and restoration.

What is a Satanic Covenant?

A satanic covenant refers to an agreement or pact made with demonic or satanic forces, either consciously or unconsciously, which typically involves a commitment, allegiance, or binding arrangement with malevolent spiritual entities. These covenants can take various forms, including blood oaths, rituals, or other practices that align with satanic or occult beliefs.

Context and Implications

Satanic covenants are often associated with occult practices, rituals, or ceremonies that aim to invoke or align with demonic powers. Such covenants might be established through rituals involving blood sacrifices, recitations, or binding ceremonies. In many religious and spiritual contexts, particularly within Christianity, satanic covenants are seen as a grave spiritual danger, leading to bondage, oppression, and separation from God's grace.

Why They're Concerning

1. Spiritual Bondage: Entering into a satanic covenant can lead to spiritual bondage, where individuals are bound to the demonic entities with whom they've made agreements. This can manifest in oppressive influences, compulsive behaviors, or other signs of demonic control.
2. Legal Ground for Oppression: In spiritual warfare contexts, satanic covenants can be seen as providing legal ground for demonic forces to oppress or exert control over an individual, family, or community.
3. Impact on Relationships and Legacy: These covenants may have far-reaching effects, potentially impacting relationships, family dynamics, and generational legacies. It's believed that the consequences of these agreements can be passed down, affecting future generations.
4. Spiritual Consequences: For those who believe in the Christian gospel, entering into a satanic covenant represents a fundamental turning away from God's will and grace, leading to spiritual consequences like loss of salvation, inner turmoil, and spiritual separation from God.

Examples and Origins

Satanic covenants can originate from various sources:

- Occult Practices: Involvement in occult activities, witchcraft, or rituals that explicitly invite demonic entities.
- Unintentional Agreements: Individuals may enter into covenants without realizing it, through practices that seem benign but are spiritually dangerous.
- Inherited or Ancestral Covenants: Covenants that have been established by ancestors or family members, impacting subsequent generations.

Breaking Free from Satanic Covenants

Breaking satanic covenants typically involves a combination of various actions that you have to take to set yourself free:

1. Repentance and Renunciation: Acknowledging the covenant, confessing it to God, and renouncing any allegiance to demonic forces.
2. Prayer and Spiritual Warfare: Engaging in prayer, invoking the name of Jesus, and utilizing biblical principles to break the legal ground of the covenant.
3. Community and Support: Involving other believers, church leaders, and spiritual mentors in the process to provide guidance, support, and accountability.

Overall, the concept of a satanic covenant underscores the gravity of spiritual decisions and the need for discernment and spiritual protection.

Different forms and manifestations of satanic covenants

Satanic covenants, in the context of spiritual warfare and religious beliefs, can take many forms and have varied manifestations. Here is an overview of the different types and their common characteristics:

1. Blood Covenants

Blood covenants involve rituals where blood is used as a sign of agreement or binding. The continuous practice of these rituals is the feeding of demons and strengthening the covenant. Hence, the need for persons who are seeking deliverance to desist from doing these things. This can be done through:

- Sacrifices: Offering animal or human blood to satanic or demonic entities.
- Self-Harm: Using one's own blood to seal an agreement, such as in blood oaths or rituals that use cuts or other forms of self-injury. Sometimes you will hear of people cutting themselves with razor or something sharp, that's because they are already under the influence of demons and the demons need blood. So, when they cut themselves, they are feeding demons to empower them and strengthening the covenant at the same time.
- Ceremonial Agreements: Involving blood as part of a formalized ritual, often with occult symbols or language.

2. Soul Ties

Soul ties are emotional or spiritual connections that bind individuals to others or to demonic entities. These can occur through:

- Sexual Relationships: Engaging in sexual activities with individuals involved in satanic or occult practices, creating a spiritual bond.
- Emotional Attachments: Developing deep emotional or psychological connections with those involved in dark or satanic practices.
- Spiritual Linkages: Joining in rituals or practices that create spiritual connections with demonic forces.

3. Spiritual Pacts

These covenants are formalized agreements or pacts with demonic entities. They often involve:

- Vows and Promises: Making specific promises to serve or worship a demonic entity in exchange for power, wealth, or other worldly benefits.
- Commitment Ceremonies: Rituals where individuals pledge allegiance to satanic or demonic forces, often marked by specific symbols, tattoos, or other identifying signs.
- Written Contracts: In some cases, there might be physical documents or symbols that represent the covenant.

4. Occult Practices

These are covenants formed through participation in occult activities, which can include:

- Magic and Witchcraft: Engaging in practices that seek to manipulate spiritual forces, often invoking demonic entities.
- Divination: Using tools like tarot cards, Ouija boards, or other methods to communicate with spirits or demons.
- Ritualistic Ceremonies: Participating in ceremonies that involve invocations, enchantments, or other activities that align with satanic beliefs.

5. Ancestral Covenants

These are covenants passed down through family lines, often established by ancestors. They can manifest in:

- Inherited Rituals: Family traditions or rituals that have satanic or occult origins.
- Generational Curses: Patterns of misfortune, sickness, or spiritual bondage that affect family members across generations.
- Spiritual Inheritance: Receiving items, symbols, or practices from ancestors that connect to demonic entities.

6. **Unintentional Covenants**

These are covenants entered into without explicit intent, often through:

- Influence and Exposure: Being around or influenced by individuals involved in occult or satanic practices, leading to spiritual connections.
- Participation in Activities: Taking part in events or activities that appear harmless but have hidden satanic or occult elements. E.g. taking part in challenges on social media, many of them come in the form of games but in fact have a satanic origin, your participation is your initiation and an open door to the enemy.
- False Teachings: Adhering to religious or spiritual teachings that subtly promote satanic or demonic ideologies.

The various forms and manifestations of satanic covenants highlight the complex and sometimes subtle ways in which these agreements can be formed. Awareness and discernment are crucial in recognizing and addressing them, and the process of breaking free often involves prayer, fasting, spiritual warfare, and community support.

The Impact of Satanic Covenants on Individuals, Families, and Communities

Satanic covenants, as agreements or bonds with demonic or wicked spiritual forces, can have far-reaching and detrimental effects on various levels of life. Let's explore these impacts on individuals, families, and communities.

Impact on Individuals

Satanic covenants can profoundly affect an individual's life, influencing their thoughts, behaviors, health, and spiritual well-being.

Spiritual Bondage and Oppression

- Loss of Spiritual Freedom: Individuals under satanic covenants often experience a sense of spiritual bondage, feeling controlled or oppressed by demonic forces.
- Diminished Faith: These covenants can weaken an individual's faith, leading to spiritual confusion or disorientation.

Emotional and Mental Distress

- Anxiety and Depression: Many individuals report increased levels of anxiety, depression, and other mental health issues.
- Isolation and Despair: Satanic covenants can lead to a sense of isolation and despair, with individuals feeling cut off from supportive communities. This is why it is important to seek help from others, and don't allow yourself to be in lonely places because that is what Satan wants so he can have his way with you. Loneliness and isolation are not from God. Psalm 68:6 says God puts the solitary in families, Hebrews 10:25 reminds us that we must not forsake the assembling of ourselves.

Physical Manifestations

Satan has nothing good to offer anyone, only that which is bad, and he seeks to destroy you (John 10:10). The bible reminds us that all good and perfect things come from our father (James 1:17).

- Chronic Illness and Unexplained Symptoms: Physical ailments, chronic pain, and other unexplained symptoms can be linked to satanic covenants.
- Self-Destructive Behaviors: Individuals may engage in substance abuse, self-harm, or other risky behaviors because of spiritual oppression.

Impact on Families

The effects of satanic covenants often extend beyond individuals, impacting their families and relationships.

Generational Curses and Patterns

- Family Strife: Satanic covenants can lead to increased conflict, estrangement, and breakdowns in family relationships.
- Generational Patterns: These covenants can create patterns of misfortune, addiction, or other destructive behaviors that persist through generations.

Hindrance of Family Unity

- Disrupted Relationships: Families may struggle with maintaining unity and harmony due to spiritual oppression and bondage.

- Estrangement and Isolation: Members of the family may feel isolated or estranged from each other, leading to a breakdown in communication and relationships.

Influence on Children

- Spiritual Vulnerability: Children born into families with satanic covenants may be more vulnerable to spiritual attacks or influences.
- Behavioral Problems: These covenants can lead to behavioral issues, educational difficulties, or other developmental challenges in children.

Impact on Communities

Satanic covenants can also affect broader communities, influencing social dynamics, cultural norms, and spiritual climates.

Spiritual Darkness and Oppression

- Community Division: Satanic covenants can create division within communities, leading to conflict and unrest.
- Spiritual Despair: A community's spiritual climate can be affected, leading to a sense of darkness or hopelessness.

Impact on Culture and Society

- Cultural Corruption: The influence of satanic covenants can contribute to the erosion of moral values and ethical principles within a community.
- Increased Crime and Violence: Communities affected by satanic covenants may experience higher rates of crime, violence, or other forms of social decay.

Breakdown of Social Structures

- Weakening of Institutions: Satanic covenants can undermine social and religious institutions, weakening their ability to promote positive change.
- Loss of Social Cohesion: The cohesion and unity of communities can be compromised, leading to increased fragmentation and disorder.

The impact of satanic covenants on individuals, families, and communities can be profound and destructive. Addressing these effects requires a combination of spiritual warfare, prayer, community support, and, often, professional help or therapy. By breaking these covenants and restoring spiritual freedom, individuals and communities can begin the journey toward healing and restoration.

Providing Biblical Insights into Satanic Covenants

This chapter seeks to explore the biblical understanding of covenants and how satanic covenants can form, either intentionally or unintentionally.

The Nature of Covenants

Covenants play a central role in biblical theology, representing a binding agreement between parties. Understanding the concept of covenants is crucial when exploring the formation and implications of satanic covenants. Let's explore these topics in detail.

What are Covenants in a Biblical Context?

A covenant in the biblical context is a sacred agreement or contract, often between God and humanity, that is both relational and legally binding. It signifies a commitment and involves promises, stipulations, and consequences for breaking the covenant. The Hebrew word for covenant, *"berith,"* and the Greek word, *"diathēkē,"* emphasize the binding nature of these agreements. Covenants often involve symbols or rituals that signify the formalization of the agreement.

Types of Biblical Covenants

- **Covenants with Individuals**: God made covenants with key figures like Noah, Abraham, and David. Each covenant had specific promises and responsibilities.
- **Covenants with Nations**: God established covenants with the nation of Israel, notably through Moses, detailing laws and regulations (e.g., the Mosaic Covenant).
- **The New Covenant**: In the New Testament of the bible, the New Covenant through Jesus Christ represents the ultimate covenant, emphasizing forgiveness, redemption, and a new relationship with God.

Characteristics of Biblical Covenants

- **Mutual Commitments**: Biblical covenants typically involve commitments from both sides, with God providing promises and individuals or nations required to uphold specific obligations.
- **Symbols and Rituals**: Biblical covenants often involve symbols, such as the rainbow for Noah's covenant, or rituals, such as circumcision in the covenant with Abraham, and the new covenant of the Lord's Supper in the New Testament with Jesus and his disciples.
- **Blessings and Curses**: Covenants come with blessings for obedience and curses or consequences for breaking the covenant (Deuteronomy 28).

Formation of Satanic Covenants

Satanic covenants are agreements with demonic or satanic forces, made consciously or unconsciously. They can be formed through:

- Occult Rituals: Involvement in rituals that invoke demonic powers, often requiring a symbolic or literal sacrifice.
- Pacts and Vows: Making formal promises to demonic entities, sometimes for personal gain or power.
- Inherited or Ancestral Covenants: Covenants passed down from previous generations, often established through family traditions or occult practices.
- Unintentional Formation: Through exposure to occult practices or joining groups with hidden satanic influences.

Maintenance of Satanic Covenants

Satanic covenants are maintained through continued engagement with demonic practices, further ritualistic commitments, or a persistent refusal to repent and renounce the covenant.

- Binding Symbols and Artifacts: These covenants may involve physical symbols or artifacts that serve as reminders or reinforcement of the agreement.
- Reinforcement through Rituals: Regular participation in occult ceremonies or rituals can strengthen the covenant.

- Influence and Control: Demonic entities often maintain control over individuals through fear, manipulation, or intimidation, keeping the covenant intact.

The Spiritual and Legal Implications

Spiritual Implications

- Spiritual Bondage: Satanic covenants create spiritual bondage, limiting individuals' freedom and exposing them to demonic oppression.
- Separation from God: Such covenants represent a turn away from God, resulting in spiritual separation and a disrupted relationship with Him.
- Emotional and Mental Turmoil: The spiritual oppression associated with these covenants often leads to emotional and mental distress.

Legal Implications

In the context of spiritual warfare, satanic covenants can be seen as giving "legal ground" to demonic forces, allowing them to oppress or control individuals.

- Binding Contracts: If these covenants involve formalized agreements or symbols, they can act as binding contracts, requiring a deliberate and intentional process to break.
- Generational Impact: The legal implications may extend to future generations, leading to patterns of bondage, curses, or inherited spiritual oppression.

Understanding the nature of covenants in a biblical context provides a framework for comprehending how satanic covenants are formed and maintained, along with their profound spiritual and legal implications. Breaking these covenants requires focused spiritual warfare, prayer, and the transformative power of God's grace through Jesus Christ.

Satanic covenants, whether entered into intentionally or not, can have profound effects on an individual's life, as well as on their family and community. Recognizing the signs of these covenants is crucial for identifying the presence of demonic oppression and taking steps toward spiritual deliverance.

Signs of the existence of Satanic covenants

Satanic covenants can manifest in a variety of symptoms affecting a person's body, mind, and spirit. Here are common signs to watch for:

Physical Symptoms

- Chronic Illness and Unexplained Ailments: Recurrent or chronic health issues without clear medical explanations.
- Fatigue and Lethargy: Persistent tiredness or lack of energy, despite adequate rest.
- Unusual Physical Sensations: Sensations like burning, tingling, or heaviness that lack a medical basis.

Emotional Symptoms

- Anxiety and Depression: High levels of anxiety, depression, or emotional instability.
- Sudden Mood Swings: Rapid shifts in mood without apparent cause.
- Fear and Paranoia: Unexplained feelings of fear or paranoia, particularly regarding spiritual matters.

Spiritual Symptoms

- Loss of Spiritual Joy: A sense of spiritual dryness, with little or no joy in faith-based activities.
- Resistance to Prayer and Worship: A strong aversion to prayer, worship, or other spiritual disciplines.
- Spiritual Confusion: Difficulty discerning God's voice or experiencing consistent doubt in one's faith.

Patterns of Misfortune or Recurring Negative Experiences

Satanic covenants can create patterns of misfortune or recurring negative experiences that can be challenging to break. These patterns might include:

- Repeated Financial Hardship: Continuous financial struggles or business failures, despite best efforts.
- Relationship Issues: Recurrent conflicts, breakdowns in relationships, or an inability to maintain healthy relationships.
- Legal Problems: Frequent legal issues or encounters with law enforcement.

- Accidents and Injuries: Unusual frequency of accidents or injuries, affecting oneself or family members.

Discerning Demonic Oppression and Influence

Recognizing demonic oppression involves discernment, often requiring a combination of spiritual insight and objective observation. Here are signs that suggest demonic influence:

- Voices and Hallucinations: Hearing voices or experiencing visual hallucinations that encourage harmful or destructive behavior.
- Unusual Phenomena: Unexplained occurrences, such as objects moving, electrical disturbances, or other paranormal events.
- Compulsion and Addiction: Strong compulsions toward destructive behaviors, like substance abuse, self-harm, or other addictions.
- Violent Outbursts: Uncharacteristic or extreme anger and violence without clear provocation.

Recognizing the signs of satanic covenants is a crucial step toward addressing their impact. The symptoms and patterns mentioned above can indicate the presence of demonic oppression, requiring focused spiritual intervention, prayer, and deliverance. If you or someone you know exhibits these signs, it's essential to seek spiritual guidance, engage in prayer, and consider professional help if needed. Please note, as a born-again Christian you also have the ability to break covenants off your life. Ultimately, breaking satanic covenants involves addressing the root cause and relying on the power and authority of Jesus Christ for deliverance and healing.

The Authority of Christ

The foundation of our Christian faith clearly explains and emphasizes that Jesus Christ defeated Satan through His death and resurrection. Here's how this victory establishes authority over satanic forces:

- The Cross and Resurrection: Jesus's crucifixion and resurrection symbolize the ultimate triumph over sin and death, including Satan's power. Through these events, Jesus rendered Satan's hold on humanity null and void.
- Fulfilment of Prophecy: Biblical prophecies, such as Genesis 3:15, foreshadow the defeat of Satan through the "seed of the woman." Jesus's victory is the fulfilment of these prophecies, confirming His dominion over all demonic forces.
- Christ's Reconciliation with God: Jesus reconciled humanity to God, removing the barrier of sin and enabling a restored relationship. This reconciliation empowers believers to reclaim spiritual authority and reject satanic covenants.

The Power of His Name in Spiritual Warfare

The name of Jesus carries immense power in spiritual warfare. This power is derived from His identity as the Son of God and His victory over Satan. Here's how the name of Jesus is used to confront demonic forces:

- Authority to Cast Out Demons: Throughout the New Testament, Jesus's name is used to drive out demons and break spiritual strongholds. The apostles and early believers often invoked His name to confront and defeat evil spirits.
- Promises in Scripture: Passages like Philippians 2:9-11 declare that Jesus's name is above all names, reinforcing His supreme authority. John 14:13-14 and Matthew 28:18-20 also affirm the power of His name in prayer and spiritual action.
- The Weapon of Prayer: Invoking the name of Jesus during prayer and spiritual warfare aligns believers with His authority. This practice is a powerful tool for breaking satanic covenants and reclaiming spiritual freedom.

Biblical Examples of Deliverance from Demonic Forces

The Bible is filled with accounts of Jesus and His disciples delivering people from demonic oppression. These stories illustrate the power of Jesus's authority and the effectiveness of His name in spiritual warfare. Here are key examples:

- The Gerasene Demoniac (Mark 5:1-20): Jesus encounters a man possessed by a legion of demons. By

His command, Jesus drives the demons into a herd of swine, demonstrating His supreme authority over even the most formidable demonic forces.
- The Syrophoenician Woman's Daughter (Mark 7:24-30): A Gentile woman seeks Jesus's help for her demon-possessed daughter. Jesus heals the daughter with a word, showing that faith in His authority is sufficient for deliverance.
- The Boy with a Demon (Matthew 17:14-21): When the disciples struggle to cast out a demon from a boy, Jesus steps in and delivers him. This event underscores that faith and reliance on Jesus's authority are key to successful deliverance.
- Paul and the Slave Girl (Acts 16:16-18): The Apostle Paul encounters a slave girl with a spirit of divination. Using the name of Jesus, he commands the spirit to leave, demonstrating that believers can exercise spiritual authority through Jesus's name.

Understanding the authority of Christ is critical for engaging in spiritual warfare and breaking satanic covenants. His victory over Satan, the power of His name, and the biblical examples of deliverance form a solid foundation for confronting and overcoming demonic forces. By embracing these truths, believers can confidently move forward in their journey toward deliverance and spiritual freedom.

Scriptural Promises for Freedom

One of the key elements in breaking satanic covenants and experiencing deliverance is understanding and claiming the scriptural promises for freedom. This chapter delves into the Bible's assurances of liberation, guides you on how to claim these promises, and highlights the crucial role of faith in the process.

Promises of Liberation and Freedom in the Bible

The Bible is filled with promises that affirm God's desire for His people to live in spiritual freedom, liberated from the bondage of sin and demonic oppression. Here are some significant scriptural promises that emphasize this:

- Freedom in Christ (John 8:36): "So if the Son sets you free, you will be free indeed." This verse encapsulates the essence of freedom through Jesus Christ. It assures us as believers that true liberation comes from Christ alone.
- Deliverance from Bondage (Colossians 1:13-14): "For he has rescued us from the dominion of darkness and brought us into the kingdom of the Son he loves, in whom we have redemption, the forgiveness of sins." This passage speaks to God's deliverance from the dominion of darkness into the kingdom of light.
- Victory Over Satan (Romans 16:20): "The God of peace will soon crush Satan under your feet." This promise is a declaration of God's ultimate victory over Satan,

reinforcing that believers can claim victory over satanic covenants.
- Freedom from Fear (2 Timothy 1:7): "For God has not given us a spirit of fear, but of power and love and a sound mind." This verse emphasizes that fear has no place in the life of a believer, further strengthening the call to spiritual freedom.

How Believers Can Claim These Promises

Claiming scriptural promises for freedom involves both understanding and applying them to one's life. Here are steps believers can take to claim these promises:

- Identify the Promises: Study the Bible to identify verses and passages that speak to freedom, liberation, and deliverance. A comprehensive understanding of these promises provides a solid foundation for faith-based action.
- Pray with Authority: When praying for deliverance or to break satanic covenants, use the scriptural promises as a basis for your prayers. Declare God's promises with confidence, knowing that they are rooted in His word.
- Renounce Satanic Agreements: As part of claiming God's promises, believers must renounce any ties or agreements with demonic forces. This involves confessing and repenting of any involvement in satanic covenants, whether intentional or unintentional.
- Invoke the Name of Jesus: The name of Jesus is powerful in spiritual warfare. Invoke His name when

claiming scriptural promises, reinforcing the authority He has over all demonic forces.
- Stand in Faith: Claiming promises requires unwavering faith. Even when circumstances seem challenging, stand firm in the belief that God's promises are true and effective.

The Role of Faith in Breaking Covenants

Faith plays a central role in breaking satanic covenants and experiencing spiritual deliverance. Here's why faith is crucial:

- Faith as the Foundation: The Bible emphasizes that faith is the foundation for a relationship with God and the means by which we as believers access His promises. Hebrews 11:1 defines faith as "confidence in what we hope for and assurance about what we do not see."
- Faith in Action: Faith is not passive; it requires action. James 2:17 states that "faith by itself, if it is not accompanied by action, is dead." To break satanic covenants, believers must act on their faith through prayer, repentance, and renunciation.
- Faith Overcomes Fear: Faith enables believers to overcome fear and doubt, key obstacles in breaking satanic covenants. When believers trust in God's promises, they gain the courage to confront and defeat spiritual darkness.
- Faith Leads to Victory: The Bible consistently shows that faith leads to victory over spiritual forces. 1 John 5:4 declares, "For everyone born of God overcomes the

world. This is the victory that has overcome the world, even our faith."

Scriptural promises for freedom are powerful tools in the battle against satanic covenants. By understanding these promises, claiming them with authority, and standing firm in faith, believers can experience deliverance and spiritual freedom. The role of faith is paramount in this process, as it provides the confidence and assurance needed to break free from satanic covenants and embrace the freedom that Christ offers.

Understanding Prayer as Spiritual Warfare

Prayer is central to the Christian life and plays a critical role in breaking satanic covenants and achieving spiritual deliverance. This chapter explores the significance of prayer, its power in spiritual warfare, and various types of prayer that can be used to break covenants and bring about deliverance.

The Importance of Prayer in the Christian Life

Prayer is more than just communication with God—it is a spiritual lifeline that connects believers to the divine and provides strength, guidance, and support. Here's why prayer is crucial in the Christian life:

- Relationship with God: Prayer is the primary way believers build and maintain their relationship with God. It allows for intimacy, communication, and a deeper connection with the divine.
- Expression of Faith: Prayer demonstrates a believer's faith and trust in God's power and promises. It is a declaration of dependence on God for guidance and strength.
- Source of Strength and Comfort: Through prayer, believers receive comfort, encouragement, and strength, especially in times of spiritual warfare and personal challenges.

- Channel for God's Will: Prayer aligns believers with God's will and allows them to seek divine guidance and wisdom. It is through prayer that believers can discern God's purposes and direction for their lives.

How Prayer Can Break Satanic Covenants

Prayer is a powerful tool in breaking satanic covenants, as it connects us to the ultimate source of spiritual authority: Jesus Christ. Here are ways in which prayer can break these covenants:

- Invoking the Name of Jesus: When we pray in the name of Jesus, we are invoking His authority and power. This act is key to breaking satanic covenants, as it reminds demonic forces of their ultimate defeat.
- Renouncing and Repenting: Prayer allows us to renounce any ties or agreements with demonic forces and repent of any involvement in satanic covenants. This act breaks the spiritual and legal ground that these covenants hold.
- Engaging in Spiritual Warfare: Prayer is a form of spiritual warfare that allows us to combat demonic oppression and reclaim spiritual territory. Through prayer, we can confront and overcome satanic forces.
- Seeking God's Protection: Prayer serves as a means to seek God's protection and covering, essential when breaking satanic covenants. We can pray for divine protection over themselves, our families, and our communities.

Different Types of Prayer (Intercessory, Warfare, etc.)

Prayer comes in various forms, each with a unique role in spiritual warfare and breaking satanic covenants. Here are some common types of prayer and how they contribute to deliverance:

- **Intercessory Prayer**: This type of prayer involves praying on behalf of others. Intercessory prayer is powerful in spiritual warfare, as it allows us to stand in the gap for those who may be struggling with satanic covenants or oppression. Through intercession, we can call upon God's power to bring deliverance to others.
- **Warfare Prayer**: Warfare prayer is aggressive and focused on confronting and defeating demonic forces. This type of prayer involves using spiritual authority to rebuke and cast out demonic entities, often accompanied by declarations of God's promises and the authority of Jesus.
- **Confession and Repentance**: These prayers involve confessing sins, repenting of wrongdoings, and seeking God's forgiveness. In the context of satanic covenants, confession and repentance are vital for breaking spiritual bondage and restoring a right relationship with God.
- **Prayers of Protection**: These prayers seek God's protection and covering. They are crucial when confronting satanic covenants, as they help to shield us from spiritual retaliation or attacks.
- **Prayers of Thanksgiving and Praise**: Giving thanks and praising God is a powerful form of prayer that shifts the focus from fear to faith. These prayers affirm God's

goodness and reinforce a sense of victory over satanic forces.

Understanding prayer as spiritual warfare is essential for breaking satanic covenants and achieving spiritual deliverance. Prayer connects believers to the power and authority of Jesus Christ, allowing them to confront and defeat demonic forces. By embracing different types of prayer—intercessory, warfare, confession, and others—believers can effectively engage in spiritual warfare and break free from the bondage of satanic covenants. Ultimately, prayer is the key to reclaiming spiritual freedom and experiencing the transformative power of God's grace and deliverance.

Introduction to the 8 Prayer Watches

In spiritual warfare and deliverance, timing is everything. Throughout Scripture, we see that God moves at appointed times—and so does the enemy. Understanding the 8 prayer watches equips believers to strategically position themselves in prayer, intercession, and warfare according to divine timing.

The Bible divides the day and night into eight three-hour segments—what we now call the 8 prayer watches. These watches mark specific times where God moved mightily, angels intervened, and the enemy launched attacks. Jesus Himself referenced these watches, and the early Church used them to align with the rhythms of heaven.

This section is designed to help you discern the spiritual atmosphere of each watch and respond accordingly—whether it be through worship, warfare, intercession, prophetic declaration, or rest. Each watch carries its own purpose and prophetic power, offering unique opportunities to engage with God, cancel the assignments of darkness, and birth His promises.

As you study and pray through these watches, remember this: you are not just praying randomly—you are standing watch, as a spiritual gatekeeper over your life, family, ministry, and territory. These insights are not laws, but spiritual tools to help you walk in greater victory, strategy, and intimacy with God.

Use this guide to help you:

- Strengthen your prayer life
- Identify divine timing
- Understand the movement of spiritual forces
- Position yourself for breakthrough, protection, and divine alignment

Let the Holy Spirit lead you into deeper revelation as you discover the power of praying within God's appointed times. Deliverance is not just about what you pray—but *when* you pray. Here's a breakdown of the 8 Prayer Watches:

🕐 First Watch (6 PM – 9 PM)

Evening Watch / Time of Quiet Reflection

> **Scriptural reference**: Genesis 24:63, Mark 1:32
> **Purpose**:

- Time to meditate on the Word and reflect on the day
- Offer thanksgiving for the day

- Pray for peace, protection, and rest through the night
- Seal your evening with worship and preparation for dreams and divine downloads

🕒 Second Watch (9 PM – 12 AM)

Watch of Deepening Intimacy / Warfare Watch

Scriptural reference: Exodus 12:29, Judges 16:3
Purpose:
- Engage in spiritual warfare, dismantling plans of the enemy
- Pray against demonic activity, witchcraft, and generational curses
- Ask God for insight through dreams and night visions
- Cover your household in protection

🕐 Third Watch (12 AM – 3 AM)

Watch of Power / Witching Hour

Scriptural reference: Acts 16:25-26, Luke 12:38
Purpose:
- This is a highly spiritual time (both demonic and divine activity peak)
- Time for deliverance prayers, intercession, and decrees
- Bind and cast down strongholds
- Worship and cry out for mercy, breakthrough, and divine intervention

🕒 Fourth Watch (3 AM – 6 AM)

Divine Visitations / Early Morning Watch

> **Scriptural reference**: Matthew 14:25, Exodus 14:24
> **Purpose**:

- Watch for angelic visitations, instructions, and impartation
- Pray for the dawning of new mercies and fresh anointing
- Declare God's promises and command your morning (Psalm 5:3)
- Birth new things in the spirit (e.g., ministry, healing, revival)

🕘 Fifth Watch (6 AM – 9 AM)

Resurrection Power / Blessing the Day

> **Scriptural reference**: Mark 16:2, Psalm 2:7-9
> **Purpose**:

- Pray for resurrection power and new life
- Declare the will of God over your day
- Speak blessings, favor, and strength over your family, workplace, and community
- Time to receive divine downloads for daily assignments

🕐 Sixth Watch (9 AM – 12 PM)

Holy Spirit Empowerment / Harvest Time

Scriptural reference: Acts 2:15, Matthew 27:45
Purpose:
- Ask for the infilling of the Holy Spirit
- Pray for divine appointments, souls to be saved
- Call in the harvest and evangelistic power
- War for righteousness and justice in your nation or community

🕐 Seventh Watch (12 PM – 3 PM)

Hour of the Cross / Forgiveness & Rest

Scriptural reference: Matthew 27:45-50
Purpose:
- Reflect on the sacrifice of Jesus
- Intercede for salvation and deliverance for others
- Pray prayers of repentance and forgiveness
- Release bitterness, offenses, and burdens

🕒 Eighth Watch (3 PM – 6 PM)

Hour of Rejoicing / Preparation for Night

Scriptural reference: Acts 3:1, Matthew 27:46
Purpose:
- Time of miracles and healing (Peter healed the lame man)
- Prepare spiritually for the night
- Rejoice in answered prayers
- Pray for alignment with God's evening plans

Introduction to Fasting Plans

Fasting is a powerful, biblical discipline that opens the door to divine intervention, spiritual clarity, personal transformation, and supernatural deliverance. In Scripture, fasting was often used in times of desperation, warfare, consecration, and preparation. Whether to seek God's direction, break strongholds, or usher in revival, fasting has always been a sacred act of humility before God.

This section of *Nuggets of Deliverance* provides practical fasting plans to help you go deeper in your spiritual walk and gain strategic victories in key areas of your life. These plans are not meant to be rigid rules but spiritual guides—designed to help you engage in intentional prayer and fasting that is rooted in Scripture and led by the Holy Spirit.

Each fasting plan addresses different issues such as deliverance from generational bondage, healing, marital alignment, financial breakthrough, clarity in purpose, and activation of spiritual gifts. You'll find:

- The type and duration of the fast
- Dietary guidelines
- Specific prayer focuses and scriptures
- Suggested prayer watch times for each day

Fasting, when combined with focused prayer and the Word of God, sharpens your spiritual discernment and helps dismantle the plans of the enemy. As you embark on these fasts, seek the Lord earnestly. Allow the Holy Spirit to direct your heart and adjust these plans according to your physical capacity, spiritual maturity, and divine leading.

Remember:

"Is not this the fast that I have chosen? To loose the bands of wickedness, to undo the heavy burdens, and to let the oppressed go free..." (Isaiah 58:6)

Let this guide serve as a tool for empowerment, alignment, and freedom as you grow in your authority and victory through Christ. You are not fasting in vain—God will respond.

1. **Esther Fast (3-Day Absolute Fast)**

Duration: 3 days

Purpose: Deliverance, favor, divine intervention

Issues: Life-threatening situations, court cases, major decisions

Type: Absolute (No food or water unless medically unable)

Dietary Plan: Water only (if not doing absolute); resume light fruits/vegetables afterward

Scriptures: Esther 4:16, Joel 2:12-13

Prayer Watches:

- 6 AM–9 AM: Surrender, consecration
- 9 PM–12 AM: War against spiritual opposition

2. Daniel Fast (21-Day Consecration Fast)

Duration: 21 days

Purpose: Clarity, revelation, spiritual growth, breaking strongholds

Issues: Mental fog, spiritual stagnation, addiction, generational bondage

Type: Partial Fast

Dietary Plan:

- No meat, sweets, dairy, bread, or processed foods
- Eat fruits, vegetables, nuts, legumes, whole grains, and water

Scriptures: Daniel 10:2–3, Isaiah 58

Prayer Watches:

- 3 AM–6 AM: Seek divine strategies
- 12 PM–3 PM: Declare breakthroughs over family, ministry

3. Elijah Fast (40-Day Purpose Fast)

Duration: 40 days

Purpose: Strength, prophetic insight, re-alignment with divine destiny

Issues: Depression, burnout, unclear purpose

Type: Progressive (Liquid fast for 3 days, Daniel for 7 days, 1 meal/day for remainder)

Dietary Plan:

- Days 1–3: Fresh juices and broths
- Days 4–10: Daniel Fast
- Days 11–40: 1 light plant-based meal in the evening

Scriptures: 1 Kings 19:7-8, Romans 12:1–2

Prayer Watches:

- 12 AM–3 AM: Personal transformation
- 6 PM–9 PM: Receive fresh vision

4. Watchman Fast (7-Day Intercessory Fast)

Duration: 7 days

Purpose: Prophetic intercession, regional breakthrough, standing in the gap

Issues: Community revival, city/nation deliverance, family salvation

Type: Time-restricted fast (Eat one meal after sunset)

Dietary Plan: Light protein-rich meal, no sweets or caffeine

Scriptures: Ezekiel 3:17, Isaiah 62:6-7

Prayer Watches:

- 12 AM–3 AM: Binding spiritual wickedness
- 6 AM–9 AM: Release of angelic help

5. Healing & Wholeness Fast (10-Day Fast)

Duration: 10 days

Purpose: Physical healing, inner healing, emotional restoration

Issues: Chronic illness, trauma, forgiveness, grief

Type: Daniel Fast

Dietary Plan: High alkaline diet (greens, fruit, herbal teas, lots of water)

Scriptures: Isaiah 58:8, James 5:16, 3 John 1:2

Prayer Watches:

- 6 AM–9 AM: Command healing scriptures
- 3 PM–6 PM: Anoint and decree wholeness over body and soul

6. Marital Destiny Fast (14-Day Fast)

Duration: 14 days

Purpose: Divine alignment for marriage, restoration, healing from past relationships

Issues: Marital delay, spouse alignment, healing from heartbreak, marriage preparation

Type: Sunrise to Sunset Fast

Dietary Plan: Light plant-based meal at sunset (avoid fried, sugary foods)

Scriptures: Genesis 2:18, Proverbs 18:22, Ruth 3, Isaiah 34:16

Prayer Watches:

- 3 AM–6 AM: Cancel spiritual spouses, declare divine alignment
- 6 PM–9 PM: Decree God-ordained relationships

7. Ministry Activation Fast (7-Day Fast)

Duration: 7 days

Purpose: Activation of spiritual gifts, launching into ministry, clarity in calling

Issues: Confusion, stagnation, fear of launching, doubt

Type: Juice or liquid fast, or 1-meal Daniel

Dietary Plan: Light soups, juices, herbal teas

Scriptures: Acts 13:2-3, 2 Timothy 1:6, Luke 4:1-14

Prayer Watches:

- 3 AM–6 AM: Receive downloads from God
- 12 PM–3 PM: Pray over assignments, mantle, and open 127oorstop of Form

Intercessory Prayer for Deliverance

Intercessory prayer plays a vital role in spiritual warfare and breaking satanic covenants. It involves standing in the gap for others and appealing to God on their behalf. This chapter explores how intercessory prayer can be used to break covenants, the role of the church and community in this process, and specific prayers and declarations for deliverance.

Praying for Others Who Are Bound by Satanic Covenants

Intercessory prayer is the act of praying for others, particularly those who cannot or do not know how to pray for themselves. When praying for people bound by satanic covenants, consider the following:

- Understanding the Need for Intercession: Individuals bound by satanic covenants may be spiritually oppressed, making it difficult for them to seek help or even recognize their need for deliverance. Intercessory prayer is crucial for breaking through this spiritual barrier.

- Praying for Deliverance and Freedom: When praying for those under demonic bondage, the focus is on breaking covenants, renouncing demonic ties, and seeking God's intervention. This involves praying for their freedom and for the chains of spiritual oppression to be broken.
- Praying for Healing and Restoration: After deliverance, individuals may need healing and restoration, both spiritually and emotionally. Intercessory prayer should encompass these aspects, seeking God's healing touch and restoration in the lives of those delivered.
- Praying for Spiritual Protection: People who have experienced deliverance may be vulnerable to spiritual attacks or retaliation from demonic forces. Intercessory prayer should include requests for divine protection and covering for these individuals.

The Role of the Church and Community in Intercessory Prayer

Intercessory prayer is most effective when it involves the collective faith and support of the church and broader spiritual community. Here's how the church and community contribute to this process:

- Corporate Prayer and Fasting: The church can engage in corporate prayer and fasting to break satanic covenants and seek deliverance for those bound by them. This collective effort can be a powerful force in spiritual warfare.
- Community Support and Accountability: After deliverance, the church and community play a critical role in providing support, accountability, and

encouragement to those seeking to maintain their spiritual freedom.
- Teaching and Discipleship: The church can offer teaching and discipleship programs to help those who have been delivered grow in their faith, understand biblical principles, and build spiritual resilience.
- Outreach and Evangelism: The church can engage in outreach and evangelism to reach those who may be bound by satanic covenants, offering them hope and guidance toward deliverance through intercessory prayer.

Recommended Scriptures for Spiritual Warfare

The Bible contains numerous passages that address spiritual warfare, offering guidance, encouragement, and assurance of God's victory over darkness. These scriptures can serve as powerful tools for those engaged in spiritual warfare, breaking satanic covenants, and seeking deliverance. Here is a collection of recommended scriptures to guide you in your study and prayer life.

Scriptures Affirming God's Authority and Power

- **Ephesians 6:10-12**-"Finally, be strong in the Lord and in his mighty power. Put on the full armor of God, so that you can take your stand against the devil's schemes. For our struggle is not against flesh and blood, but against the rulers, against the authorities, against the

powers of this dark world and against the spiritual forces of evil in the heavenly realms."
- **1 John 4:4-**"You, dear children, are from God and have overcome them, because the one who is in you is greater than the one who is in the world."
- **James 4:7-8-**"Submit yourselves, then, to God. Resist the devil, and he will flee from you. Come near to God and he will come near to you."
- **Colossians 2:13-15-**"When you were dead in your sins and in the uncircumcision of your flesh, God made you alive with Christ. He forgave us all our sins, having canceled the charge of our legal indebtedness, which stood against us and condemned us; he has taken it away, nailing it to the cross. And having disarmed the powers and authorities, he made a public spectacle of them, triumphing over them by the cross."

Scriptures for Spiritual Armor and Warfare

- **Ephesians 6:13-18-**"Therefore put on the full armor of God, so that when the day of evil comes, you may be able to stand your ground, and after you have done everything, to stand. Stand firm then, with the belt of truth buckled around your waist, with the breastplate of righteousness in place, and with your feet fitted with the readiness that comes from the gospel of peace. In addition to all this, take up the shield of faith, with which you can extinguish all the flaming arrows of the evil one. Take the helmet of salvation and the sword of the Spirit, which is the word of God. And pray in the

Spirit on all occasions with all kinds of prayers and requests."

- **2 Corinthians 10:3-5-**"For though we live in the world, we do not wage war as the world does. The weapons we fight with are not the weapons of the world. On the contrary, they have divine power to demolish strongholds. We demolish arguments and every pretension that sets itself up against the knowledge of God, and we take captive every thought to make it obedient to Christ."
- **Romans 8:37-39-**"No, in all these things we are more than conquerors through him who loved us. For I am convinced that neither death nor life, neither angels nor demons, neither the present nor the future, nor any powers, neither height nor depth, nor anything else in all creation, will be able to separate us from the love of God that is in Christ Jesus our Lord."

Scriptures on Deliverance and Freedom

- **John 8:36-**"So if the Son sets you free, you will be free indeed."
- **Psalm 91:1-4-**"Whoever dwells in the shelter of the Most High will rest in the shadow of the Almighty. I will say of the Lord, 'He is my refuge and my fortress, my God, in whom I trust.' Surely he will save you from the fowler's snare and from the deadly pestilence. He will cover you with his feathers, and under his wings you will find refuge; his faithfulness will be your shield and rampart."

- **Isaiah 54:17-** "No weapon formed against you will prevail, and you will refute every tongue that accuses you. This is the heritage of the servants of the Lord, and this is their vindication from me,' declares the Lord."

Living in Freedom and Restoration

After Deliverance: Walking in Freedom

Breaking free from satanic covenants is a significant victory, but the journey doesn't end with deliverance. Living in freedom and maintaining spiritual restoration require ongoing effort and commitment. This chapter explores how to establish a daily walk with God, build spiritual disciplines to maintain freedom, and harness the power of community and support.

Establishing a Daily Walk with God

A daily walk with God is foundational for maintaining spiritual freedom and growing in faith. Here's how to cultivate this essential relationship:

- Regular Prayer and Meditation: Establish a daily routine of prayer and meditation on God's word. This practice helps to strengthen your connection with God and provides spiritual guidance and strength.
- Bible Study and Reflection: Consistently engage with Scripture, allowing it to shape your thoughts, attitudes, and behaviors. Regular Bible study helps to keep you grounded in truth and focused on God's promises.
- Listening to the Holy Spirit: Be open to the leading of the Holy Spirit, allowing Him to guide your steps and reveal God's will for your life. This attentiveness to the Spirit's voice is crucial for ongoing spiritual growth.

- Journaling and Reflection: Keep a spiritual journal to document your journey with God. Writing about your experiences, insights, and answered prayers can be a source of encouragement and a reminder of God's faithfulness.

Building Spiritual Disciplines to Maintain Freedom

Spiritual disciplines are habits and practices that help believers grow in faith and maintain spiritual freedom. Here's how to build these disciplines:

- Worship and Praise: Engage in regular worship and praise, both individually and with a church community. Worship helps to focus your heart on God and reinforces His presence in your life.
- Fasting and Spiritual Cleansing: Periodic fasting is a powerful spiritual discipline, helping to break strongholds and cleanse the soul. Fasting, combined with prayer, yields greater results than prayer alone would do, and allows for deeper spiritual focus and renewal.
- Accountability and Mentorship: Seek out a spiritual mentor or accountability partner to help guide you in your walk with God. Having someone to share your journey with can provide encouragement and support.
- Acts of Service and Giving: Practice acts of service and generosity, which help to keep you grounded in God's love and demonstrate faith in action. Serving others reinforces the values of compassion and humility.

- Consistent Repentance and Confession: Maintain a heart of repentance, regularly examining your life and confessing any sins. This discipline helps to keep your spiritual walk pure and free from the encumbrances of sin.

The Importance of Community and Support

Community and support are vital for maintaining spiritual freedom after deliverance. Here's why they are crucial and how to cultivate them:

- Engagement with a Church Community: Join a church community where you can worship, learn, and grow with other believers. The church provides spiritual nourishment, encouragement, and accountability.
- Small Groups and Bible Studies: Participate in small groups or Bible studies to foster deeper relationships and spiritual growth. These groups offer a safe space for sharing, learning, and prayer.
- Regular Fellowship and Social Connections: Build friendships and social connections within the faith community. Regular fellowship helps to strengthen your sense of belonging and provides a support network in times of need.
- Seeking Help When Needed: If you face challenges or spiritual setbacks, don't hesitate to seek help from trusted church leaders or members. Getting support early can prevent further spiritual distress and keep you on the path to freedom.

Walking in freedom after deliverance involves a commitment to a daily relationship with God, the cultivation of spiritual disciplines, and the embrace of community and support. These practices not only help to maintain spiritual freedom but also foster continued growth in faith and character. By establishing a solid foundation of prayer, Bible study, worship, and fellowship, believers can experience the fullness of life that God intends and continue to live in the freedom and restoration that come through Jesus Christ.

Restoration and Healing

Deliverance from satanic covenants marks the beginning of a new journey toward restoration and healing. This chapter explores God's promise of restoration, the process of healing emotional and spiritual wounds, and practical steps to rebuild one's life after deliverance.

God's Promise of Restoration

The Bible is filled with promises of restoration, offering hope to those who have been broken or oppressed. Here are some key scriptural references that affirm God's commitment to restoration:

- Restoration of Joy and Peace (Psalm 51:12): "Restore to me the joy of Your salvation and uphold me with a willing spirit." This verse emphasizes that God restores joy and inner peace to those who turn to Him.

- Healing and Renewal (Isaiah 61:1-3): This passage speaks of God healing the broken-hearted, proclaiming freedom to captives, and comforting those who mourn. It promises beauty for ashes and joy instead of mourning.
- Restoration of Relationships (Joel 2:25): "I will repay you for the years the locusts have eaten." This promise speaks to the restoration of lost time, resources, and relationships, assuring that God can restore what has been lost or destroyed.
- Renewed Strength (Isaiah 40:31): "But those who hope in the Lord will renew their strength." This promise indicates that God restores strength to those who trust in Him, allowing them to rise above past struggles.

Healing Emotional and Spiritual Wounds

Healing emotional and spiritual wounds is a critical aspect of restoration. These wounds can result from oppression, trauma, or past involvement with satanic covenants. Here are key steps to facilitate healing:

- Acknowledging the Wounds: Healing begins with acknowledging the presence of emotional and spiritual wounds. This involves recognizing the impact of past traumas, betrayals, or spiritual attacks on one's well-being.
- Seeking God's Healing Touch: Pray for God's healing touch to mend emotional and spiritual wounds. Ask for His comfort, peace, and restoration in the areas that have been damaged or broken.

- Professional Counselling and Support: In some cases, seeking professional counselling or therapy can aid in healing deep emotional wounds. A faith-based counsellor can offer guidance while incorporating spiritual principles into the healing process.
- Forgiveness and Reconciliation: Healing often involves forgiving those who have caused harm, including oneself. This act of forgiveness can be liberating and is key to the healing process. Reconciliation with others, when possible, can also contribute to emotional healing.
- Building Spiritual Resilience: Developing spiritual resilience through prayer, Bible study, and community support helps to strengthen the spirit and promote ongoing healing. This resilience aids in overcoming future challenges and setbacks.

Steps to Rebuild One's Life After Deliverance

After deliverance from satanic covenants, rebuilding your life involves practical steps that lead to restoration and renewal. Here are key actions to take in this process:

- Redefining Priorities: Reassess your life priorities in light of your newfound freedom. Focus on what aligns with God's will and contributes to spiritual growth and well-being.
- Establishing New Habits: Replace old habits associated with spiritual bondage with new, healthy ones. This could involve spiritual disciplines like prayer, Bible study, and fellowship, as well as lifestyle changes that promote overall health and wellness.

- Rebuilding Relationships: Work on rebuilding relationships that may have been damaged by past involvement in satanic covenants. Seek reconciliation and healing where possible, and invest in meaningful connections with family and friends.
- Finding Purpose and Direction: Explore God's purpose and calling for your life. Engage in activities and work that align with your values and contribute to personal growth and fulfillment.
- Serving Others and Giving Back: A key aspect of rebuilding involves serving others and giving back to the community. This service helps to reinforce a sense of purpose and fosters a spirit of gratitude and humility.

Restoration and healing after deliverance from satanic covenants are essential to reclaiming the fullness of life that God intends. Through God's promises, emotional and spiritual wounds can be healed, and lives can be rebuilt. By taking practical steps to rebuild relationships, establish new habits, and find purpose, individuals can experience ongoing restoration and the joy of living in spiritual freedom. Ultimately, this journey toward restoration is a testament to God's transformative power and His ability to bring beauty out of ashes.

Sharing Testimonies

One of the most powerful tools in spiritual warfare and breaking satanic covenants is the testimony—the personal story of God's deliverance and transformation in a person's life. This chapter explores the power of sharing testimonies, the impact they have on encouraging others to seek freedom through prayer, and the role of testimony in overcoming the enemy.

The Power of Sharing Personal Stories of Deliverance

Personal stories of deliverance resonate deeply with others, offering hope, encouragement, and a tangible example of God's power at work. Here's why sharing these stories is so impactful:

- Evidence of God's Power: Testimonies provide concrete evidence of God's power to transform lives, break satanic covenants, and bring about spiritual freedom. They show that deliverance is possible for anyone who seeks it.
- Creating a Connection: When people share their stories, they create a connection with others who may be experiencing similar struggles. This connection fosters empathy and opens the door for meaningful conversations about faith and deliverance.
- Breaking Stigma and Isolation: Sharing testimonies helps to break the stigma often associated with spiritual oppression. It reassures those who feel isolated or

ashamed that they are not alone and that there is a way out.
- Inspiring Hope and Courage: Hearing stories of deliverance inspires hope and courage in others, motivating them to seek their own path to freedom. It serves as a reminder that no situation is too difficult for God to overcome.

Encouraging Others to Seek Freedom Through Prayer

Testimonies are a powerful means of encouraging others to seek freedom through prayer and spiritual warfare. Here's how personal stories can inspire others to take action:

- Modelling the Power of Prayer: When someone shares their story of deliverance, they often highlight the role of prayer in their journey. This act demonstrates the effectiveness of prayer and encourages others to adopt similar practices.
- Providing Practical Guidance: Testimonies often include practical steps that individuals took to achieve deliverance. This guidance can serve as a roadmap for others seeking freedom, offering concrete actions they can take.
- Fostering a Community of Support: Sharing testimonies can create a community of support where people feel safe to share their own stories and seek help. This sense of community can be a significant source of strength and encouragement.
- Highlighting God's Faithfulness: Testimonies underscore God's faithfulness in answering prayers and

bringing deliverance. This emphasis on God's reliability encourages others to trust in Him and seek freedom through prayer.

The Role of Testimony in Overcoming the Enemy

In the context of spiritual warfare, testimonies play a crucial role in overcoming the enemy. Here's how they contribute to spiritual victory:

- Defeating the Accuser (Revelation 12:11): The Bible says, "They triumphed over him by the blood of the Lamb and by the word of their testimony." Testimonies are a powerful weapon against Satan, the accuser, demonstrating that he has no hold over those who have been redeemed by the blood of Jesus.
- Establishing Spiritual Authority: Sharing testimonies reaffirms the authority of Jesus Christ in the lives of believers. It is a declaration that demonic forces have been defeated and that God has the final say in every situation.
- Empowering Others for Spiritual Warfare: Testimonies equip others for spiritual warfare by demonstrating that the enemy can be defeated. They offer practical examples of how to stand firm in faith and use spiritual weapons to combat satanic covenants.
- Encouraging Perseverance: Overcoming the enemy often requires perseverance and endurance. Testimonies serve as a source of encouragement, reminding believers that they can overcome any challenge through God's strength.

Sharing the testimony is a powerful act of faith that has the potential to transform lives, encourage others, and overcome the enemy. Personal stories of deliverance inspire hope, foster connections, and demonstrate the power of prayer and spiritual warfare. By sharing their testimonies, believers can create a ripple effect that reaches others who are seeking freedom and restoration. Ultimately, the testimony is a testament to God's faithfulness and a vital tool in the ongoing battle against spiritual darkness and satanic covenants.

Deliverance from satanic covenants is not just a momentary event but a profound turning point that leads to a transformed life. This final section offers a call to action, encouraging readers to seek deliverance, break free from spiritual bondage, and embrace the life of freedom and restoration that God promises. It also provides words of hope and inspiration to those on this journey.

Encouragement for Readers to Pursue Deliverance

Pursuing deliverance is a bold and courageous step that requires determination, faith, and the support of a spiritual community. Here's why I am encouraging you to take this step:

- Breaking Free from Bondage: Satanic covenants create spiritual bondage, restricting you from experiencing the fullness of life. Deliverance is the pathway to breaking these chains and reclaiming spiritual freedom.
- Finding Spiritual Healing: Pursuing deliverance opens the door to healing emotional and spiritual wounds

caused by demonic oppression. It allows individuals to experience God's healing touch and restoration.
- Restoring Relationships and Purpose: Breaking satanic covenants can lead to the restoration of broken relationships and a renewed sense of purpose. It creates the opportunity for reconciliation and a fresh start.
- Embracing a New Life in Christ: Deliverance is a step toward embracing a new life in Christ, characterized by spiritual growth, joy, and freedom. It signifies a commitment to live according to God's will and walk in His ways.

An Invitation to Seek God's Help in Breaking Any Satanic Covenants

The journey to deliverance begins with an invitation to seek God's help in breaking satanic covenants. This invitation is extended to anyone who feels bound, oppressed, or hindered by demonic influences. Here's what this invitation involves:

- Recognizing the Need for God's Help: The first step is recognizing that breaking satanic covenants requires divine intervention. God's power is needed to break the spiritual and legal hold these covenants have on individuals.
- Turning to Jesus for Deliverance: Jesus is the ultimate source of deliverance and freedom. The invitation is to turn to Him, trust in His authority, and seek His help in breaking covenants and overcoming spiritual oppression.

- Engaging in Prayer and Spiritual Warfare: Seeking God's help involves engaging in prayer and spiritual warfare. This includes confessing sins, renouncing demonic ties, and invoking the name of Jesus to break the power of satanic covenants.
- Connecting with a Faith Community: An essential part of seeking God's help is connecting with a faith community that can provide support, guidance, and encouragement. This community can be a source of strength during the process of deliverance.

Final Words of Hope and Inspiration

Deliverance from satanic covenants is a journey filled with hope and the promise of spiritual freedom. Here are final words of hope and inspiration for those who are embarking on this journey:

- God's Love and Grace Are Unfailing: No matter how deep the bondage or how strong the covenants, God's love and grace are greater. He is willing and able to deliver and restore those who seek Him.
- You Are Not Alone: Many have walked this path before and found freedom. There is a community of believers who are ready to support and walk alongside you as you pursue deliverance.
- Victory Is Promised in Christ: Jesus has already won the victory over Satan and all demonic forces. By aligning with Him, you can access this victory and experience the freedom He offers.

- A New Life Awaits: Deliverance is not the end; it's the beginning of a new life filled with purpose, joy, and spiritual growth. Embrace this journey with faith, knowing that God is with you every step of the way.

Introduction to the Prayer Points

In the journey toward deliverance and spiritual freedom, prayer is not just a tool—it is a weapon. The Bible teaches us to *"pray without ceasing"* (1 Thessalonians 5:17) and to *"call upon the Lord in the day of trouble"* (Psalm 50:15). This section of *Nuggets of Deliverance* has been carefully designed to equip you with strategic prayer points for various areas of bondage, lack, and spiritual warfare.

These prayer points are not exhaustive or formulaic. Rather, they serve as a guide to help you engage with God intentionally and fervently about specific challenges or areas of your life. As you read and pray, you are encouraged to personalize these prayers, allow the Holy Spirit to lead you further, and stand firmly on the promises of God's Word.

For maximum effectiveness, pair these prayers with relevant Scriptures, fasting, and meditate on them, and declare them aloud in faith. The Word of God is alive and powerful—it sharpens your prayers and drives the enemy back (Hebrews 4:12).

Remember, true deliverance comes through Jesus Christ, and sustained victory is found in communion with Him. May these prayer points stir your spirit, sharpen your discernment, and empower you to walk in the freedom and authority Christ has already secured for you. You are not alone—God fights for you. Pray with boldness. Pray with fire. Pray with the Word.

Prayer Points to Break Witchcraft Powers

- Heavenly Father, I repent of every sin in my life that has given the enemy legal ground to operate against me. Cleanse me with the blood of Jesus. (1 John 1:9)
- Lord, I acknowledge that You are greater than any power of darkness. I put my trust in You alone, for You are my deliverer. (Psalm 91:1-2)
- In the name of Jesus, I break every curse, incantation, or spell spoken against me or my family. I declare them null and void by the power of the blood of Jesus. (Isaiah 54:17)
- Every assignment of witchcraft against my life, my health, my family, or my finances, I command you to be destroyed now in Jesus' name! (Luke 10:19)
- I dismantle every demonic altar speaking against my destiny. I call down fire from heaven to consume them in the mighty name of Jesus! (1 Kings 18:38)
- I bind every spirit of witchcraft, manipulation, and control operating against me, and I cast them into the abyss in Jesus' name. (Matthew 18:18)
- Every arrow of witchcraft fired against me, I command you to be broken and destroyed in Jesus' name! (Psalm 7:15-16)
- I break every soul tie and evil covenant formed through witchcraft manipulation or contact. I declare myself free by the power of the cross. (Colossians 2:14)
- Every negative word, enchantment, or incantation spoken over my life, I cancel you by the power of the blood of Jesus. You have no authority over me. (Numbers 23:23)

- Father, release Your holy fire to destroy every work of witchcraft and every demonic force opposing my life in Jesus' name. (Hebrews 12:29)
- I declare that no weapon formed against me shall prosper, and every tongue that rises against me in judgment, I condemn in Jesus' name. (Isaiah 54:17)
- I declare that I am more than a conqueror through Christ Jesus. Every power of witchcraft is defeated, and I walk in victory. (Romans 8:37)
- I cover myself, my family, and everything that concerns me with the blood of Jesus. No evil shall come near my dwelling. (Revelation 12:11)
- In the name of Jesus, I declare total freedom from every form of witchcraft. I walk in liberty, for whom the Son sets free is free indeed! (John 8:36)
- Lord, I thank You for breaking every chain of witchcraft in my life. I give You all the glory for my deliverance and victory. (Psalm 107:1-2)

Prayer Points for Fixing Foundations

- Heavenly Father, I come before You in repentance for any sins committed by me, my ancestors, or my family line that have corrupted my foundation. Cleanse me with the blood of Jesus. (1 John 1:9)
- Lord, I declare that You are my solid foundation. Every other foundation in my life is dismantled, and I stand on Christ, the Rock of my salvation. (1 Corinthians 3:11)
- I break every evil foundation laid in my life through ancestral covenants, idol worship, or occult practices.

Let those foundations be uprooted in the name of Jesus. (Jeremiah 1:10)

- Father, I invite You to rebuild every area of my life on the foundation of Your Word, righteousness, and truth. Establish me in Your ways. (Psalm 127:1)
- Every negative pattern, failure, or limitation in my life caused by faulty foundations, I command them to be destroyed by fire in the name of Jesus. (Ezekiel 18:20)
- I break and nullify every generational curse affecting my foundation, and I declare that they have no hold over my life in Jesus' name. (Galatians 3:13)
- Lord, uproot every evil seed planted in my life by the enemy or through my bloodline. Replace them with seeds of righteousness and blessings. (Matthew 15:13)
- Father, heal every damaged or broken foundation in my life. Restore what the enemy has stolen and bring me into alignment with Your perfect will. (Isaiah 58:12)
- I close every gateway and portal that the enemy has used to attack my foundation. I seal them with the blood of Jesus. (Revelation 12:11)
- I renounce and break every evil covenant tied to my foundation. Let every agreement with darkness be cancelled by the power of the cross. (Colossians 2:14)
- Every error in my foundation causing setbacks or failures in my life, be reversed now by the power of God in Jesus' name. (Isaiah 43:19)
- Lord, I repair every faulty foundation in my marital life. Let Your peace, love, and unity be the cornerstone of my home. (Ephesians 5:31)

- Father, rebuild the financial foundations of my life. Let every devourer of my finances be rebuked and establish me in abundance. (Malachi 3:10-11)
- Every foundational issue that has delayed or diverted my destiny, I command restoration now in Jesus' name. My destiny shall be fulfilled! (Jeremiah 29:11)
- I declare that my foundation is rebuilt in Christ, and I am free from every bondage and limitation caused by faulty foundations. I walk in victory! (John 8:36)
- I plead the blood of Jesus over my foundation, my family, and my life. Let Your protection and blessings flow in every area. (Exodus 12:13)
- Lord, I thank You for repairing and restoring my foundation. I give You all the glory for the victory You have given me. (Psalm 107:1-2)

Prayer Points for Restoration of Soul Fragments

- Heavenly Father, I come before You with a heart of repentance. Forgive me for any sin, disobedience, or wrong choices that have caused my soul to be fragmented. Cleanse me with the blood of Jesus and make me whole again. (Psalm 51:10)
- Lord, I declare that You are my shepherd and restorer. Restore my soul and heal every broken part of me. (Psalm 23:3)
- In the name of Jesus, I break every ungodly soul tie formed through relationships, trauma, or spiritual covenants. I sever these ties completely and reclaim every fragment of my soul. (1 Corinthians 6:17)

- Father, I call back every part of my soul that has been taken, stolen, or fragmented through hurt, abuse, rejection, or sin. Let every piece of my soul be restored to its rightful place in Jesus' name. (Joel 2:25)
- Lord, heal every emotional wound that caused my soul to fragment. Pour Your healing balm over my mind, will, and emotions, and bring wholeness to my being. (Jeremiah 30:17)
- I release every trauma, fear, and pain that caused my soul to break. I declare that I am free from every chain of past hurts in Jesus' name. (Isaiah 61:1)
- In the name of Jesus, I break every curse, covenant, or agreement with darkness that has caused my soul to be bound or fragmented. I nullify their power over my life by the blood of Jesus. (Colossians 2:14)
- Father, I renounce every open door in my life that allowed the enemy to steal parts of my soul. I close these doors now by the power of the Holy Spirit. (Ephesians 4:27)
- Lord, I declare that I am whole, complete, and restored in You. Let Your peace guard my heart and mind. (Colossians 2:10)
- Father, I speak peace over my mind and emotions. I command every spirit of confusion, anxiety, and unrest to leave me now in Jesus' name. (Philippians 4:7)
- Every spiritual bondage that has captured fragments of my soul, I break your hold over me now by the power of the Holy Spirit. I declare my complete freedom in Jesus' name. (Isaiah 49:24-25)

- Lord, I renounce every form of manipulation, control, or abuse that has taken parts of my soul. Restore my strength and identity in You. (Psalm 34:18)
- Father, I seal every restored fragment of my soul in Christ Jesus. Let no power of darkness access or disrupt my being again. (Ephesians 1:13)
- Holy Spirit, fill every empty space in my life where soul fragments have been lost. Restore me with Your love, power, and presence. (Romans 8:26)
- I declare that my soul belongs to the Lord Jesus. The enemy has no claim or access to my being. I am fully restored and rooted in Christ Jesus. (Ezekiel 18:4)
- Lord, I thank You for restoring every broken part of my soul. I praise You for making me whole and filling me with Your peace and joy. (Psalm 103:1-5)

Prayer Points for Destroying Demonic Altars

- Heavenly Father, I repent of any sin in my life, my family, or my bloodline that has empowered demonic altars to operate against me. Cleanse me by the blood of Jesus. (1 John 1:9)
- Lord, I declare that You are the only true and living God. Every other altar that opposes Your will in my life is powerless before You. (Exodus 20:3)
- In the name of Jesus, I renounce and reject every evil altar erected against me or my family, knowingly or unknowingly. I cancel their influence over my life. (Colossians 2:14)

- Father, I break every covenant, agreement, or dedication made on any demonic altar that speaks against my destiny. I nullify them by the blood of Jesus. (Galatians 3:13)
- I command every ancestral altar operating in my bloodline to be destroyed by fire. I disconnect myself from every evil inheritance in Jesus' name. (Lamentations 5:7)
- Lord, release Your consuming fire to destroy every demonic altar and its sacrifices working against my life. Let them be reduced to ashes in Jesus' name. (1 Kings 18:38)
- Every priest or agent assigned to service demonic altars against me, I silence and nullify their works now in Jesus' name. (Isaiah 54:17)
- Every word, curse, or enchantment spoken from demonic altars against my life, I reverse and render powerless in Jesus' name. (Numbers 23:23)
- Father, uproot every territorial altar in my home, workplace, or community that is opposing Your plans. Let Your authority reign in these places. (Jeremiah 1:10)
- Every chain, bondage, or captivity enforced by demonic altars in my life, I command you to break now in the name of Jesus. (Isaiah 10:27)
- I declare that every demonic altar has been defeated through the cross of Jesus. No altar of darkness can prevail against me. (Colossians 2:15)
- Father, I establish Your altar in my life, my home, and my family. Let Your presence, power, and blessings flow continually in these places. (Genesis 12:7)

- I cover myself, my family, and everything concerning me with the blood of Jesus. Let the blood speak against every demonic altar on my behalf. (Revelation 12:11)
- I seal every prayer and victory with the blood of Jesus. No power of darkness can rebuild or reactivate what God has destroyed in my life. (Nahum 1:9)
- Lord, I thank You for destroying every demonic altar working against me. I give You all the glory for my deliverance and freedom. (Psalm 107:1-2)

Prayer Points for Bloodline Cleansing

- Heavenly Father, I repent on behalf of my ancestors for any sins, iniquities, or evil covenants they entered into knowingly or unknowingly. Forgive us, Lord, and cleanse my bloodline with the blood of Jesus. (Leviticus 26:40-42)
- Lord, I thank You for the blood of Jesus that cleanses and purifies. I apply the blood of Jesus over my life and family, breaking every generational curse. (Hebrews 9:14)
- In the name of Jesus, I break every generational curse operating in my bloodline. I declare that every cycle of failure, sickness, poverty, and delay is broken now! (Galatians 3:13)
- Father, I nullify every evil covenant or agreement made by my ancestors that is affecting my bloodline. I declare these covenants null and void by the power of the blood of Jesus. (Colossians 2:14)

- Lord, I dismantle every evil altar in my family line. Let every sacrifice or dedication made at these altars be destroyed by fire in Jesus' name. (1 Kings 18:38)
- Father, uproot every evil seed planted in my family line that is bearing bad fruit in my life. Replace them with seeds of righteousness and blessings. (Matthew 15:13)
- Every sickness, disease, or affliction that has flowed through my bloodline, I command it to stop now in Jesus' name. By His stripes, I am healed. (Isaiah 53:5)
- I cancel every negative word, curse, or pronouncement spoken over my bloodline. I declare that no weapon formed against my family shall prosper. (Isaiah 54:17)
- In the name of Jesus, I sever every ungodly soul tie connected to my family line that is hindering my progress. I declare my freedom now! (2 Corinthians 6:17)
- Father, I reclaim every godly blessing, inheritance, and destiny that the enemy has stolen from my bloodline. Restore what has been lost in Jesus' name. (Joel 2:25)
- Every pattern of failure, delay, or stagnation in my bloodline, I command you to be broken now in the name of Jesus. I declare progress and prosperity over my life. (Deuteronomy 28:12)
- Lord, I renew my covenant with You. I declare that my bloodline belongs to Jesus Christ, and no power of darkness can claim ownership over me or my family. (Joshua 24:15)
- Father, sanctify my bloodline by Your Holy Spirit. Let Your power flow through my family tree, bringing

healing, deliverance, and restoration. (1 Thessalonians 5:23)
- Lord, I establish a new godly foundation for my bloodline. Let righteousness, peace, and joy in the Holy Spirit be the portion of my family. (Isaiah 58:12)
- Father, I thank You for cleansing my bloodline and breaking every chain. I declare that my family and I are free, restored, and blessed in Jesus' name. (Psalm 107:1-2)

Prayer Points Against Visual Hallucinations

- Heavenly Father, I repent of any sin, disobedience, or involvement in ungodly activities, knowingly or unknowingly, that may have opened the door to visual attacks. Cleanse me with the blood of Jesus. (1 John 1:9)
- Lord, I declare that You alone are Lord over my mind, eyes, and spirit. Every vision or image that is not from You, I reject and rebuke in Jesus' name. (Philippians 2:10-11)
- I bind every spirit of deception, fear, or confusion working to manipulate my vision. I command you to leave my life now in the name of Jesus. (Matthew 18:18)
- Father, I sanctify my physical and spiritual eyes with the blood of Jesus. Let my eyes see only what You desire for me to see. (Psalm 119:18)
- I plead the blood of Jesus over my mind, eyes, and thoughts. Let every evil image or hallucination be erased and rendered powerless by the blood of Jesus. (Revelation 12:11)

- I cast down every evil imagination, vision, or high thing that exalts itself against the knowledge of God. I bring every thought into obedience to Christ. (2 Corinthians 10:5)
- Lord Jesus, shine Your light into every dark area of my mind and vision. Let every work of darkness flee from me in Your mighty name. (John 8:12)
- In the name of Jesus, I break every assignment of the enemy to torment me through visual hallucinations. I declare these attacks null and void by the power of the cross. (Colossians 2:14-15)
- Father, I ask for Your peace that surpasses all understanding to guard my heart and mind. Let Your calmness take over every area of my life. (Philippians 4:7)
- Lord, I close every door that the enemy has used to access my vision, whether through trauma, fear, or occult involvement. I seal these doors with the blood of Jesus. (Ephesians 4:27)
- Father, strengthen my faith to reject the lies and illusions of the enemy. Help me to stand firm in Your truth. (Ephesians 6:16)
- I declare that I have the mind of Christ, and every attack on my vision is defeated. I am whole and complete in Jesus. (1 Corinthians 2:16)
- I rebuke the spirit of fear and its manifestations. I declare that God has given me a spirit of power, love, and a sound mind. (2 Timothy 1:7)

- Lord, release Your angels to surround me and guard me against all forms of spiritual or mental attacks. Protect me from every assault of the enemy. (Psalm 91:11)
- I declare that I am victorious through Jesus Christ. Every plan of the enemy to torment me with visual hallucinations is destroyed in Jesus' name. (Romans 8:37)
- Father, I thank You for delivering me from visual hallucinations. I praise You for the peace, clarity, and restoration You have brought to my life. (Psalm 107:1-2)

Prayer Points Against Satanic Delusions

- Heavenly Father, I repent of any sin or disobedience that may have opened the door to satanic delusions in my life. Cleanse me with the blood of Jesus and renew my mind. (1 John 1:9)
- Lord, I declare that You are the Lord of my life. No lie or deception of the enemy will take root in my mind or heart. (Psalm 24:1)
- In the name of Jesus, I bind every spirit of deception, delusion, and confusion sent to manipulate my mind. I cast you out now in Jesus' name. (Matthew 18:18)
- Father, I cast down every false imagination, thought, or argument that exalts itself against the knowledge of God. I bring every thought into captivity to Christ. (2 Corinthians 10:5)

- I plead the blood of Jesus over my mind, emotions, and spirit. Let every satanic delusion be destroyed by the power of the blood. (Revelation 12:11)
- Lord, I declare that I have the mind of Christ. I reject every thought, vision, or belief that does not align with Your truth. (1 Corinthians 2:16)
- Father, I destroy every satanic stronghold in my mind that the enemy has used to plant lies. Let Your Word and Spirit uproot them completely. (Jeremiah 1:10)
- In the name of Jesus, I cancel every assignment of satanic delusions designed to mislead, confuse, or hinder my spiritual walk. I declare them null and void. (Isaiah 54:17)
- I rebuke the spirit of fear and confusion. God has given me a spirit of power, love, and a sound mind. I stand in His peace and authority. (2 Timothy 1:7)
- Lord, give me discernment to recognize and reject satanic delusions. Let Your Spirit guide me into all truth. (John 16:13)
- I renounce and reject every false belief, lie, and illusion that I have ever accepted or entertained. I replace them with Your truth, Lord. (John 8:32)
- Father, fill my mind with Your Word and truth. Let Your Word dwell richly in me and expose every lie of the enemy. (Colossians 3:16)
- I declare that the Word of God is my foundation, my shield, and my guide. I reject anything contrary to it in Jesus' name. (Hebrews 4:12)

- Lord, open my spiritual eyes and ears to see and hear clearly from You. Remove every veil of delusion in Jesus' name. (Ephesians 1:17-18)
- I declare that I am victorious over every satanic delusion. No weapon formed against my mind shall prosper. I stand in the truth and freedom of Christ. (Romans 8:37)
- Father, let Your peace, which surpasses all understanding, guard my heart and mind. I will not be shaken by lies or confusion. (Philippians 4:7)
- Lord, I thank You for delivering me from satanic delusions. I praise You for clarity, truth, and freedom in Christ. (Psalm 107:1-2)

Prayer Points Against Destiny Thieves

- Heavenly Father, I repent of any sin, disobedience, or actions that may have opened the door for destiny thieves to operate in my life. Cleanse me with the blood of Jesus and restore me. (1 John 1:9)
- Lord Jesus, I declare that You are the Lord of my life and destiny. No power of darkness can tamper with what You have ordained for me. (Jeremiah 29:11)
- In the name of Jesus, I bind every spirit of theft, delay, and diversion operating against my destiny. I command you to release what you have stolen now! (John 10:10)
- Father, I declare that everything the enemy has stolen from my lifetime, opportunities, relationships, and blessings—is restored sevenfold in Jesus' name. (Proverbs 6:31)

- Lord, uproot every evil seed and plantation the enemy has sown into my destiny to hinder my progress. Let them be consumed by Your fire. (Matthew 15:13)
- In the name of Jesus, I cancel every evil covenant or agreement made to divert or delay my destiny. I replace them with the covenant of life and purpose in Christ. (Colossians 2:14)
- Every chain of delay and stagnation holding my destiny captive, break now by the power of the Holy Spirit in Jesus' name. (Isaiah 61:1)
- Father, I release my destiny helpers wherever they may be hindered or delayed. Let them locate me now and assist me in fulfilling my purpose. (Isaiah 60:10)
- I destroy every evil altar raised to manipulate or exchange my destiny. Let the fire of God consume these altars now in Jesus' name. (1 Kings 18:38)
- Lord, sever every ungodly connection, relationship, or influence that is draining my strength and purpose. Let me walk in divine alignment. (2 Corinthians 6:14)
- Father, I recover every opportunity, blessing, and resource that the enemy has stolen from my life. I claim divine restoration in Jesus' name. (Joel 2:25)
- I cover my destiny with the blood of Jesus. Let every attack against my purpose be rendered powerless by the blood. (Revelation 12:11)
- Lord, release Your fire to consume every demonic force working to steal, delay, or destroy my destiny. Let them be scattered now! (Psalm 97:3)
- I rebuke and cast out the spirit of failure, disappointment, and frustration sent to derail my

destiny. I declare that I will succeed in Jesus' name. (Deuteronomy 28:13)

- Father, I declare divine acceleration over my life. Every wasted year, month, or day is restored with supernatural speed in Jesus' name. (Amos 9:13)
- I speak life over my destiny. I declare that I will walk in my divine purpose and bring glory to God. (Ezekiel 37:4-5)
- Every evil verdict or pronouncement against my destiny, I overturn it by the authority of Jesus Christ. Only God's plan for my life will stand. (Isaiah 54:17)
- I declare that I am victorious through Jesus Christ. No power of darkness can steal or destroy my God-ordained destiny. (Romans 8:37)
- Lord, anoint me with fresh oil to overcome every obstacle and barrier to my destiny. Strengthen me to walk boldly in Your purpose. (Psalm 92:10)
- Father, I thank You for giving me victory over destiny thieves. I praise You for restoring, accelerating, and securing my purpose in Jesus' name. (Psalm 107:1-2)

Prayer for Restoration of Destiny

- Heavenly Father, I come before You in repentance. I ask for Your forgiveness for any sins, disobedience, or choices that may have hindered or diverted the path You have set for me. Cleanse me with the precious blood of Jesus and restore me to Your divine purpose. (1 John 1:9)

- Lord, I declare that You are the Creator of my destiny, and You alone have the authority to restore it. I acknowledge that You know the plans You have for me, plans to prosper me and not to harm me, plans to give me a future and a hope. (Jeremiah 29:11)
- In the name of Jesus, I renounce and break every curse, covenant, or stronghold that the enemy has placed on my destiny. I cancel every assignment to steal, delay, or destroy what God has ordained for me. I command every power working against my divine destiny to be paralyzed by the blood of Jesus. (John 10:10)
- Father, I ask that You restore every opportunity that has been lost or stolen from me. I declare that every door that has been closed against me is now opened by Your mighty hand. Bring back the opportunities, favor, and relationships that are in alignment with Your will for my life. (Joel 2:25)
- Lord, I declare that I will walk in the fullness of the purpose You have for my life. I take back every part of my vision and destiny that has been diverted. Let Your Holy Spirit guide me into all truth, helping me to fulfil my divine calling. (Proverbs 16:9)
- I break every chain of limitation, delay, and stagnation that has held me back from fulfilling my destiny. I declare that no weapon formed against my destiny shall prosper, and I will rise to all that God has called me to be. (Isaiah 54:17)
- Father, I pray for divine acceleration over my destiny. Every area where I have been delayed or hindered, let Your Spirit speed up the process. Let everything that

was meant to come to me in due season manifest quickly in Jesus' name. (Amos 9:13)

- Lord, I pray that every step of my life aligns with Your will. Lead me by Your Holy Spirit and direct my paths in the way that will fulfill Your plan for me. I submit my desires, my plans, and my future to Your divine will. (Proverbs 3:5-6)
- Father, I reclaim my true identity in Christ. I declare that I am fearfully and wonderfully made, created in Your image, with a destiny to impact the world for Your glory. I reject any false identity or labels placed upon me by the enemy. (Psalm 139:14)
- Father, in the name of Jesus I release Your angels to assist me in the restoration and fulfilment of my destiny. Let them go before me, clearing the way and bringing about divine connections, opportunities, and favor. (Psalm 91:11)
- I declare that I am free from every oppression, torment, and lie of the enemy concerning my destiny. The enemy will not steal my joy, my purpose, or my future. I stand firm in the victory that Christ has won for me. (Romans 8:37)
- I speak life to every area of my destiny. I declare that my destiny is being restored and will manifest according to God's perfect timing. Every dry bone, vision, and dream in my life will come to life through the power of the Holy Spirit. (Ezekiel 37:4-6)
- Lord, I thank You for restoring my destiny. I give You all the praise and glory for bringing me into alignment with Your perfect plan. I trust you, Father, to continue

guiding me into the fullness of my purpose. (Psalm 107:1)

Prayer Points Against Strongman of the Family

- Heavenly Father, I come before You in repentance for any sins or iniquities committed by me or my ancestors that have allowed the strongman of the family to have influence over my bloodline. I ask for Your forgiveness and cleanse me with the blood of Jesus. (1 John 1:9)
- I declare that Jesus Christ is the Lord over my life, my family, and my destiny. I renounce and break every stronghold that the strongman of the family has held over my bloodline. No power of darkness will dominate my life or my family in Jesus' name. (Philippians 2:10-11)
- In the name of Jesus, I bind the strongman of the family that has been causing generational curses, oppression, stagnation, and delay. I command you to be bound and cast out of my life and bloodline now. (Matthew 18:18)
- Father, I break every generational curse or evil pattern of behavior that has been passed down through my family. I declare that my family will no longer be a vessel for these curses in the name of Jesus. (Galatians 3:13)
- Lord, I declare that my family and I are free from the bondage of the strongman. Every area of my life where the enemy has held control is now released in Jesus' name. (John 8:36)

- In the name of Jesus, I destroy every evil altar and idol that the strongman of the family has used to operate in our lives. Let these altars be consumed by the fire of God. (1 Kings 18:38)
- I renounce every spirit of inherited bondage that has been affecting my family. I declare that my bloodline is delivered and sanctified by the blood of Jesus. (2 Corinthians 5:17)
- I stand in the gap for my family and declare total deliverance from the strongman's hold. I declare that every chain of oppression, poverty, failure, and sickness is broken by the power of the Holy Spirit. (Isaiah 61:1)
- I cancel every evil covenant or agreement that the strongman has made with my ancestors that is affecting my family. I break every ungodly alliance in the name of Jesus. (Colossians 2:14)
- Father, I declare the restoration of every blessing that has been stolen by the strongman of the family. Let financial, marital, and spiritual blessings be restored sevenfold in Jesus' name. (Proverbs 6:31)
- Lord, release Your fire to consume every power of darkness operating in my family. Let every demonic stronghold be broken, and every enemy that has been hindering our progress be destroyed. (Hebrews 12:29)
- I declare victory over every strongman that has been tormenting my family. No power of darkness shall hold us back. We are free in Christ and will fulfil our God-ordained purpose. (Romans 8:37)
- Father, I pray for the salvation of every family member who has been under the influence of the strongman.

Bring them to the knowledge of Your truth and deliver them from the lies of the enemy. (Acts 16:31)

- Lord, anoint my family with fresh oil for breakthrough. Let every area of our lives that has been stagnant be revived and experience supernatural progress. (Psalm 92:10)
- I declare that my family is protected from every attack of the enemy. We are shielded by the blood of Jesus, and no weapon formed against us shall prosper. (Isaiah 54:17)
- Father, I thank You for delivering my family from the strongman's hold. I praise You for the victory You have given us, and for the new season of blessings and freedom in our lives. (Psalm 107:1)

Prayer Points Against Monitoring Spirits

- Heavenly Father, I come before You in repentance for any sin, disobedience, or agreement with the enemy that has allowed monitoring spirits to operate in my life. I ask for Your forgiveness and cleansing through the blood of Jesus. (1 John 1:9)
- Lord, I declare that You are the Lord of my life. No spirit, power, or entity can monitor or track my movements, thoughts, or actions unless You permit it. I stand in the authority of Jesus Christ over every monitoring spirit. (Philippians 2:9-10)
- In the name of Jesus, I bind every monitoring spirit that has been sent to observe, manipulate, or hinder my

progress. I command you to be rendered powerless and paralyzed by the blood of Jesus. (Matthew 18:18)

- Father, I break every spirit of tracking, surveillance, and observation that has been following me, my family, or my destiny. I declare that every plan and surveillance of the enemy against me is nullified and destroyed. (Psalm 91:5-6)
- Lord, I command every evil eye that is watching, tracking, or monitoring my life to be blind in the name of Jesus. Let every demonic eye be consumed by the fire of God. (Psalm 35:8)
- Father, I declare Your divine protection over my life, my family, and my destiny. I cover myself with the precious blood of Jesus, and no monitoring spirit shall track or invade my privacy. (Isaiah 54:17)
- I declare that every spirit sent to monitor me, my family, or my ministry will be confused and disoriented by the power of the Holy Spirit. Let their plans be scattered and nullified. (Genesis 11:7)
- Lord, I sever every connection between me and monitoring spirits. I break every link or spiritual tether that has allowed them access to my life. I declare that no demonic power shall have access to my affairs. (Luke 10:19)
- In the name of Jesus, I dismantle every network of monitoring spirits that has been assigned to spy on me. Let their plans be destroyed and let their activities cease now. (Matthew 12:25-26)
- Lord, make me invisible to every monitoring spirit. Let my life and destiny be hidden under the shadow of Your

wings, where the enemy cannot find me or hinder me. (Psalm 91:1)

- I break and cancel every covenant, agreement, or alliance that I or my ancestors have made with monitoring spirits, knowingly or unknowingly. I renounce all their works in Jesus' name. (2 Corinthians 6:14)
- I declare that the anointing of the Holy Spirit protects me from all monitoring spirits. I walk under the full covering of God's protection, and no evil can penetrate this covering. (Psalm 105:15)
- Father, I send confusion to every demonic agent sent to monitor or spy on me. Let them be confused, their communications disrupted, and their plans foiled in the name of Jesus. (1 Samuel 14:20)
- Lord, expose every monitoring spirit and demonic agent assigned to hinder or manipulate my life. Bring their hidden agendas to light and frustrate their efforts in Jesus' name. (Luke 8:17)
- Let the fire of God consume every demonic entity sent to monitor, track, or hinder me. I command them to be burnt by the fire of God right now. (Hebrews 12:29)
- I declare that I have victory over every monitoring spirit. No weapon of surveillance or tracking can succeed against me. I am secure in Christ, and I walk in divine freedom. (Romans 8:37)
- Father, I thank You for protecting me from every monitoring spirit and for giving me victory over all forms of surveillance from the enemy. I praise You for Your constant covering over my life. (Psalm 34:7)

Prayer Points Against Sexual Unclean Spirits

- Heavenly Father, I come before You in repentance for any sin, disobedience, or agreement with sexual unclean spirits in my life. I ask for Your forgiveness for indulging in lust, masturbation, pornography, and any form of sexual immorality. Cleanse me with the precious blood of Jesus and remove all defilement from my heart, mind, and body. (1 John 1:9)
- In the name of Jesus, I break the power of every sexual unclean spirit, including lust, masturbation, pornography, spirit spouses, homosexuality, incest, and transgender spirits. I renounce every bond with these spirits and declare freedom in Christ. (1 Corinthians 6:18-20)
- I renounce and break every covenant, contract, or relationship with spirit spouses (marine spirits, incubus, succubus) that have been assigned to my life. I command you to leave me now and never return in the name of Jesus. (Isaiah 54:5)
- Father, I ask You to destroy every root of lust, sexual addiction, and unclean desires within me. I bind every spirit of lust, masturbation, and pornography. I declare that I am set free from sexual sin by the power of the Holy Spirit. (Matthew 5:28)
- Lord, I declare that my mind is purified, and my heart is cleansed from all impure thoughts, fantasies, and desires. Let the power of the Holy Spirit take control of my thoughts and emotions, leading me into purity. (Philippians 4:8)

- In the name of Jesus, I destroy the spirits of homosexuality and incest that have taken root in my life, family, or bloodline. I declare that these spirits have no power over me or my family, and I break every stronghold of sexual perversion in Jesus' name. (Leviticus 18:22, Romans 1:26-27)
- Father, I renounce every spirit of confusion regarding my identity, especially the spirit of transgender confusion. I declare that I am created in Your image, male and female, and I accept the identity You have given me in Christ. (Genesis 1:27, 1 Corinthians 6:9-11)
- In the name of Jesus, I sever every ungodly soul tie formed through past sexual relationships, pornography, and immoral acts. I break every emotional, spiritual, and physical bond with these spirits. Let the blood of Jesus cleanse and break every chain of attachment. (1 Corinthians 6:16)
- Father, I ask for total deliverance from every sexual unclean spirit that has influenced my life. Let every spirit of perversion, immorality, and confusion be cast out and bound by the power of the Holy Spirit. I declare complete freedom in Christ Jesus. (Luke 4:18)
- I receive the purity and holiness that comes from God. Holy Spirit, I ask You to fill me with the power to resist temptation and walk in sexual purity. Let me reflect the image of Christ in my thoughts, words, and actions. (1 Thessalonians 4:3-4)
- Let the fire of God purify my life from every defilement, especially sexual perversion. I command every evil spirit that has defiled me sexually to be consumed by the fire of God. (Hebrews 12:29)

- Lord, I pray for the restoration of my sexual integrity, that I may walk in the holiness You have called me to. I declare that my body is the temple of the Holy Spirit, and I will honor God with my body. (1 Corinthians 6:19-20)
- I break the spirit of shame, guilt, and condemnation that has been attached to my sexual struggles. I declare that there is no condemnation for those who are in Christ Jesus. I receive the forgiveness and freedom You have given me. (Romans 8:1)
- Father, I pray for the renewal of my mind. I choose to think on things that are pure, lovely, and praiseworthy. Let Your Word transform my mind and heart, so that I may walk in sexual purity and honor You with my life. (Romans 12:2, Philippians 4:8)
- Father, I stand in the gap for my family and bloodline. I break every generational stronghold of sexual sin, including lust, perversion, spirit spouses, homosexuality, incest, and transgender confusion. I declare freedom and purity for my family in Jesus' name. (Exodus 20:5-6)
- Father, I thank You for the complete restoration and freedom You have granted me. I praise You for delivering me from all sexual unclean spirits and for renewing my mind, body, and spirit. I commit to walking in purity and holiness, by Your grace. (Psalm 107:1)

Prayer Points Against Marine Spirits

- Heavenly Father, I come before You in repentance for any sin or iniquity that may have opened the door for marine spirits to operate in my life or my bloodline. I ask for Your forgiveness and cleanse me with the precious blood of Jesus. (1 John 1:9)
- In the name of Jesus, I break every covenant, agreement, or alliance with marine spirits, including water spirits, mermaids, and spirit spouses. I renounce every connection with them and declare that they have no legal right to operate in my life or family. (2 Corinthians 6:14-18)
- I command every marine spirit, including marine powers, strongholds, and entities that have been assigned to monitor or control my life, to leave now in the name of Jesus. I declare that you are bound and rendered powerless. (Matthew 18:18)
- Father, I declare my freedom from every water spirit that has been assigned to delay, confuse, or hinder my progress. I declare that I am free from the grip of marine spirits and every form of bondage they have placed on me. (John 8:36)
- I renounce every spirit spouse that has been sent by marine spirits to defile me, including the spirits of incubus and succubus. I break every soul tie and covenant with these spirits and declare my total deliverance in the name of Jesus. (Isaiah 54:5)
- I cancel and nullify every dream and attack from marine spirits, including dreams of water, drowning, or sexual encounters in dreams. I bind every marine attack against

my spiritual and physical life and command it to stop in Jesus' name. (Job 33:15-18)

- Father, I come against the spirit of financial stagnation and poverty brought on by marine spirits. I break the hold of water spirits that have been causing financial setbacks, and I release divine provision and breakthroughs in my finances. (Deuteronomy 8:18)

- In the name of Jesus, I destroy every marine altar that has been set up against me, my family, or my destiny. Let every evil altar and its powers be consumed by the fire of the Holy Spirit and rendered powerless. (1 Kings 18:38)

- I break every generational curse of marine spirits affecting my family and bloodline. I declare that every spiritual contract, covenant, and influence with marine spirits is null and void in my family. I declare my lineage free from their influence. (Exodus 20:5)

- In the name of Jesus, I command every marine spirit to release my blessings, destiny, and promises that have been stolen or held captive by them. I declare that my spiritual, emotional, and physical blessings are released now. (Isaiah 43:2-3)

- I command every marine demon operating in my life, my family, or my destiny to be destroyed by the fire of God. Let every spirit sent to cause destruction, delays, or confusion be consumed by the Holy Spirit's fire. (Psalm 18:8)

- I declare victory over every influence and power of marine spirits in my life. I declare that no weapon formed against me by these spirits shall prosper. I am more than a conqueror through Christ who strengthens me. (Romans 8:37)

- In the name of Jesus, I break every spirit of lust, perversion, and sexual immorality that marine spirits have placed upon me or my family. I declare that I am cleansed and set free from every unclean spirit. (1 Corinthians 6:18-20)

- I apply the blood of Jesus over my life, my family, my home, and my destiny. I declare that the blood of Jesus speaks against every marine spirit and gives me victory over all their attacks and plans. (Revelation 12:11)

- Father, I ask You to build a wall of fire and a hedge of protection around me and my family, preventing marine spirits from accessing our lives. Keep us safe from all evil and covered under Your divine protection. (Zechariah 2:5)

- Father, I thank You for delivering me from the influence and control of marine spirits. I praise You for the freedom You have given me, and I declare that I will walk in the fullness of my destiny, free from all demonic influence. (Psalm 34:7)

Prayer Points Against Evil Covenants

- Heavenly Father, I come before You in repentance for any sin or disobedience that has opened the door for evil covenants in my life or bloodline. Forgive me, cleanse me with the blood of Jesus, and make me whole. (1 John 1:9)

- In the name of Jesus, I break every evil covenant knowingly or unknowingly entered into by me or my ancestors. I nullify their power and declare them void and powerless over my life. (Isaiah 28:18)
- I plead the blood of Jesus over every area of my life. Let the blood of Jesus cleanse me from every evil covenant and break its hold over me completely. (Hebrews 12:24)
- Lord, I cancel and nullify every covenant made in my dreams, whether through eating, drinking, sex, or any other activity. I reject their power and influence in Jesus' name. (Matthew 13:25)
- I renounce and break every covenant made with marine spirits, whether by me, my ancestors, or through ungodly altars. I declare freedom from their influence and assignments in Jesus' name. (Ezekiel 29:3)
- Father, I break every generational covenant passed down through my bloodline. I declare that no evil covenant from my ancestors will have power over me or my descendants. (Exodus 20:5-6)
- In the name of Jesus, I break every evil covenant made through witchcraft, sorcery, divination, or occult practices. I declare their power null and void over my life. (Leviticus 19:31)
- Lord, I renounce and break every covenant made through the worship of idols or false gods. I declare that I serve the one true God, and no other power has dominion over me. (Deuteronomy 5:7-10)
- I nullify every evil covenant sealed with blood, whether animal or human, in my life or family. I declare that the

blood of Jesus speaks better things over my life. (Hebrews 9:14)
- Father, I break every evil covenant formed through ungodly soul ties, relationships, or agreements. I sever their influence and declare myself free in Jesus' name. (2 Corinthians 6:14)
- Lord, let Your fire consume every evil altar that was raised to enforce evil covenants against my life or destiny. Let those altars be destroyed now in Jesus' name. (1 Kings 18:38)
- I bind and destroy every monitoring spirit assigned to enforce evil covenants in my life. I command them to be blinded and destroyed by the fire of God. (Psalm 35:8)
- Father, restore everything that has been stolen or delayed in my life due to evil covenants. I reclaim my blessings, breakthroughs, and purpose in Jesus' name. (Joel 2:25-26)
- I release the judgment of God against every power, principality, or human agent enforcing evil covenants in my life. Let their plans and schemes come to nothing. (Isaiah 54:17)
- Father, I declare that I am in a new covenant with You through the blood of Jesus. No evil covenant has power over my life, for I am redeemed by the blood of the Lamb. (Luke 22:20)
- I renounce and break every covenant made by my ancestors dedicating me or my family to demonic powers, altars, or false gods. I declare my total freedom in Jesus' name. (Galatians 3:13)

- I bind the strongman assigned to enforce evil covenants in my life. I cast them out and render them powerless in the name of Jesus. (Matthew 12:29)
- Lord, I nullify every token, symbol, or object used to seal or enforce evil covenants in my life or home. Let them lose their power and be destroyed by fire. (Isaiah 44:25)
- Father, release Your angels to fight on my behalf and destroy every stronghold, altar, or power enforcing evil covenants against my life. (Psalm 91:11)
- Lord, I thank You for breaking every evil covenant and setting me free. I walk in the liberty of Christ, and I declare total victory over every scheme of the enemy. (Psalm 107:1-2)

Prayer Points for Breaking Curses

- Heavenly Father, I come before You in repentance for any sin in my life or my family that may have opened the door for curses to operate. Forgive me and cleanse me with the blood of Jesus. (1 John 1:9)
- In the name of Jesus, I renounce and reject every curse spoken over my life, my family, or my destiny. I declare that I am no longer under any curse but under the blessings of God. (Galatians 3:13-14)
- I break every generational curse operating in my bloodline. I declare that I am set free from the sins, iniquities, and curses of my ancestors through the blood of Jesus. (Exodus 34:7)

- Father, I cancel every negative word, curse, or declaration spoken over my life by others or myself. I declare that only Your Word will stand in my life. (Proverbs 18:21)
- In the name of Jesus, I break every curse, spell, or enchantment placed upon me by witchcraft or occult powers. Let every chain be broken and destroyed by the fire of God. (Numbers 23:23)
- I command every altar enforcing curses against my life to be destroyed by the fire of God. Let every power behind those altars be rendered powerless in Jesus' name. (1 Kings 18:38)
- I cover myself and my family with the blood of Jesus. I declare that the blood of Jesus speaks better things than the blood of any curse, and it sets me free completely. (Hebrews 12:24)
- I come against every curse of delay, stagnation, and backwardness in my life. I declare progress and divine acceleration in the name of Jesus. (Deuteronomy 28:13)
- Lord, I break every curse of poverty, financial struggle, and lack in my life. I declare that I am blessed, and my finances are under divine blessing and favor. (Deuteronomy 8:18)
- In the name of Jesus, I break every curse causing delays, confusion, or failure in my relationships and marriage. I declare restoration and divine alignment in Jesus' name. (Isaiah 62:4)
- I renounce and break every curse brought about by idolatry, whether in my life or my family. I declare that I

serve the one true God, and no idol has power over me. (Deuteronomy 5:8-9)

- I bind the strongman assigned to enforce curses in my life. I render their power useless and cast them out in the name of Jesus. (Matthew 12:29)
- I cancel and nullify every curse or demonic covenant formed in my dreams. I declare that no evil dream will take root in my life. (Matthew 13:25)
- I declare that I am blessed and not cursed. I am the head and not the tail, above and not beneath, and I walk in the blessings of Abraham through Christ Jesus. (Deuteronomy 28:2-6)
- Father, release Your angels to fight for me and destroy every curse, stronghold, or power working against my life. Let every demonic chain be broken now in Jesus' name. (Psalm 91:11)
- I reclaim every blessing, opportunity, and breakthrough stolen from me by curses. I declare total restoration in Jesus' name. (Joel 2:25-26)
- I reject the spirit of fear and intimidation brought on by curses. I walk in boldness and power, knowing that God has not given me a spirit of fear. (2 Timothy 1:7)
- Lord, I break every curse of sickness, infirmity, and untimely death over my life and family. I declare healing and divine health in Jesus' name. (Isaiah 53:5)
- I bind and blind every monitoring spirit enforcing curses in my life. Let their devices and assignments be destroyed by the fire of God. (Psalm 35:8)
- Father, I thank You for breaking every curse in my life and setting me free. I declare that I am walking in Your

blessings, favor, and victory in Christ Jesus. (Psalm 107:1-2)

Prayer Points Against Financial Stagnation

- Heavenly Father, I repent of any sin or disobedience that has opened the door to financial stagnation in my life. Forgive me and align my finances with Your will. (1 John 1:9)
- In the name of Jesus, I break every curse of financial stagnation, lack, and poverty operating in my life. I declare that I am set free by the power of the blood of Jesus. (Galatians 3:13-14)
- Father, I nullify every evil covenant or agreement working against my financial progress. Let every demonic altar enforcing stagnation in my finances be destroyed by fire. (Isaiah 28:18)
- Lord, I declare that every closed financial door in my life is opened now in the name of Jesus. I receive divine opportunities and breakthroughs. (Revelation 3:8)
- I bind and destroy the spirit of delay, hindrance, and frustration assigned to my financial progress. I command it to leave my life in Jesus' name. (Matthew 16:19)
- Father, rebuke every devourer, waster, or destroyer of my finances. Let every hole in my pocket or source of income be sealed in Jesus' name. (Malachi 3:11)
- Lord, grant me divine wisdom and understanding to manage my finances according to Your principles.

Teach me to make wise decisions and investments. (Proverbs 3:13-14)

- I recover every financial blessing, opportunity, and breakthrough stolen by the enemy. I declare total restoration in Jesus' name. (Joel 2:25-26)
- Father, release Your angels to go before me and bring favor, divine connections, and financial resources into my life. Let Your angels fight every force hindering my prosperity. (Psalm 91:11)
- I break every generational curse or pattern of financial stagnation and poverty in my bloodline. I declare that I am set free, and my family is released into divine abundance. (Exodus 20:5-6)
- Lord, let Your favor rest upon me and my endeavors. Cause me to find favor with You and with people in every area of my life. (Psalm 5:12)
- In the name of Jesus, I command every chain of financial limitation, restriction, and bondage to be broken. I declare freedom in my finances. (Isaiah 10:27)
- I blind and destroy every monitoring spirit assigned to track and hinder my financial progress. Let their plans and devices be destroyed in Jesus' name. (Psalm 35:8)
- Lord, let the heavens open over my life, and pour out financial blessings and abundance that I will not have room to contain. (Malachi 3:10)
- Father, send destiny helpers and divine connections into my life. Connect me to people and opportunities that will lead to my financial upliftment. (Psalm 121:1-2)

- I cancel every shame and reproach connected to my finances. I declare that I will walk in abundance and not lack. (Psalm 34:5)
- In the name of Jesus, I bind and cast out the spirit of poverty operating in my life and family. I declare that poverty has no place in my destiny. (2 Corinthians 8:9)
- Lord, I reject the spirit of fear and doubt concerning my finances. I trust in Your provision and walk in boldness, knowing You are my source. (2 Timothy 1:7)
- I declare that my finances are blessed, and I will experience increase, overflow, and abundance. I will lend to many and borrow from none. (Deuteronomy 28:12)
- Father, I thank You for breaking the chains of financial stagnation and for the breakthroughs You have released in my life. I give You all the glory for my financial restoration. (Psalm 107:1-2)

Prayer Points for Covering a Singing Ministry and Its Success

- Heavenly Father, I dedicate my singing ministry to You. Let it be a vessel for Your glory and an instrument to draw souls to Your kingdom. Take complete control over this ministry. (Romans 12:1)
- Holy Spirit, saturate my ministry with Your presence. Let Your anointing rest upon every song, every performance, and every moment of worship. Without You, I can do nothing. (Zechariah 4:6)

- Lord, inspire my songs with Your Word and Spirit. Let the lyrics, melodies, and messages be in alignment with Your will and speak life to those who hear them. (2 Timothy 3:16-17)
- In the name of Jesus, I come against every hindrance, limitation, and opposition to the growth and success of my singing ministry. Let every plan of the enemy be destroyed. (Isaiah 54:17)
- I cover myself, my team, and my singing ministry with the blood of Jesus. Let no weapon formed against us prosper. (Exodus 12:13)
- Father, connect me with the right people who will support, mentor, and elevate this ministry according to Your purpose. Bring divine helpers and kingdom partners into my life. (Proverbs 18:16)
- Lord, grant me the spirit of excellence in my singing and ministry. Help me to grow in skill, discipline, and dedication to reflect Your glory. (Daniel 6:3)
- Father, let Your favor rest upon me and my ministry. Open doors of opportunity for me to minister in places where Your name will be glorified. (Psalm 5:12)
- Lord, expand the reach of my ministry. Let it touch lives across nations, breaking barriers and bringing hope, healing, and salvation to people everywhere. (Psalm 96:3)
- I bind and cancel every spirit of discouragement, fear, or doubt that may come against me. Strengthen me to stand firm in faith and press on toward my calling. (2 Timothy 1:7)

- Father, shield me and my ministry from spiritual attacks. Protect my mind, heart, and voice from any harm or manipulation by the enemy. (Psalm 91:1-2)
- Lord, release a fresh anointing upon my voice and ministry. Let Your power flow through every song, bringing deliverance, healing, and salvation to the listeners. (Luke 4:18)
- In the name of Jesus, I break every spirit of lack and financial limitation over my ministry. I declare that resources will flow freely for the work of the kingdom. (Philippians 4:19)
- Lord, keep me humble as You elevate me. Let pride have no place in my heart and help me to always point others to You as the source of my success. (James 4:6)
- Father, I commit every project, album, song release, and performance into Your hands. Let each endeavor succeed and bring glory to Your name. (Psalm 37:5)
- Lord, grant unity and harmony among everyone involved in this ministry. Let there be love, understanding, and a shared vision for glorifying You. (Psalm 133:1)
- I reject the spirit of unhealthy competition or comparison in my ministry. Let my focus always remain on You and the unique calling You have placed on my life. (Galatians 6:4)
- Father, let my ministry be a tool for saving souls. Let my songs lead people to repentance, deliverance, and a closer relationship with You. (Luke 15:10)

- Lord, establish my ministry and sustain it for Your glory. Let it stand the test of time and continue to bear fruit for generations to come. (Psalm 92:12-14)
- Father, I thank You for the gift of this ministry and for what You are doing through it. I trust You for its growth and success, and I give You all the glory. (Psalm 100:4-5)

Prayer Points for the Ministry of Authorship

- Heavenly Father, I dedicate my gift of writing and the ministry of authorship to You. Let every word I write glorify You and edify others. Take control of my thoughts and creativity for Your kingdom. (Romans 12:1)
- Lord, I ask for divine inspiration and creativity. Fill me with Your Spirit so that the words I write will carry power, wisdom, and truth. Let my writing be a reflection of Your heart and purpose. (2 Timothy 3:16-17)
- In the name of Jesus, I come against every spirit of procrastination, distraction, and writer's block. I declare that I will write with focus, discipline, and purpose. (Philippians 4:13)
- Father, grant me clarity of thought and understanding as I write. Let the message You want to communicate through me be clear and impactful to the readers. (Proverbs 2:6)
- I bind and reject every spirit of fear and self-doubt that seeks to hinder my writing ministry. I declare that I am

confident in the calling You have placed on my life. (2 Timothy 1:7)

- Lord, anoint every word I write. Let my books, articles, and content minister life, healing, and encouragement to all who read them. (Luke 4:18)
- Father, I cover every manuscript, idea, and project under the blood of Jesus. Protect them from theft, destruction, or any form of attack by the enemy. (Psalm 91:11)
- Lord, lead the right readers to my writings. Let the words You inspire in me reach those who need them most and bring transformation to their lives. (Isaiah 55:11)
- Father, I pray for divine provision and resources to publish and promote my writings. I trust You to meet all my needs according to Your riches in glory. (Philippians 4:19)
- In the name of Jesus, I break every limitation and barrier that may hinder the success of my writing ministry. I declare that I will reach global platforms for Your glory. (Psalm 18:29)
- Lord, grant me favor with publishers, editors, readers, and platforms. Open doors for opportunities and divine connections in the publishing industry. (Psalm 5:12)
- Father, let my writings bring salvation, healing, deliverance, and hope to those who encounter them. Use my books to touch and transform lives for Your glory. (Romans 10:14-15)
- Lord, grant me a spirit of excellence in my writing. Help me to produce work that is clear, professional, and pleasing in Your sight. (Daniel 6:3)

- I bind every spirit of discouragement and frustration that may arise in the writing process. Strengthen me to press on and complete every project You have placed in my hands. (Galatians 6:9)
- Father, establish my writing ministry and let it stand the test of time. Let the words You inspire in me have a lasting impact on generations to come. (Psalm 90:17)
- Lord, I reject the spirit of competition or comparison in my writing ministry. Help me to focus on my unique calling and trust in the path You have set for me. (Galatians 6:4)
- Lord, expand the reach of my writings. Let them go to the nations, touching lives and spreading the message of Your kingdom across the globe. (Matthew 28:19)
- Father, help me to walk in Your timing. Let every book, article, or piece of writing be released at the right time to fulfil Your divine purpose. (Ecclesiastes 3:1)
- Lord, let my writing always align with Your truth. Guard me from compromise or writing anything that does not reflect Your Word and character. (Colossians 3:23-24)
- Father, I thank You for entrusting me with the gift of writing. I give You all the glory for the impact it will have and the lives it will change. Let Your name be glorified through this ministry. (1 Thessalonians 5:18)

Prayer Points for Mentorship and Purpose Coaching Ministry

- Heavenly Father, I dedicate this mentorship and purpose coaching ministry to You. Let it be an instrument for guiding others into their God-ordained destinies. Take full control of every aspect of this ministry. (Proverbs 3:5-6)
- Lord, grant me divine wisdom, knowledge, and understanding to lead, mentor, and guide others effectively. Help me to speak words that will inspire and uplift. (James 1:5)
- Father, order my steps in this ministry. Let every plan and decision align with Your will and purpose for my life and the lives of those I mentor. (Psalm 37:23)
- Lord, anoint me afresh for this ministry. Let Your power flow through every session, conversation, and activity, bringing transformation and clarity to those I coach. (Isaiah 61:1)
- In the name of Jesus, I come against every spirit of distraction, discouragement, and opposition that may rise against this ministry. I declare that no weapon formed against it shall prosper. (Isaiah 54:17)
- Lord, connect me with the people You have ordained for me to mentor and coach. Let them come with open hearts, ready to grow and fulfil their God-given purpose. (Proverbs 27:17)
- Father, help me to guide others to discover and walk in their divine purpose. Let every session bring clarity and alignment with their God-ordained destinies. (Jeremiah 29:11)

- I cover this mentorship and coaching ministry with the blood of Jesus. Protect it from spiritual attacks, envy, and sabotage. Shield me and those I mentor under Your divine covering. (Psalm 91:1-2)
- In the name of Jesus, I reject every spirit of fear and doubt that seeks to undermine the confidence and growth of those I mentor. Let faith and courage arise in their hearts. (2 Timothy 1:7)
- Lord, let this ministry bear much fruit. Let the lives of those I mentor reflect transformation, growth, and alignment with Your Word. (John 15:5)
- Father, keep me humble as I mentor and coach others. Help me to always remember that this ministry is about serving You and glorifying Your name. (James 4:6)
- Lord, grant this ministry favor with individuals, organizations, and platforms that will help expand its reach and impact. Open doors of opportunity for growth and collaboration. (Psalm 5:12)
- Father, I pray for divine provision and resources for this ministry. Remove every financial limitation and send kingdom helpers to support this work. (Philippians 4:19)
- Lord, help me to operate with a spirit of excellence in all areas of this ministry. Let everything, I do reflect professionalism, diligence, and Your glory. (Daniel 6:3)
- Father, strengthen me physically, emotionally, and spiritually as I pour into others. Let me find rest and renewal in You so I can continue to serve effectively. (Matthew 11:28-30)
- Lord, let every mentoring session, workshop, or program be conducted in Your perfect timing. Help me

to move according to Your pace and direction. (Ecclesiastes 3:1)

- Father, let the seeds I plant in the lives of others through this ministry bear fruit for generations. Let their lives become testimonies of Your grace and purpose. (Psalm 92:12-14)
- Lord, grant me the gift of discernment to understand the unique needs, challenges, and opportunities of those I mentor. Help me to guide them wisely and truthfully. (1 Corinthians 12:10)
- In the name of Jesus, I reject the spirit of comparison and competition in this ministry. Help me and those I mentor to focus on our unique callings and paths. (Galatians 6:4-5)
- Father, I thank You for the privilege of being a vessel in this mentorship and purpose coaching ministry. I give You all the glory for the lives You have entrusted to me and the transformation You will bring. (1 Thessalonians 5:18)

Prayer Points Against Attacks on Marital Destiny

- Heavenly Father, I thank You for Your perfect plan for my marital destiny. I thank You because marriage is Your divine institution, created for companionship, love, and purpose. (Genesis 2:18)
- Lord, I surrender my marital destiny to You. Take full control and let Your will alone be done in my life. Lead me to the partner You have ordained for me. (Proverbs 3:5-6)

- In the name of Jesus, I break every generational curse affecting my marital destiny. I declare that I will not inherit any pattern of marital failure from my bloodline. (Galatians 3:13)
- Father, I cancel every negative word or evil pronouncement spoken against my marital destiny. I decree that no evil word shall stand in my life. (Isaiah 54:17)
- Lord, I break every ungodly soul tie that is hindering my marital progress. I sever every emotional or spiritual connection that is not of You. (2 Corinthians 6:14)
- In the name of Jesus, I come against every spirit spouse attacking my marital destiny. I renounce and reject every covenant or agreement with such spirits, and I declare my total deliverance. (Nahum 1:13)
- Father, I come against every spirit of delay assigned to frustrate my marital destiny. I declare that my marriage will happen in Your perfect timing without any hindrance. (Habakkuk 2:3)
- In the name of Jesus, I destroy every monitoring spirit assigned to sabotage my relationships and marital progress. Let every evil eye be blinded permanently. (Numbers 23:23)
- Lord, I rebuke every satanic manipulation aimed at confusing me or diverting me from the partner You have chosen for me. Let all evil plots be exposed and destroyed. (Psalm 35:1)
- Father, restore my marital glory and honor. Let everything that has been stolen from me be returned sevenfold. (Joel 2:25-26)

- Lord, grant me the wisdom and discernment to identify and align with the partner You have ordained for me. Help me to avoid counterfeits and wrong associations. (Proverbs 2:6)
- In the name of Jesus, I break every spirit of marital stagnation. I declare that my marital destiny is moving forward, and I shall experience progress and fulfillment. (Psalm 40:2)
- Father, I renounce and break every ancestral covenant working against my marital breakthrough. By the blood of Jesus, I set myself free from their influence. (Colossians 2:14-15)
- Lord, destroy every power or force that seeks to bring division or misunderstanding in my relationships. I declare that my marriage will be built on love, unity, and peace. (Mark 10:9)
- Father, shield my marital destiny from every attack of the enemy. Surround me and my future spouse with Your divine protection and let no evil come near us. (Psalm 91:1-2)
- I rebuke every spirit of fear, anxiety, or doubt concerning my marital future. I trust in Your plans for my life, and I walk in faith and confidence. (2 Timothy 1:7)
- Lord, I declare that my marriage will be fruitful and filled with purpose. I shall experience joy, peace, and fulfilment in my marital union. (Genesis 1:28)
- In the name of Jesus, I destroy every demonic altar raised against my marital destiny. Let the fire of God consume them now. (Deuteronomy 7:5)

- Father, grant me favor in the eyes of my future spouse and their family. Let Your favor pave the way for a joyful and successful marriage. (Proverbs 18:22)
- Lord, I thank You in advance for my marital breakthrough. I believe that You have heard and answered my prayers, and I await the manifestation of Your promises. (1 Thessalonians 5:18)

Prayer Points for a Kingdom Spouse

- Heavenly Father, I thank You for Your divine plan for marriage and the blessing of a kingdom spouse. I trust that Your plans for my life are good and perfect. (Jeremiah 29:11)
- Lord, guide my steps to meet the spouse You have ordained for me. Lead me in the right direction and help me to recognize them when the time comes. (Proverbs 3:5-6)
- Father, I surrender the timing of my marriage to You. Let it happen in Your perfect season. Remove every spirit of impatience and help me to wait on You. (Ecclesiastes 3:1)
- Lord, prepare a God-fearing spouse for me—someone who loves You above all else and walks in obedience to Your Word. Let their heart be fully yielded to You. (Psalm 112:1)
- Father, work on my heart and character so I can be the spouse my future partner needs. Mold me into someone who reflects Your love, patience, and humility. (Galatians 5:22-23)

- In the name of Jesus, I break every generational curse and pattern that seeks to hinder my marital destiny. I declare that I am free to fulfil God's plan for my life. (Galatians 3:13)
- Lord, I break every covenant with spirit spouses and renounce their hold on my life. I command them to leave me now in the name of Jesus. (Nahum 1:13)
- Father, protect me from counterfeit relationships. Give me discernment to recognize and avoid anyone who is not aligned with Your purpose for my life. (Proverbs 4:23)
- Lord, let Your favor rest upon me and my kingdom spouse. Surround us with grace and open doors for our connection to be established and blessed. (Proverbs 18:22)
- Father, prepare my heart and my spouse's heart to be compatible in purpose, vision, and values. Let there be unity in all areas of our lives. (Amos 3:3)
- In the name of Jesus, I come against every spirit of delay and stagnation in my marital destiny. I declare that every obstacle is removed, and my marriage will manifest in God's perfect time. (Isaiah 60:22)
- Lord, I cover my kingdom spouse with prayer, even before I meet them. Protect their heart, mind, and spirit. Let them grow in their relationship with You daily. (Ephesians 6:18)
- Father, heal every wound and brokenness in me and my future spouse. Let us both enter marriage whole and free from past hurts or baggage. (Psalm 147:3)

- In the name of Jesus, I bind every spirit of confusion or manipulation that may try to interfere with my marital destiny. Let clarity and peace reign in my heart. (1 Corinthians 14:33)
- Lord, let my marriage be a union that glorifies You and fulfil Your kingdom purpose. Use us to serve You and impact others for Your glory. (Matthew 6:33)
- In the name of Jesus, I destroy every monitoring spirit assigned to hinder or sabotage my relationship. Let them be blinded and rendered powerless. (Numbers 23:23)
- Father, I declare that my marriage will be filled with love, peace, prosperity, and fruitfulness. Let it be a testimony of Your goodness. (Jeremiah 32:27)
- Lord, connect me with people and environments that will lead me closer to meeting my kingdom spouse. Remove any distractions or relationships that are not from You. (Isaiah 45:2)
- Father, grant me patience and unwavering faith as I wait for my kingdom spouse. Help me to trust You completely and not be anxious. (Philippians 4:6-7)
- Lord, I thank You in advance for the manifestation of my kingdom marriage. I give You all the glory, knowing that Your plans will come to pass in my life. (1 Thessalonians 5:18)

Prayer Points for the Deliverance of your Kingdom Spouse

- Heavenly Father, I thank You for Your power to deliver and set captives free. I thank You for the life of my kingdom spouse and the deliverance You are about to perform. (Psalm 107:20)
- Lord, I plead the blood of Jesus over my kingdom spouse's life. Let the blood of Jesus cleanse and purify them from every defilement of sin, curses, or spiritual contamination. (Revelation 12:11)
- In the name of Jesus, I break every curse and spell placed upon my kingdom spouse. Every word spoken against their life to hinder their destiny is nullified now by the power of God. (Galatians 3:13)
- Father, I come against every power of witchcraft working against my kingdom spouse. Let every satanic manipulation and enchantment be destroyed by the fire of the Holy Spirit. (Numbers 23:23)
- Lord, I break every evil covenant my kingdom spouse has entered into knowingly or unknowingly. By the blood of Jesus, I declare them free from every ungodly agreement. (Colossians 2:14-15)
- Father, I renounce and uproot every evil foundation in my kingdom spouse's life. I decree that they are no longer bound by ancestral powers or generational patterns. (Psalm 11:3)
- Lord, I pray for a cleansing of my kingdom spouse's bloodline. Let every contamination, iniquity, and transgression inherited from their forefathers be removed by the power of the blood of Jesus. (Isaiah 53:5)

- In the name of Jesus, I bind and overthrow every strongman operating in my kingdom spouse's life. I command them to release their hold and leave forever. (Mark 3:27)
- Father, I destroy every evil altar raised against my kingdom spouse's life and destiny. Let the fire of God consume these altars and their sacrifices. (Deuteronomy 7:5)
- Lord, I declare that my kingdom spouse is set free from every spiritual captivity. Every chain holding them down is broken now in Jesus' name. (Isaiah 49:25)
- Father, I pray for a hedge of protection around my kingdom spouse. Let no evil come near them and frustrate every attack of the enemy against their life. (Psalm 91:1-2)
- In the name of Jesus, I break every yoke of oppression and bondage upon my kingdom spouse. Let every burden be lifted and destroyed by the anointing. (Isaiah 10:27)
- Lord, I blind every monitoring spirit assigned to watch and frustrate my kingdom spouse's progress. Let their plans be nullified by the power of God. (Job 5:12)
- I declare that my kingdom spouse is delivered from every spirit of stagnation and delay. Let their life and destiny begin to move forward according to God's plan. (Isaiah 40:31)
- Father, I come against every spirit of fear, doubt, or confusion operating in my kingdom spouse's life. Let them walk boldly in faith and victory. (2 Timothy 1:7)

- Lord, align my kingdom spouse's life with Your divine purpose. Let every area of their life be brought under the Lordship of Jesus Christ. (Jeremiah 29:11)
- Father, restore every area of my kingdom spouse's life that has been broken or damaged by the enemy. Let them experience Your healing and wholeness. (Joel 2:25)
- In the name of Jesus, I destroy every barrier and hindrance to the manifestation of our marriage. Let nothing stand in the way of God's perfect plan for us. (Isaiah 62:4)
- Lord, I declare victory over every enemy working against my kingdom spouse. Let every adversary be put to shame and let Your glory manifest in their life. (1 Corinthians 15:57)
- Father, I thank You for the deliverance You have wrought in my kingdom spouse's life. I praise You for breaking every chain and bringing them into the fullness of Your purpose. (Psalm 107:1-2)

Prayer Points for Future Children Dedicated to Jesus Christ

- Heavenly Father, I thank You in advance for the children that will come from my marriage. I praise You for blessing my womb and for making me a steward of their lives. (Psalm 127:3)
- Lord, I covenant my children to You. I declare that they will serve You all the days of their lives and walk in Your divine purpose. (1 Samuel 1:27-28)

- Father, I pray that each of my children will have a personal encounter with You. Let them come to know and love You as their Lord and Savior at an early age. (Romans 10:9)
- Lord, I declare that my children's lives are preserved by the blood of Jesus. No weapon formed against them shall prosper, and every plan of the enemy is destroyed. (Isaiah 54:17)
- Father, I declare that my children will fulfil the destiny You have written for them. Let Your purpose for their lives stand firm forever. (Jeremiah 29:11)
- In the name of Jesus, I break every generational curse that may attempt to affect my children. I declare that they will walk in divine blessings and not inherit any evil patterns. (Galatians 3:13)
- Lord, grant my children wisdom, knowledge, and understanding in all areas of life. Let them grow in stature, favor with God and man, just as Jesus did. (Luke 2:52)
- Father, shield my children from negative influences and ungodly associations. Surround them with godly mentors, friends, and teachers who will lead them closer to You. (Psalm 1:1-3)
- In the name of Jesus, I come against every spiritual attack aimed at my children. Let every arrow of the enemy be destroyed and let no harm come near them. (Psalm 91:10-11)
- Lord, I declare that my children will serve You with their gifts, talents, and time. Let them find joy and

fulfilment in worshiping and working for Your kingdom. (Joshua 24:15)

- Father, I commit my children's education and future careers into Your hands. Guide their steps, open doors of opportunity, and grant them success in their endeavors. (Proverbs 16:3)
- Lord, I speak divine health over my children. Let no sickness or disease have power over their bodies. Strengthen them physically, emotionally, and spiritually. (Exodus 15:26)
- Father, I pray that the spiritual gifts You have deposited in my children will be nurtured and used for Your glory. Let them walk in their divine calling with boldness. (1 Corinthians 12:4-7)
- Lord, I declare that my children will live victorious lives. No stronghold, oppression, or temptation will overcome them, for they are more than conquerors in Christ. (Romans 8:37)
- Father, I pray for my children's future friendships, mentors, and spouses. Let each relationship align with Your will and bring them closer to fulfilling their destiny. (Proverbs 27:17)
- Lord, equip my children with unwavering faith in You. Give them courage to stand firm in the face of trials and to boldly declare their allegiance to Christ. (2 Timothy 1:7)
- Father, grant my children hearts full of compassion and a desire to serve others. Let their lives be a reflection of Your love and grace. (Matthew 22:37-39)

- Lord, fill my children's lives with joy and peace that surpasses all understanding. Let them find their strength and satisfaction in You alone. (Philippians 4:7)
- Father, I release generational blessings upon my children and their descendants. Let them walk in prosperity, righteousness, and favor all their days. (Deuteronomy 28:1-14)
- Lord, I thank You for Your faithfulness in answering these prayers for my children. I trust that You will guide, protect, and bless them abundantly. (1 Thessalonians 5:24).

Prayer Points Against Satanic Dreams, Dream Contamination, Not Remembering Dreams, and Dream Manipulation

- Heavenly Father, I thank You for the gift of dreams through which You speak and reveal Your will. I honor You as the One who protects and guides me even in my sleep. (Job 33:14-16)
- Lord, I plead the blood of Jesus over my dreams. Let Your blood cleanse my dream life and protect it from every satanic contamination or manipulation. (Revelation 12:11)
- In the name of Jesus, I cancel and nullify every satanic dream sent to harm, oppress, or confuse me. Let such dreams be rendered powerless and ineffective. (Isaiah 54:17)
- Father, I come against every spirit of manipulation seeking to distort or control my dreams. I rebuke them

now in the name of Jesus and declare my dreams under Your divine authority. (2 Corinthians 10:4-5)

- Lord, I reject and renounce every demonic seed planted in my life through contaminated dreams. Let every evil deposit be uprooted and destroyed by fire in Jesus' name. (Matthew 15:13)
- Father, grant me clarity and discernment in my dream life. Let me distinguish between dreams from You and those from the enemy. Help me to interpret and act on Your divine revelations. (Daniel 2:22)
- Lord, restore my ability to remember dreams that come from You. I rebuke every spirit of forgetfulness assigned to steal divine revelations and instructions. (John 14:26)
- In the name of Jesus, I recover every blessing, virtue, and destiny stolen from me through satanic dreams. Let what the enemy meant for harm be turned into good. (Joel 2:25)
- Father, I break every evil covenant, agreement, or transaction entered into through my dreams. By the blood of Jesus, I am set free from every demonic attachment. (Colossians 2:14-15)
- Lord, I bind every spirit of fear, terror, or oppression that attacks me in my dreams. I declare that I shall lie down in peace and safety, for You are my refuge. (Psalm 4:8)
- In the name of Jesus, I break every connection with spirit spouses or any demonic entity appearing in my dreams. I command them to leave me now and never return. (Nahum 1:9)

- Father, release Your consuming fire into my dream life. Let every demonic power operating in my dreams be destroyed completely. (Hebrews 12:29)
- Lord, place a divine shield around me as I sleep. Let Your angels encamp around me and protect me from every spiritual attack in the night. (Psalm 34:7)
- In the name of Jesus, I cancel every negative decree, prophecy, or pronouncement made against me in the dream realm. I declare that they shall not stand or come to pass. (Isaiah 7:7)
- Lord, I declare victory over every power working against my dream life. I am more than a conqueror through Christ, and no weapon of the enemy shall prevail. (Romans 8:37)
- Father, I open my heart to receive divine dreams and visions from You. Speak to me clearly as You guide me in the path of righteousness. (Joel 2:28)
- In the name of Jesus, I command every demonic agent operating in my dreams to depart now. I declare my dream life off-limits to every work of darkness. (James 4:7)
- Lord, I rebuke every satanic dream aimed at causing delay, stagnation, or confusion in my life. I declare that I shall move forward and fulfil my divine destiny. (Isaiah 40:31)
- Father, I declare that my dream life is a channel of blessing, revelation, and breakthrough. I reject every form of corruption and invite Your Spirit to take control. (Genesis 37:5-7)

- Lord, I thank You for protecting my dream life and giving me the victory over every attack of the enemy. I praise You for the clarity, peace, and revelations I will experience in my sleep. (1 Thessalonians 5:18)

Prayer Points to Break Satanic Covenants and Initiations in the Dream

- Heavenly Father, I thank You for Your power to deliver and set captives free. Thank You for Your authority that breaks every yoke and satanic covenant. (Isaiah 10:27)
- Lord, I plead the blood of Jesus over my life. Let Your blood nullify every satanic covenant or initiation made in my dreams. (Revelation 12:11)
- In the name of Jesus, I renounce and reject every evil covenant entered into in my dreams, whether knowingly or unknowingly. I sever myself from these agreements completely. (2 Corinthians 6:14-15)
- Father, I break every chain of spiritual bondage tied to satanic initiations in the dream. Let every evil attachment and connection be destroyed by the power of the Holy Spirit. (Nahum 1:13)
- Lord, I command every evil deposit planted in my life through dreams to be uprooted and destroyed by Your fire. Let nothing from the enemy take root in my life. (Matthew 15:13)
- In the name of Jesus, I cancel every agreement, transaction, or vow made with demonic spirits during dreams. Let such agreements be null and void now. (Colossians 2:14-15)

- Father, I break every covenant with spirit spouses or any demonic entity seeking to claim ownership over me. I declare myself free by the blood of Jesus. (Isaiah 54:5)
- Lord, I reverse every satanic transaction conducted in my dreams. I reclaim everything stolen from me and declare that no loss shall prevail in my life. (Joel 2:25)
- In the name of Jesus, I destroy every demonic altar raised against me in the dream realm. Let the fire of God consume these altars and their sacrifices. (Deuteronomy 7:5)
- Father, I reject and renounce every demonic symbol, mark, or token received in my dreams. Let them be erased completely by the blood of Jesus. (Galatians 6:17)
- Lord, I command every demonic spirit that gained access to my life through dreams to leave now in the name of Jesus. Let no evil spirit find a foothold in me. (James 4:7)
- Father, I pray for a hedge of protection over my life. Let Your angels guard me as I sleep and let no demonic force invade my dreams again. (Psalm 91:10-11)
- In the name of Jesus, I nullify every negative word spoken over my life in dreams. Let every curse, decree, or pronouncement be overturned and replaced with Your blessings. (Isaiah 8:10)
- Lord, I reject every false covenant presented to me in the dream realm. I choose to align myself only with Your divine covenant through Jesus Christ. (Hebrews 8:6)
- Father, I break every ancestral covenant tied to my bloodline that manifests through dreams. Let Your blood

cleanse my lineage and deliver me from every generational bondage. (Lamentations 5:7)
- In the name of Jesus, I rebuke every spirit of manipulation working against my dreams. I take authority over my dream life and declare it fully surrendered to You, Lord. (2 Timothy 1:7)
- Lord, I recover every blessing, virtue, and opportunity stolen from me through satanic dreams. Let nothing be missing or lost in my destiny. (Obadiah 1:17)
- Father, I bind and destroy every monitoring spirit operating in my dreams. Let their plans be frustrated, and their assignments terminated now in Jesus' name. (Job 5:12)
- Lord, sanctify my dream life and let it be a channel for Your divine revelations and blessings. Let only the Holy Spirit have access to my dreams. (Joel 2:28)
- Heavenly Father, I thank You for delivering me from every satanic covenant and initiation in dreams. I praise You for the victory You have given me through Christ. (1 Corinthians 15:57)

Prayer Points for the Blood Covenant of Jesus Christ to Speak in Your Life

- Heavenly Father, I thank You for the precious blood of Jesus Christ that was shed for my redemption, justification, and victory. Thank You for the eternal covenant established through His sacrifice. (Hebrews 13:20-21)

- Lord, I acknowledge the blood covenant of Jesus Christ over my life. I declare that I belong to You and no other power has authority over me. (Colossians 1:13-14)
- Father, I plead the blood of Jesus over my spirit, soul, and body. Let Your blood sanctify me and speak better things than any other covenant. (Hebrews 12:24)
- In the name of Jesus, I cancel and nullify every negative covenant or agreement made against my life, knowingly or unknowingly. Only the blood covenant of Jesus will speak in my life. (Colossians 2:14-15)
- By the power of the blood of Jesus, I break every curse, evil pattern, and stronghold operating in my life and family. I declare freedom through the covenant of Jesus' blood. (Galatians 3:13)
- Lord, I declare that the blood of Jesus is my shield and protection. Let no weapon of the enemy prosper against me and let every evil plan be destroyed. (Isaiah 54:17)
- Father, let the blood of Jesus silence every voice of accusation, condemnation, or judgment speaking against me in the spiritual realm. Let His blood speak mercy, grace, and victory over me. (Revelation 12:11)
- Lord, let Your blood continually sanctify me and cleanse me from all unrighteousness. Purify my thoughts, words, and actions to align with Your will. (1 John 1:7)
- I declare that through the blood covenant of Jesus, I have life, restoration, and wholeness. Let the power of His blood restore everything the enemy has stolen from me. (John 10:10)
- In the name of Jesus, I break every demonic blood covenant or sacrifice speaking against my life. I declare

that only the blood of Jesus has power over me. (Leviticus 17:11)

- Father, I declare that the blood of Jesus has given me victory over sin, death, and hell. I am no longer bound by fear or guilt but walk in the freedom of Christ. (Romans 8:1-2)
- Lord, let the blood of Jesus speak better things over my destiny. Let it proclaim favor, blessings, and divine alignment in every area of my life. (Hebrews 12:24)
- By the blood of Jesus, I destroy every evil altar and monitoring spirit assigned against my life. Let the blood of Jesus erase every mark or claim they have on me. (1 Peter 1:18-19)
- Father, through the blood of Jesus, I receive healing and restoration in my body, mind, and spirit. Let every sickness bow to the power of His blood. (Isaiah 53:5)
- Lord, I declare that I am redeemed, justified, and made righteous through the blood of Jesus. No accusation or condemnation can stand against me. (Romans 5:9)
- In the name of Jesus, I break every ancestral or generational covenant that contradicts the blood covenant of Christ. Let His blood cleanse my bloodline and establish righteousness. (2 Corinthians 5:17)
- Father, I secure my future, family, and generations to come with the blood of Jesus. Let His covenant of peace, provision, and protection speak over us continually. (Isaiah 26:3)
- Lord, I declare that I overcome every trial, temptation, and attack by the blood of Jesus and the word of my testimony. (Revelation 12:11)

- Lord, let the blood of Jesus form a hedge of protection around me and my family. Let no evil come near us and let every attack be thwarted by the power of His blood. (Exodus 12:13)
- Father, I thank You for the blood of Jesus that has redeemed, restored, and reconciled me to You. I give You all the glory for the eternal victory I have through Him. (Ephesians 1:7)

Prayer Points Against Food Covenants in the Dream

- Heavenly Father, I thank You for Your power to deliver me from every form of spiritual defilement and covenant. Thank You for Your mercy and the authority You've given me through Christ Jesus. (Psalm 34:17)
- Lord, I plead the blood of Jesus over my spirit, soul, and body. Let Your blood cleanse me from every defilement caused by consuming food in dreams. (Revelation 12:11)
- In the name of Jesus, I nullify and cancel every demonic covenant entered into through food in dreams. Let every satanic agreement be broken and rendered powerless by the blood of Jesus. (Isaiah 28:18)
- Father, I reject and vomit every demonic food I consumed in my dreams. Let it have no effect on my life or destiny in Jesus' name. (Jeremiah 30:16)
- Lord, I command every evil deposit planted in my life through eating in dreams to be uprooted and destroyed by fire in the name of Jesus. (Matthew 15:13)

- Father, every spiritual poison I consumed in my dreams is neutralized by the blood of Jesus. I declare that my body is cleansed and healed in Jesus' name. (Mark 16:18)
- In the name of Jesus, I bind and cast out every spirit of manipulation, witchcraft, and control operating through dream food. Let their assignments against me be destroyed. (2 Corinthians 10:4-5)
- Lord, purify my spiritual and physical systems. Let every contamination or defilement caused by eating in dreams be flushed out by the power of the Holy Spirit. (Psalm 51:7)
- Father, I break every agreement or covenant made with satanic hosts or personalities through dream food. I sever myself from their influence in Jesus' name. (2 Corinthians 6:14-15)
- In the name of Jesus, I destroy every ancestral covenant tied to food and sacrifices in my lineage. Let the blood of Jesus cleanse my foundation and set me free. (Lamentations 5:7)
- Lord, I cancel every spirit of lack, poverty, or stagnation introduced into my life through dream food. Let Your blessings flow freely in my life. (Philippians 4:19).
- Father, I receive divine strength and renewal in my body, spirit, and soul. Let every weakness introduced through dream food be replaced by Your power and vitality. (Isaiah 40:31)
- Lord, I reclaim every virtue, blessing, and breakthrough stolen from me through eating in dreams. Let everything the enemy has taken be restored sevenfold. (Joel 2:25)

- In the name of Jesus, I bind and cast out every monitoring spirit or familiar spirit responsible for feeding me in my dreams. Let them be destroyed by fire. (Job 5:12)
- Father, I break every stronghold of witchcraft and occult power working against my destiny through food in dreams. I declare myself free in Jesus' name. (Micah 5:12)
- Lord, I declare deliverance over my dream life. Let my dreams be sanctified and protected from every satanic intrusion. (Joel 2:28)
- Father, I ask that You nourish me with Your Word, power, and presence. Let every spiritual hunger be satisfied by You alone. (Matthew 4:4)
- In the name of Jesus, I command every altar where food sacrifices were made against me to be destroyed by fire. Let no evil altar prevail over my life. (Deuteronomy 7:5)
- Lord, I cancel every negative effect of consuming food in dreams. Let sickness, spiritual weakness, delay, and confusion depart from my life now in Jesus' name. (Isaiah 54:17)
- Heavenly Father, I thank You for delivering me from every satanic food covenant. I declare that I am free, and only the covenant of the blood of Jesus will speak in my life. (John 8:36)

Prayer Points Against Evil Altars and Covenants Formed from Child Molestation

Child molestation is a wicked attack from the enemy, often used to create demonic covenants, altars, and bondage in the life of victims. These prayer points will break every evil connection, destroy satanic altars, and establish complete healing and restoration in Jesus' name.

- Father, I thank You because You are my Deliverer and Restorer! (Psalm 34:17-18)

- Lord, I acknowledge that You are my Redeemer, and no evil altar can have power over me! (Job 19:25)

- Thank You, Jesus, for shedding Your blood to set me free from every evil covenant! (Revelation 12:11)

- By the blood of Jesus, I break every covenant made through child molestation, knowingly or unknowingly! (Colossians 2:14-15)

- I renounce and reject any demonic soul tie formed through sexual abuse—I am free in Jesus' name! (2 Corinthians 6:14-15)

- Every evil altar where my name or destiny was submitted through molestation, be destroyed by fire! (Isaiah 49:24-26)

- Father, let Your fire consume every altar that was erected through my pain and innocence! (1 Kings 18:38)

- I command every demonic priest officiating over these altars to be judged by fire! (Exodus 22:18)

- Every altar of shame, oppression, and bondage fighting my life, catch fire now in Jesus' name! (Nahum 1:9)

- I plead the blood of Jesus over my body, mind, and emotions—let every defilement be washed away! (Leviticus 17:11)

- Jesus, cleanse my spirit from every contamination caused by this wicked act! (Ezekiel 36:25-26)

- I receive total emotional, mental, and spiritual healing in the mighty name of Jesus! (Psalm 147:3)

- Every spirit of fear, shame, and guilt linked to molestation, I cast you out in Jesus' name! (2 Timothy 1:7)

- I destroy every demonic pattern of rejection, brokenness, or immorality caused by this attack! (Isaiah 61:7)

- Every spiritual chain that was placed on my life through this evil act, break by fire now! (Psalm 107:14)

- I stand in the gap for my family and renounce every generational curse of sexual perversion! (Exodus 20:5-6)

- Every ancestral altar of molestation, incest, or abuse, be destroyed by the fire of God! (Jeremiah 1:10)

- I cancel every demonic agreement made by my ancestors that opened doors to this attack! (Lamentations 5:7)

- Every word spoken against my destiny through this experience, I cancel it by the blood of Jesus! (Isaiah 54:17)

- I break free from every identity distortion, confusion, or manipulation caused by molestation! (2 Corinthians 5:17)
- My destiny is realigned to God's purpose, and no demonic altar can divert my life! (Jeremiah 29:11)
- Father, restore every blessing stolen from me due to this attack! (Joel 2:25-26)
- I decree that I will not live under the shadow of my past—I am free in Jesus' name! (Romans 8:1)
- I declare that my testimony shall bring healing and deliverance to others in Jesus' name! (Revelation 12:11)
- I declare that I am an overcomer, and the enemy has no hold over me! (1 John 4:4)
- No evil altar from my past shall have any legal ground over my future! (Isaiah 43:18-19)
- I cover my future, my relationships, and my children under the blood of Jesus! (Exodus 12:13)

Prayer Points to Command Your Morning

- Heavenly Father, I thank You for the gift of life and for waking me up this morning. Thank You for Your mercies that are new every morning. Great is Your faithfulness. (Lamentations 3:22-23)
- Lord, I dedicate this day to You. Take pre-eminence over every activity, plan, and decision. Let Your will be done in my life today. (Proverbs 16:3)

- Father, I plead the blood of Jesus over my life, family, and this entire day. Let Your blood speak protection, blessings, and favor in every area of my life. (Revelation 12:11)
- I command this morning and the rest of the day to align with God's divine plan and purpose for my life. Let every element of creation cooperate with me and favor me today. (Job 38:12-13)
- Lord, I declare that no weapon formed against me today shall prosper. I cancel every plan of the enemy concerning my life and my family. (Isaiah 54:17)
- Father, I release Your angels to go ahead of me and prepare the way. Let them guard, guide, and protect me in all my ways today. (Psalm 91:11)
- Lord, I declare that Your favor surrounds me like a shield today. I walk into divine opportunities, open doors, and supernatural breakthroughs. (Psalm 5:12)
- Father, in the name of Jesus I declare that I will be productive and successful in all that I do today. I receive wisdom, strength, and excellence to carry out my assignments. (Philippians 4:13)
- In the name of Jesus, I cancel every negative word, curse, or pronouncement spoken against me or my day. Only Your promises and blessings will prevail. (Numbers 23:23)
- I bind every power of darkness assigned against my life today. Let every demonic agenda be frustrated and destroyed in Jesus' name. (Matthew 18:18).

- Lord, guide my steps today. Order my thoughts, words, and actions according to your word Lead me on the path of righteousness. (Psalm 37:23)
- I declare that today, I will experience the peace and joy of the Lord in every area of my life. Nothing will steal my peace or cause me to fear. (John 14:27)
- Father, I sanctify the atmosphere around me with the power of the Holy Spirit. Let Your presence fill my home, workplace, and everywhere I go today. (Exodus 33:14)
- Lord, I reclaim every lost opportunity and wasted time. Let there be restoration and acceleration in my life today. (Joel 2:25)
- I declare that I am more than a conqueror through Christ Jesus. Every challenge I face today will turn into a testimony. (Romans 8:37)
- Father, I pray for my family and loved ones. Protect, bless, and prosper them today. Let Your hand rest upon each of them. (3 John 1:2)
- Lord, I declare that Your Word will guide me today. Let it be a lamp to my feet and a light to my path. (Psalm 119:105)
- I release this day into Your capable hands, Lord. Let all things work together for my good according to Your purpose. (Romans 8:28)
- I take authority over this day and declare that it will cooperate with my divine destiny. Nothing will happen by accident; everything will align with God's will in Jesus' name. (Luke 10:19)

- Father, I thank You for hearing my prayers. I give You all the glory, honor, and praise for the blessings, protection, and breakthroughs You will manifest today. (1 Thessalonians 5:18)

Prayer Points for Commanding the Year

- Father, I thank You for bringing me into this new year. Thank You for Your grace, mercy, and unfailing love that has sustained me. I dedicate this year to You, Lord. (Psalm 100:4-5)
- Lord, I acknowledge You as the Alpha and Omega, the beginning and the end of this year. Take full control of every aspect of my life throughout this year. (Revelation 22:13)
- In the name of Jesus, I declare this year blessed. Every day, week, and month of this year will bring divine favor, breakthroughs, and testimonies. (Psalm 65:11)
- I plead the blood of Jesus over this year. Let His blood speak protection, victory, and deliverance over my life, family, and all that concerns me. (Revelation 12:11)
- In the name of Jesus, I cancel every plan, scheme, or agenda of the enemy against me and my family this year. No weapon formed against us shall prosper. (Isaiah 54:17)
- Father, let the heavens be open over my life this year. Pour out Your blessings, wisdom, and guidance in abundance. (Deuteronomy 28:12)

- Lord, I declare that this year I will recover every lost opportunity and wasted time. Let there be divine restoration in every area of my life. (Joel 2:25)
- Father, in the name of Jesus I declare that Your favor will surround me like a shield this year. Let doors of opportunity, promotion, and blessings open for me wherever I go. (Psalm 5:12)
- In the name of Jesus, I bind every spirit of delay, stagnation, and backwardness in my life this year. I declare supernatural progress and advancement. (Isaiah 40:31)
- Lord, I break every limitation, barrier, or obstacle standing in the way of my progress and purpose this year. I declare that nothing will hold me back. (Philippians 4:13)
- Father, I declare that You will protect and preserve me and my family throughout this year. No evil will come near us. (Psalm 91:1-2)
- Lord, I decree that this year I will walk in financial abundance. Bless the work of my hands and establish me in prosperity. (Philippians 4:19)
- Father, I pray that this year I will grow deeper in my relationship with You. Help me to walk in holiness, righteousness, and obedience to Your Word. (Colossians 2:6-7)
- Lord, I declare that this year I will fulfil my divine purpose and destiny. Lead me in the path You have ordained for me. (Jeremiah 29:11)

- I declare that this year I will experience the peace and joy of the Lord in every area of my life. Nothing will steal my peace. (John 14:27)
- In the name of Jesus, I command fruitfulness in every area of my life this year—spiritually, financially, relationally, and professionally. (Genesis 1:28)
- Lord, I release Your angels to go before me and prepare the way. Let them protect, guide, and fight on my behalf throughout this year. (Psalm 91:11)
- I declare that this year will be filled with divine breakthroughs, miracles, and answered prayers. (Micah 2:13)
- Father, I consecrate this year to You. Let Your will alone be done in my life and family. Take all the glory for every testimony and blessing this year. (Matthew 6:10)
- Lord, I thank You in advance for a victorious and successful year. I give You all the glory for what You have done and will do. (1 Thessalonians 5:18)

Prayer Points Against Sickness and Diseases

- Heavenly Father, I thank You for the gift of life and the promise of divine health. Thank You for being my healer and sustainer. (Exodus 15:26)
- I plead the blood of Jesus over my body, spirit, and soul. Let the blood of Jesus flush out every sickness, disease, and infirmity from my life. (Revelation 12:11)

- Lord, You are Jehovah Rapha, my healer. I declare that by Your stripes, I am healed and made whole in Jesus' name. (Isaiah 53:5)
- In the name of Jesus, I cancel every arrow of sickness, disease, or infirmity sent by the enemy against me or my family. Let it return to the sender. (Psalm 91:10)
- Father, I break every yoke of infirmity operating in my body. I declare that sickness has no power over me in Jesus' name. (Matthew 8:17)
- I come against every generational curse of sickness and disease in my bloodline. I declare that I am set free by the blood of Jesus. (Galatians 3:13)
- Lord, my body is Your temple. Let no sickness, disease, or contamination defile it. Cleanse and restore me completely in Jesus' name. (1 Corinthians 6:19-20)
- Father, I pray for divine immunity against every sickness, infection, and disease. Let my immune system be strengthened by Your power. (Deuteronomy 7:15)
- In the name of Jesus, I bind every spirit of sickness, disease, and infirmity working against my health. I cast it out of my life by the authority of Christ. (Matthew 18:18)
- Lord, I declare that every organ, tissue, and system in my body is healed and restored to perfect function in Jesus' name. (Jeremiah 30:17)
- Father, I reject every fear of sickness or disease. I declare that I will walk in boldness, trusting in Your promises of health and life. (2 Timothy 1:7)

- I rebuke every chronic illness or recurring sickness in my body. I declare an end to its affliction in the name of Jesus. (Nahum 1:9)
- Lord, I pray that every hidden sickness or disease in my body, whether known or unknown, be exposed and destroyed by Your power. (Luke 8:17)
- Father, I stand on Your promises of healing. Let Your Word bring life and health to every part of my being. (Proverbs 4:20-22)
- In the name of Jesus, I cancel every assignment of sickness or disease targeted at my destiny. I declare that my purpose will not be cut short. (Psalm 118:17)
- Lord, I pray for divine strength in my body. Let weakness and fatigue be replaced with Your supernatural energy and vitality. (Isaiah 40:29)
- I declare that I am free from every sickness and disease because the Son has set me free. I walk in liberty and perfect health in Jesus' name. (John 8:36)
- Father, protect me and my family from any epidemic, pandemic, or outbreak of disease. Let no plague come near my dwelling. (Psalm 91:3-7)
- Lord, I pray for divine healing over every member of my family. Let Your healing power flow through our household in Jesus' name. (3 John 1:2)
- Father, I thank You for healing me and restoring my health. I declare that I will live in divine health and testify of Your goodness. (Psalm 103:2-3)

Prayer Points Against Untimely/Premature Death

- Heavenly Father, I thank You for the gift of life and for preserving me and my family thus far. I give You all the glory for Your protection and mercy. (Psalm 103:1-5)
- Lord, I stand on Your promise in Psalm 91:16 that You will satisfy me with long life and show me Your salvation. I declare that I will fulfil the number of my days in Jesus' name.
- I plead the blood of Jesus over my life, family, and loved ones. Let the blood speak protection and preservation for us against the spirit of death. (Revelation 12:11)
- In the name of Jesus, I cancel every spirit of untimely death assigned against me or my family. I declare that the plans of the enemy are destroyed. (Isaiah 54:17)
- Father, I break every generational curse of untimely death in my bloodline. Let every covenant of premature death be destroyed by the blood of Jesus. (Galatians 3:13)
- Lord, I declare that no weapon formed against me shall prosper. I will dwell under the shadow of the Almighty and no harm shall come near me. (Psalm 91:1-7)
- I decree that no accident, calamity, or tragedy will come near me or my family. The angels of the Lord will guard and protect us in all our ways. (Psalm 34:7)
- In the name of Jesus, I cancel every dream of death, burial, or mourning. I declare that those evil plans are null and void. (Job 5:12)

- I speak life over my destiny and purpose. I will live to fulfil every divine assignment and promise ordained for me. (Psalm 118:17)
- In Jesus' name, I command every monitoring spirit or agent of death to be consumed by the fire of the Holy Ghost. I declare my life is hidden in Christ. (Colossians 3:3)
- Father, I reject every spirit of fear and anxiety concerning untimely death. I declare that God has not given me the spirit of fear but of power, love, and a sound mind. (2 Timothy 1:7)
- Lord, I cover my family with the blood of Jesus. No member of my household will die untimely. We will all live to declare the works of the Lord. (Exodus 12:13)
- In the name of Jesus, I bind every spirit of sickness or disease assigned to cut my life short. I declare divine health and healing over my body. (Jeremiah 30:17)
- Father, in the name of Jesus, release Your angels to encamp around me and my family. Let them protect us from every form of harm and danger. (Psalm 91:11)
- I destroy every evil altar speaking death against my life. Let every sacrifice made against me be nullified by the blood of Jesus. (1 Kings 18:38)
- I declare that my household will not experience sorrow, mourning, or premature death. We will enjoy divine peace and joy. (Isaiah 65:20)
- In Jesus' name, I cancel every negative word or pronouncement of death made against me or my loved ones. Only the Word of God will prevail in my life. (Numbers 23:23)

- Lord, grant me the wisdom to avoid every trap or snare of the enemy. Order my steps and keep me from evil. (Proverbs 3:5-6)
- I declare that death has been swallowed up in victory through Jesus Christ. I will live and not die, and I will proclaim the works of the Lord. (1 Corinthians 15:55-57)
- Father, I thank You for preserving my life and the lives of my loved ones. I give You all the glory for the testimonies of divine protection and long life. (1 Thessalonians 5:18)

Prayer Points Against Cancer of Any Kind

- Father, I thank You for being the Lord who heals all diseases. I praise You for Your love, mercy, and power over sickness and infirmities. (Exodus 15:26)
- Lord, I stand on Your Word that by the stripes of Jesus, I am healed. I declare that cancer has no place in my body. (Isaiah 53:5)
- I plead the blood of Jesus over every part of my body. Let the blood of Jesus flush out every cancerous cell and purify my body. (Revelation 12:11)
- In the name of Jesus, I command every cancerous cell in my body to die by fire. I speak life and restoration to every affected organ. (Mark 11:23)
- I bind the spirit of infirmity behind cancer in Jesus' name. I command it to loose its hold over me and my loved ones. (Luke 13:12)

- Father, I break every generational curse or pattern of cancer in my family line. Let it be destroyed by the power of the Holy Spirit. (Galatians 3:13)
- Lord, my body is Your temple. I declare that no disease or infirmity will defile it. Cancer has no legal right to operate in my body. (1 Corinthians 6:19)
- Father, I pray for total healing and restoration of my body. Let every organ, tissue, and cell be renewed by Your power. (Jeremiah 30:17)
- In the name of Jesus, I cancel every negative medical report and declare that only the report of the Lord will stand concerning my health. (Isaiah 53:1)
- I declare that I am free from the bondage of cancer and every associated pain, weakness, and suffering. (John 8:36)
- I reject every spirit of fear and anxiety about cancer. I trust in the Lord for healing and deliverance. (2 Timothy 1:7)
- Lord, strengthen my immune system to fight against every form of cancer. Let my body align with divine health and wholeness. (Deuteronomy 7:15)
- In Jesus' name, I rebuke every spirit of death working through cancer. I declare that I will live and not die, and I will proclaim the works of the Lord. (Psalm 118:17)
- Father, I destroy every evil altar speaking sickness, disease, or cancer into my life. Let those altars be consumed by fire in Jesus' name. (1 Kings 18:38)
- In the name of Jesus, I declare that cancer will not return to my body. I seal my healing with the blood of Jesus. (Nahum 1:9)

- I declare that cancer is defeated in my life. I walk in the victory that Christ has already won for me. (1 Corinthians 15:57)
- Lord, guide the doctors and caregivers involved in my treatment. Let their decisions align with Your will and let all treatments bring success. (James 1:5)
- Father, release Your healing power into every fiber of my being. Let Your resurrection power flow through my body, destroying every trace of cancer. (Romans 8:11)
- Lord, grant me supernatural strength, peace, and joy as I walk through this healing journey. Let Your grace be sufficient for me. (2 Corinthians 12:9)
- Father, I thank You in advance for healing me and restoring my health. I give You all the glory for the testimony of my deliverance. (Psalm 103:2-3)

Prayer Points Against Schizophrenia

- Heavenly Father, I thank You because You are a God of healing, peace, and deliverance. I praise You for the power in Your name to set the captives free. (Psalm 107:20)
- Lord, You are Jehovah Rapha, the God who heals. I declare that schizophrenia is not above Your power. By Your stripes, I claim healing and restoration. (Isaiah 53:5)
- I plead the blood of Jesus over my mind, emotions, and spirit. Let the blood of Jesus wash away every oppression and disorder in my life. (Revelation 12:11)

- In the name of Jesus, I bind and cast out every spirit of mental torment, confusion, delusion, and hallucination working against me. (2 Timothy 1:7)
- I declare that I am free from every yoke of schizophrenia or mental illness. Jesus Christ has set me free, and I will not be enslaved again. (Galatians 5:1)
- Father, I rebuke every spirit of fear and anxiety operating in my mind. I declare that You have given me power, love, and a sound mind. (2 Timothy 1:7)
- Lord, I break every generational curse of mental illness, schizophrenia, or emotional instability in my family. I declare that I am redeemed by the blood of Jesus. (Galatians 3:13)
- I command my mind to align with the Word of God. I have the mind of Christ, and every thought contrary to God's truth is cast down. (2 Corinthians 10:5)
- In the name of Jesus, I destroy every evil altar speaking mental affliction into my life. Let the fire of the Holy Ghost consume it now. (1 Kings 18:38)
- Father, I pray for complete healing and restoration of my mind, emotions, and thoughts. Let every broken part of my soul be made whole. (Jeremiah 30:17)
- I pull down every mental stronghold and argument that exalts itself against the knowledge of God. I bring every thought into obedience to Christ. (2 Corinthians 10:4-5)
- Lord, I declare Your peace over my mind. Let every storm raging in my mind be still, and let Your peace that surpasses all understanding guard my heart and mind. (Philippians 4:7)

- In Jesus' name, I rebuke and expel every spirit of schizophrenia, confusion, or double-mindedness. I declare that it has no place in my life. (James 1:8)
- Father, protect my mind from every attack of the enemy. I cover my thoughts and emotions with the blood of Jesus. (Isaiah 26:3)
- Lord, I release the Spirit of soundness, clarity, and stability over my life. Let my mind be fully restored to operate in alignment with Your will. (Romans 12:2)
- In the name of Jesus, I silence every negative, demonic voice speaking lies, accusations, or confusion into my mind. I hear only the voice of the Holy Spirit. (John 10:27)
- Lord, I come against the spirit of isolation and withdrawal caused by schizophrenia. Surround me with Your love, comfort, and community. (Psalm 68:6)
- I declare that I am a child of God, fearfully and wonderfully made. My identity is rooted in Christ, not in any disorder or diagnosis. (Psalm 139:14)
- Father, I pray for supernatural strength and grace to walk through the journey of healing and deliverance. Let Your joy be my strength. (Nehemiah 8:10)
- Lord, I thank You for the victory and healing You have given me. I declare that I will testify of Your goodness and mercy in my life. (Psalm 118:17)

Prayer Points Against Depression

- Heavenly Father, I thank You for Your unfailing love and faithfulness. Thank You for being my refuge and strength in times of trouble. (Psalm 46:1)
- Lord, I declare that You are greater than depression and every emotional burden in my life. You are my deliverer, and I trust in Your power. (1 John 4:4)
- I plead the blood of Jesus over my mind, heart, and emotions. Let the blood of Jesus cleanse and purify me from every form of heaviness and despair. (Revelation 12:11)
- In the name of Jesus, I command the spirit of heaviness and despair to leave me now. I put on the garment of praise for the spirit of heaviness. (Isaiah 61:3)
- Father, I cast all my burdens and anxieties upon You because You care for me. I refuse to carry the weight of depression any longer. (1 Peter 5:7)
- Lord, I declare that the joy of the Lord is my strength. Fill my heart with Your joy and peace, and let it overflow into every area of my life. (Nehemiah 8:10)
- In Jesus' name, I silence every negative thought and voice of self-condemnation. I declare that my mind is renewed and focused on the truth of God's Word. (Romans 12:2)
- Lord, I break every chain of emotional bondage and oppression over my life. I declare freedom and healing in Jesus' name. (Isaiah 10:27)
- Father, let Your peace that surpasses all understanding guard my heart and mind. I reject every spirit of worry and anxiety. (Philippians 4:6-7)

- I declare that fear has no place in my life. I have not been given a spirit of fear but of power, love, and a sound mind. (2 Timothy 1:7)
- I reject every lie of the enemy that says I am worthless, unloved, or hopeless. I declare that I am loved, chosen, and precious in God's sight. (Ephesians 1:4-5)
- Lord, restore my hope and confidence in You. Let my heart be filled with expectation for the good plans You have for my life. (Jeremiah 29:11)
- I release the spirit of praise over my life. I will bless the Lord at all times, and His praise will continually be in my mouth. (Psalm 34:1)
- Father, when I feel weak, remind me that Your strength is made perfect in my weakness. I depend on You for strength each day. (2 Corinthians 12:9)
- Lord, I break every generational curse or pattern of depression in my family line. I declare that it will not pass down to me or my descendants. (Galatians 3:13)
- Holy Spirit, You are my Comforter. Wrap me in Your loving presence and bring comfort to my soul. (John 14:26)
- I declare that I am a child of God, fearfully and wonderfully made. My identity is rooted in Christ, and I reject all feelings of inadequacy or failure. (Psalm 139:14)
- Lord, surround me with godly relationships that will encourage, uplift, and pray with me. Let me never feel alone. (Proverbs 17:17)
- In Jesus' name, I rebuke and cast out every spirit of suicide and hopelessness. I declare that I will live and

not die, and I will declare the works of the Lord. (Psalm 118:17)
- Father, I thank You for healing me from depression. I give You all the glory for setting me free and restoring my joy and peace. (Psalm 103:2-4)

Prayer Points Against Suicide

- Heavenly Father, I thank You for the gift of life that You have given me. I acknowledge that my life is precious in Your sight and a testimony of Your goodness. (Psalm 139:13-14)
- Lord, I declare that I was created for a purpose. My life is not an accident, and You have plans for me that are good and full of hope. (Jeremiah 29:11)
- I plead the blood of Jesus over my mind, emotions, and thoughts. Let the blood of Jesus break every spirit of death, hopelessness, and despair. (Revelation 12:11)
- In the name of Jesus, I bind and cast out every spirit of suicide, hopelessness, and self-destruction. I command it to leave my life now and never return. (Matthew 18:18)
- Father, I declare that I am fearfully and wonderfully made. I am chosen, loved, and valued by You. My life is a reflection of Your glory. (Psalm 139:14)
- In Jesus' name, I cancel every satanic assignment, plan, or whisper of death over my life. I declare that only the will of God will stand in my life. (Isaiah 54:17)
- Lord, I reject every lie of the enemy that says I am worthless, unloved, or a failure. I declare that I am deeply loved and cherished by You. (John 10:10)

- Holy Spirit, I ask for Your comfort and peace to surround me. Replace every feeling of sadness and despair with the joy of the Lord. (John 14:26)
- In the name of Jesus, I break every chain of depression, heaviness, and sadness over my life. I declare that I walk in freedom and joy. (Isaiah 61:3)
- Father, I cast all my burdens, worries, and anxieties on You. I trust You to carry me through every storm of life. (1 Peter 5:7)
- I declare that I will live and not die. I will fulfil the plans and purposes that God has for my life. (Psalm 118:17)
- Lord, renew my mind with Your Word. Let every negative and suicidal thought be replaced with thoughts of hope, peace, and purpose. (Romans 12:2)
- In the name of Jesus, I destroy every evil altar speaking death or self-harm over my life. Let those altars be consumed by the fire of the Holy Spirit. (1 Kings 18:38)
- Father, I declare that nothing can separate me from Your love. Your love is greater than every feeling of despair or unworthiness. (Romans 8:38-39)
- Lord, strengthen me in my weakness and restore my hope in You. Fill me with the assurance that You are with me always. (Isaiah 40:29)
- In Jesus' name, I break every generational curse of self-harm, suicide, or hopelessness in my family line. I declare that I am set free by the blood of Jesus. (Galatians 3:13)
- Father, surround me with people who will encourage, uplift, and support me in my walk with You. Let me feel Your love through others. (Proverbs 17:17)

- I rebuke every spirit of fear and anxiety that fuels suicidal thoughts. I declare that God has given me a spirit of power, love, and a sound mind. (2 Timothy 1:7)
- I declare that God's promises for my life are yes and amen. I will experience His goodness and mercy all the days of my life. (2 Corinthians 1:20)
- Lord, I thank You for delivering me from every suicidal thought and giving me a new lease on life. I will testify of Your faithfulness and goodness. (Psalm 103:2-4)

Prayer Points Against Respiratory Illnesses (Acute or Chronic)

- Father, I thank You for being my Healer and Deliverer. I praise You for the gift of life and for breathing Your breath of life into me. (Genesis 2:7)
- Lord, You are Jehovah Rapha, the God who heals. I declare that every respiratory illness in my body must bow to the power of Your name. (Exodus 15:26)
- I plead the blood of Jesus over my respiratory system. Let the blood of Jesus cleanse and heal every part of my lungs, bronchi, and airways. (Revelation 12:11)
- In the name of Jesus, I rebuke and cast out every spirit of infirmity causing respiratory illnesses in my body. I declare freedom from its grip. (Luke 13:11-12)
- Lord, I pray for the full restoration of my breathing. Let every breath I take be free and unhindered by sickness or disease. (Job 33:4)
- Father, I declare healing over every chronic respiratory condition, including asthma, COPD, bronchitis, and

allergies. I proclaim complete restoration in Jesus' name. (Jeremiah 30:17)

- In the name of Jesus, I break every generational curse of respiratory illnesses in my family line. I declare that I am redeemed by the blood of Jesus. (Galatians 3:13)
- Lord, breathe Your life-giving breath into my lungs and renew every cell, tissue, and organ in my respiratory system. (Ezekiel 37:5-6)
- I cancel every medical diagnosis of respiratory sickness and declare that only the report of the Lord will stand in my life. (Isaiah 53:1)
- Father, let Your fire consume the root of every respiratory illness in my body. Destroy it completely and remove its effects from my life. (Jeremiah 1:10)
- I declare the Word of the Lord that says by His stripes, I am healed. I receive total healing for my lungs and airways. (Isaiah 53:5)
- In Jesus' name, I rebuke every environmental factor or substance triggering respiratory issues in my life. Let me be protected from every harmful element. (Psalm 121:7-8)
- Father, strengthen my body and immune system to fight against every respiratory illness. Let my body be renewed by Your power. (Isaiah 40:29)
- I command every symptom of respiratory illness—shortness of breath, coughing, wheezing, or fatigue—to cease now in the name of Jesus. (Mark 11:23)
- Lord, I declare that my body is covered by the blood of Jesus. No infection, virus, or chronic condition will prevail against me. (Psalm 91:10)

- I rebuke every spirit of fear and anxiety over my health. I declare that I walk in faith, not fear, because God has not given me a spirit of fear. (2 Timothy 1:7)
- Lord, I anoint myself for healing in the name of Jesus. Let Your healing anointing flow through me and restore my respiratory system. (James 5:14-15)
- Father, I declare freedom from dependency on chronic medication. Heal me completely so that I can live without medical intervention. (Exodus 23:25)
- Lord, I proclaim that You have promised me long life and good health. I shall not be cut off prematurely by respiratory illnesses. (Psalm 91:16)
- Father, I thank You for healing my body and restoring my respiratory system. I give You all the glory for this miracle and declare that my testimony will glorify Your name. (Psalm 103:1-3)

Prayer Points Against Anxiety

- Heavenly Father, I thank You for being my refuge and strength. I praise You for Your faithfulness and constant presence in my life. (Psalm 46:1)
- Lord, I cast all my worries, fears, and anxieties upon You, for You care deeply for me. I refuse to carry these burdens any longer. (1 Peter 5:7)
- Father, I declare that the peace of God, which surpasses all understanding, is guarding my heart and mind in Christ Jesus. (Philippians 4:6-7)
- In the name of Jesus, I rebuke and cast out the spirit of fear and anxiety. I declare that God has not given me a

spirit of fear but of power, love, and a sound mind. (2 Timothy 1:7)

- Lord, I trust in You with all my heart and lean not on my own understanding. I acknowledge You in all my ways, and I trust You to direct my paths. (Proverbs 3:5-6)
- I declare that I will not worry about tomorrow, for tomorrow will worry about itself. I choose to live in the present, trusting God for my future. (Matthew 6:34)
- Father, I break every hold of anxiety, panic, and stress over my life. I declare that they have no power over me in Jesus' name. (John 14:27)
- Lord, renew my mind with Your Word. Let my thoughts be filled with Your truth and not with fear or doubt. (Romans 12:2)
- I declare that I am the head and not the tail, above and not beneath. God's promises for me are good, and He will never fail. (Deuteronomy 28:13)
- Father, I receive Your strength to face every challenge. I can do all things through Christ who strengthens me. (Philippians 4:13)
- Lord, I choose to replace anxiety with thanksgiving. I will focus on Your goodness and praise You for all You have done. (1 Thessalonians 5:18)
- In the name of Jesus, I speak peace into every situation causing anxiety in my life. Let every storm be stilled by Your power. (Mark 4:39)
- Father, I trust that You will supply all my needs according to Your riches in glory. I refuse to worry about lack or insufficiency. (Philippians 4:19)

- In Jesus' name, I break every generational curse or pattern of anxiety and worry in my family line. I declare freedom and peace over my life. (Galatians 3:13)
- Holy Spirit, be my Comforter in times of trouble. Wrap me in Your presence and remind me that I am never alone. (John 14:26)
- Lord, I surrender control of my life to You. I trust You to guide my steps and lead me into peace and fulfilment. (Jeremiah 29:11)
- Father, help me to think on things that are true, noble, right, pure, lovely, and praiseworthy. Let my mind be filled with Your truth. (Philippians 4:8)
- Lord, let me lie down in peace and sleep, for You alone make me dwell in safety. I rebuke every spirit of restlessness and insomnia. (Psalm 4:8)
- I declare that I am more than a conqueror through Christ. Anxiety has no power over me, and I walk in total freedom. (Romans 8:37)
- Father, I thank You for delivering me from anxiety and fear. I praise You for giving me peace, joy, and a sound mind. (Psalm 34:4)

Prayer Points Against Chronic Non-Communicable Diseases (e.g., Hypertension, Diabetes)

- Heavenly Father, I thank You for being Jehovah Rapha, my Healer. I praise You for the power in Your Word that brings restoration and wholeness to my body. (Exodus 15:26)
- Lord, I plead the blood of Jesus over my body. Let the blood of Jesus flush out every chronic illness and repair every damaged organ in my body. (Revelation 12:11)
- In the name of Jesus, I rebuke every spirit of infirmity behind hypertension, diabetes, and other chronic diseases. I cast them out of my life by the power of God. (Luke 13:11-12)
- Father, Your Word declares that by the stripes of Jesus, I am healed. I stand on this promise and declare total healing and restoration over my body. (Isaiah 53:5)
- Lord, I break the stronghold of chronic diseases in my body. I declare that they have no power over me because I am redeemed by Your blood. (Galatians 3:13)
- Father, replace every unhealthy heart, pancreas, or organ in my body with a new one. Renew my strength and restore me to perfect health. (Ezekiel 36:26)
- In Jesus' name, I destroy every root cause of hypertension, diabetes, or any chronic illness in my body. Let the fire of God consume every sickness from its foundation. (Jeremiah 1:10)
- I declare that sickness and disease will not rule over my life. I walk in divine health, for my body is the temple of the Holy Spirit. (1 Corinthians 6:19-20)

- In the name of Jesus, I break every generational curse or inherited condition that has passed down through my bloodline. I declare that I am set free by the blood of Jesus. (Lamentations 5:7)
- Lord, renew my strength like the eagle's. Restore vitality to my body and energy to every weak part of my being. (Isaiah 40:31)
- Father, guide me to make the right dietary and lifestyle decisions that will sustain my healing and glorify You through my body. (1 Corinthians 10:31)
- I rebuke every fear, anxiety, or stress contributing to these chronic conditions. I declare that the peace of God rules in my heart and mind. (Philippians 4:6-7)
- Lord, let Your creative power bring new life to every damaged cell, tissue, and organ in my body. Let my blood pressure and sugar levels normalize in Jesus' name. (Psalm 139:14)
- Father, I declare that I will not be dependent on medications for the rest of my life. Heal me completely so that I will testify of Your healing power. (Exodus 23:25)
- In the name of Jesus, I cancel every satanic assignment, plan, or covenant that has brought chronic illness into my life. I am free in Jesus' name. (Isaiah 54:17)
- Lord, I declare that I will live a long and healthy life. I shall not die prematurely because of any sickness or disease. (Psalm 91:16)
- Father, I ask for the complete restoration of every organ that has been damaged by disease. Let my body function

perfectly according to Your divine design. (Jeremiah 30:17)
- Lord, I declare that every promise of health, healing, and wholeness in Your Word will manifest in my life. Your Word never fails. (2 Corinthians 1:20)
- Father, protect me from any worsening of these conditions or new health challenges. Let Your hedge of protection surround my body. (Job 1:10)
- Lord, I thank You for healing me completely from all chronic illnesses. I declare that my testimony will glorify Your name and inspire others to trust in You. (Psalm 103:1-3)

Prayer Points Against Diseases of the Eyes

- Heavenly Father, I thank You for being the God who heals. I praise You for Your power to restore my vision and health. (Exodus 15:26)
- Lord, I plead the blood of Jesus over my eyes. Let His blood cleanse and heal every part of my eyes, removing every disease and imperfection. (Revelation 12:11)
- Father, You are Jehovah Rapha, my Healer. I declare that every disease or infirmity affecting my eyes is healed in Jesus' name. (Psalm 103:3)
- In the name of Jesus, I rebuke every spirit of blindness, glaucoma, cataracts, or any other eye condition. I command it to leave my body now! (Mark 10:51-52)
- Lord, restore perfect vision to my eyes. Let them function according to Your divine design and purpose. (Matthew 20:34)

- Father, destroy every root cause of eye diseases in my life, whether spiritual, physical, or hereditary. Uproot every infirmity by Your power. (Jeremiah 1:10)
- In the name of Jesus, I speak healing to every damaged nerve, retina, cornea, and tissue in my eyes. Let them be fully restored. (Isaiah 58:8)
- Lord, I declare that all pain, pressure, and discomfort in my eyes are gone. I receive Your peace and healing now. (Psalm 147:3)
- In the name of Jesus, I break every generational curse of eye diseases that has been passed down in my family. I am set free by the blood of Jesus. (Galatians 3:13)
- Father, strengthen my eyes and renew their function. Let my vision be restored and remain clear and sharp. (Isaiah 40:31)
- Lord, Your Word declares that by Your stripes, I am healed. I claim this promise for my eyes and declare total healing. (Isaiah 53:5)
- I rebuke every fear and anxiety of losing my vision. I declare that I will not be overcome by fear because God is with me. (2 Timothy 1:7)
- In Jesus' name, I destroy every spiritual attack or demonic assignment against my vision. Let every plan of the enemy be nullified. (1 John 3:8)
- Lord, let Your divine light shine upon my eyes. Drive out every darkness and disease, and restore clarity to my sight. (Psalm 119:105)
- Father, just as You restored sight to the blind, I declare complete restoration over my eyes. Let my testimony glorify You. (Mark 8:25)

- I cancel every negative medical report concerning my eyes in Jesus' name. Only the report of the Lord will stand in my life. (Isaiah 53:1)
- Lord, I ask for Your divine protection over my eyes. Shield me from any further damage or sickness. (Psalm 121:7-8)
- I declare life and vitality over my eyes. Let them see clearly and perform all their functions perfectly. (Proverbs 4:20-22)
- Father, I intercede for anyone suffering from diseases of the eyes. Let Your healing power touch them and restore their vision. (James 5:15)
- Lord, I thank You for healing my eyes and restoring my vision. I praise You for the miracle You have done in my life. (Psalm 103:1-3)

Prayer Points Against Low Self-Esteem

- Heavenly Father, I thank You because I am fearfully and wonderfully made in Your image. I praise You for creating me with love and purpose. (Psalm 139:14)
- In the name of Jesus, I rebuke and cast out every spirit of rejection, inferiority, and low self-worth. I declare that I am accepted in Christ. (Ephesians 1:6)
- Lord, I declare that my identity is in You. I am a child of God, chosen, loved, and called for greatness. (1 Peter 2:9)
- Father, heal every wound in my heart caused by words, actions, or experiences that made me feel less than You created me to be. (Psalm 34:18)

- In Jesus' name, I reject every negative thought about myself. I take every thought captive and make it obedient to Christ. (2 Corinthians 10:5)
- Lord, I declare that I will no longer walk in fear or self-doubt. I will walk in boldness and confidence, knowing that You are with me. (Proverbs 3:26)
- Father, I reject the spirit of fear and timidity. I receive the spirit of power, love, and a sound mind to fulfil my purpose. (2 Timothy 1:7)
- Lord, I release every past failure, mistake, and disappointment that has held me back. I embrace Your plans for my future. (Isaiah 43:18-19)
- I declare that I am more than a conqueror through Christ who loves me. I can do all things through Christ who strengthens me. (Romans 8:37; Philippians 4:13)
- In the name of Jesus, I break every lie of the enemy telling me I am unworthy, inadequate, or unloved. I declare that only God's truth will stand in my life. (John 8:32)
- Father, reveal to me the purpose You have for my life. Help me to walk boldly in my calling and live as You designed me to live. (Jeremiah 29:11)
- Lord, restore the joy of my salvation and fill my heart with Your peace that surpasses all understanding. (Philippians 4:7)
- Father, I declare that I will no longer compare myself to others. I am unique, and my worth comes from You alone. (2 Corinthians 10:12)

- Lord, teach me to love and accept myself as You love and accept me. Help me to see myself through Your eyes. (Matthew 22:39)
- In Jesus' name, I break every generational pattern of low self-esteem and insecurity in my family. I declare that I am free. (Galatians 3:13)
- Father, renew my mind and transform my thoughts. Help me to focus on what is true, noble, right, pure, lovely, and admirable. (Romans 12:2; Philippians 4:8)
- Lord, let Your perfect love cast out all fear and insecurity in my heart. Fill me with the assurance of Your unconditional love. (1 John 4:18)
- Father, surround me with people who will encourage, uplift, and affirm my God-given worth and potential. (Proverbs 27:17)
- I declare that in my weakness, God's strength is made perfect. I am strong because God's grace is sufficient for me. (2 Corinthians 12:9)
- Lord, I thank You for delivering me from low self-esteem. I praise You forgiving me confidence, boldness, and joy in who You created me to be. (Psalm 107:2)

Prayer Points Against Drug Abuse/Addiction

- Heavenly Father, I thank You for Your power to deliver and set captives free. I praise You because nothing is impossible for You. (Luke 1:37)
- Lord, I declare that You are greater than any addiction or stronghold in my life or the lives of my loved ones.

You have the power to break every chain. (Colossians 1:13)

- In the name of Jesus, I rebuke and cast out every spirit of bondage, addiction, and dependency on drugs. I declare freedom in Christ. (Romans 8:15)
- I plead the blood of Jesus over my mind, body, and spirit. Let the blood cleanse and sanctify me from all effects of drug abuse. (Revelation 12:11)
- Father, uproot every root cause of addiction, whether emotional, spiritual, or physical. Heal every wound and void that led to this struggle. (Jeremiah 30:17)
- Lord, I break every chain of cravings and dependency on drugs in Jesus' name. Let every demonic stronghold behind these cravings be destroyed. (Isaiah 10:27)
- I declare that I am free from addiction, for whom the Son sets free is free indeed. I receive the liberty Christ has given me. (John 8:36)
- Father, renew my mind and transform my thoughts. Help me to focus on things that are holy, pure, and pleasing to You. (Romans 12:2; Philippians 4:8)
- In the name of Jesus, I break every generational curse of addiction or substance abuse in my bloodline. I declare that I am a new creation in Christ. (Galatians 3:13)
- Lord, grant me the strength to resist every temptation and trigger that leads to substance abuse. Deliver me from the snare of the enemy. (1 Corinthians 10:13)
- I declare that my body is the temple of the Holy Spirit. I renounce every habit that defiles my body and commit to living a life that honors You. (1 Corinthians 6:19-20)

- Father, in the name of Jesus, heal every inner pain, trauma, or emotional wound that has contributed to this addiction. Fill me with Your peace and joy. (Psalm 147:3)
- In Jesus' name, I rebuke every spirit of death, destruction, and self-harm associated with drug addiction. I declare that I will live and not die to declare the works of the Lord. (Psalm 118:17)
- Lord, separate me from environments, relationships, or habits that fuel addiction. Replace them with godly connections and a healthy lifestyle. (2 Corinthians 6:17)
- Father, grant me the grace to develop self-control and discipline through the power of the Holy Spirit. Strengthen me to walk in obedience to Your Word. (Galatians 5:22-23)
- Lord, I break the influence of negative friendships and peer pressure that have encouraged addiction. Surround me with people who will guide me toward healing and restoration. (Proverbs 13:20)
- Father, protect me from every scheme of the enemy to cause relapse. Strengthen me to walk consistently in the freedom You have given me. (2 Thessalonians 3:3)
- Lord, replace every desire for drugs with a deep hunger for Your Word and presence. Let me find joy and satisfaction in You alone. (Matthew 5:6)
- I declare that my life is restored. My health, relationships, and purpose are renewed in Christ Jesus. (Joel 2:25)

- Father, I thank You for delivering me completely from addiction. I praise You for the new beginning and freedom I have in Christ. (Psalm 107:2)

Prayer Points Against Food Addiction

- Heavenly Father, I thank You for Your love and for the power You have given me through Jesus Christ to overcome every stronghold, including food addiction. (1 John 5:4)
- Lord, I declare that You are my ultimate source of satisfaction. I repent for seeking comfort and fulfilment in food instead of You. (Psalm 107:9)
- In the name of Jesus, I rebuke and cast out every spirit of gluttony, lack of self-control, and overeating. I declare that my appetite is under the control of the Holy Spirit. (Proverbs 23:2)
- Father, I plead the blood of Jesus over my body and mind. Let Your blood purify my desires and free me from every unhealthy attachment to food. (Hebrews 9:14)
- Lord, grant me the fruit of the Spirit, especially self-control. Empower me to make wise and healthy choices regarding my diet. (Galatians 5:22-23)
- I declare that I am no longer a slave to food addiction. Whom the Son sets free is free indeed, and I walk in the liberty of Christ. (John 8:36)
- Father, heal every emotional wound and void that has caused me to turn to food for comfort. Let Your peace

and love fill every empty space in my heart. (Philippians 4:7)
- In the name of Jesus, I renounce every generational pattern of unhealthy eating habits and food addiction in my family. I break its hold over my life by the power of the blood of Jesus. (Exodus 34:7)
- Lord, renew my mind and transform my thoughts about food. Help me to view food as nourishment for my body rather than a source of emotional fulfilment. (Romans 12:2)
- Father, I declare that my body is the temple of the Holy Spirit. I commit to honoring You by taking care of my body and resisting unhealthy eating habits. (1 Corinthians 6:19-20)
- In the name of Jesus, I break every craving and stronghold that ties me to unhealthy foods. I declare that I will no longer be controlled by these desires. (Isaiah 10:27)
- Lord, replace my unhealthy appetite for food with a hunger and thirst for righteousness and Your presence. Satisfy my soul with spiritual nourishment. (Matthew 5:6)
- Father, help me to develop discipline and wisdom in my eating habits. Teach me to listen to my body's needs and steward my health wisely. (Proverbs 3:5-6)
- I cancel every plan of the enemy to use food addiction to hinder my purpose, health, and spiritual growth. I declare victory in Jesus' name. (1 John 3:8)

- In the name of Jesus, I break the cycle of binge eating, guilt, and shame. I declare that I am free and empowered to live a healthy and balanced life. (Psalm 34:5)
- Lord, heal every part of my body that has been affected by unhealthy eating habits. Restore my metabolism, organs, and overall health. (Jeremiah 30:17)
- Father, guide me in making wise choices about what I eat and how I care for my body. Help me to rely on Your wisdom daily. (James 1:5)
- Lord, I declare that I have victory over every temptation to overeat or indulge in unhealthy foods. I will stand firm in Your strength. (1 Corinthians 10:13)
- Father, I thank You for setting me free from food addiction. I praise You for restoring my health, joy, and peace. (Psalm 107:20)
- Lord, I commit to glorifying You in my eating habits. Let every choice I make regarding food honor You and reflect my gratitude for Your goodness. (1 Corinthians 10:31)

Prayer Points Against Smoking Addiction

- Heavenly Father, I thank You for Your power to deliver and break every chain of addiction. I praise You for Your mercy and grace over my life. (Psalm 107:2)
- Lord, I acknowledge that I cannot overcome this addiction on my own. I ask for Your strength to help me conquer smoking addiction. (Philippians 4:13)

- In the name of Jesus, I rebuke and cast out the spirit of addiction that binds me to smoking. I declare freedom through the power of the Holy Spirit. (Romans 8:15)
- Father, I plead the blood of Jesus over my body, soul, and spirit. Let the blood of Jesus cleanse me from every craving for nicotine and cigarettes. (Revelation 12:11)
- Lord, heal my body from the physical dependency on smoking. Restore my health and reverse any damage caused by this addiction. (Jeremiah 30:17)
- I declare that I am no longer a slave to smoking. Every chain and stronghold of addiction is broken in Jesus' name. (Isaiah 10:27)
- Father, grant me self-control through the Holy Spirit. Help me to resist the urge to smoke and make decisions that honor You. (Galatians 5:22-23)
- Lord, uproot every root cause of this addiction, whether it is stress, anxiety, or emotional wounds. Fill those voids with Your peace and love. (Matthew 15:13)
- Father, I declare that my body is the temple of the Holy Spirit. I will no longer defile it with smoking, and I dedicate it to You. (1 Corinthians 6:19-20)
- Lord, renew my mind and transform my thinking. Replace every desire for smoking with thoughts that are pure, noble, and pleasing to You. (Romans 12:2; Philippians 4:8)
- In Jesus' name, I break every generational curse and pattern of addiction in my family. I declare that I am set free by the power of Christ. (Exodus 34:7)

- Father, strengthen me to resist every temptation to smoke. When I feel weak, remind me of Your promises and guide me to victory. (1 Corinthians 10:13)
- I declare that whom the Son sets free is free indeed. I receive my freedom from smoking addiction through Christ Jesus. (John 8:36)
- In the name of Jesus, I cancel every plan of the enemy to use smoking to harm my health, hinder my purpose, or destroy my life. (1 John 3:8)
- Lord, heal my body from the harmful effects of smoking and restore my emotional well-being. Fill me with Your peace and joy. (Isaiah 53:5)
- Father, replace my desire for smoking with a hunger for Your Word and presence. Satisfy me with the fullness of Your Spirit. (Matthew 5:6)
- Lord, surround me with people who will encourage and support me in breaking free from smoking. Help me to walk with wise and godly counsel. (Proverbs 27:17)
- I declare that I have victory over smoking addiction. I will not return to this habit, for I am more than a conqueror through Christ. (Romans 8:37)
- Father, I commit my future to You. Protect me from relapse and empower me to maintain my freedom from smoking addiction. (2 Thessalonians 3:3)
- Lord, I thank You for delivering me from smoking addiction. I praise You for the freedom, healing, and restoration You have brought into my life. (Psalm 103:1-5)

Prayer Points Against Gambling Addiction

- Heavenly Father, I thank You for Your love, mercy, and power to set captives free. I praise You for the victory I have through Jesus Christ. (Psalm 107:2)
- Lord, I confess that I have allowed gambling to take a place in my life that belongs to You. I surrender my life and decisions to You as my Lord and Savior. (Proverbs 3:5-6)
- In the name of Jesus, I rebuke and cast out the spirit of addiction to gambling. Every chain and stronghold that ties me to gambling is broken by the power of the Holy Spirit. (2 Corinthians 10:4)
- I plead the blood of Jesus over my mind, emotions, and finances. Let the blood cleanse and purify me from every connection to gambling. (Revelation 12:11)
- I declare that I am free from gambling addiction, for whom the Son sets free is free indeed. I walk in the liberty of Christ. (John 8:36)
- Father, renew my mind and transform my thoughts. Help me to reject the lies and temptations of gambling and embrace Your truth. (Romans 12:2)
- Lord, uproot every spirit of greed, covetousness, and materialism in my life. Help me to find contentment and trust in You as my Provider. (1 Timothy 6:10)
- Father, restore every financial loss caused by gambling. Teach me to manage my resources wisely and use them to honor You. (Joel 2:25)
- Lord, strengthen me to resist every temptation to gamble. Remind me of Your promises and guide me to make decisions that honor You. (1 Corinthians 10:13)

- In Jesus' name, I break every generational curse or pattern of gambling and financial mismanagement in my bloodline. I declare that it will not pass to the next generation. (Exodus 34:7)
- I renounce every belief in luck, chance, or gambling as a means of provision. I trust only in You, Lord, as my source and sustainer. (Philippians 4:19)
- I declare that my worth and identity are found in Christ, not in financial gain or losses. I am a child of God, redeemed and loved by Him. (Ephesians 1:7)
- Lord, replace my desire for gambling with a hunger for Your Word and presence. Let me find joy and satisfaction in You alone. (Matthew 5:6)
- Father, surround me with godly people who will encourage and hold me accountable in my journey to freedom from gambling. (Proverbs 27:17)
- In Jesus' name, I break every spirit of poverty and lack that has kept me trapped in the cycle of gambling. I declare abundance and provision through Christ. (Deuteronomy 28:12)
- Lord, deliver me from environments, relationships, and habits that encourage gambling. Help me to live with integrity and wisdom. (2 Corinthians 6:17)
- I declare that I have victory over gambling addiction through the power of Christ. I will not return to this habit, for I am more than a conqueror. (Romans 8:37)
- Father, I surrender my finances to You. Grant me peace and contentment, trusting that You are in control of my needs. (Isaiah 26:3)

- In the name of Jesus, I cancel every plan of the enemy to use gambling to destroy my purpose, finances, or relationships. (John 10:10)
- Lord, I thank You for setting me free from gambling addiction. I praise You for restoring my finances, relationships, and purpose in Christ. (Psalm 103:1-5)

Prayer Points Against Alcohol Addiction

- Heavenly Father, I thank You for Your mercy and love. I praise You because You are the God who sets captives free and restores broken lives. (Psalm 107:14)
- Lord, I acknowledge that I cannot overcome alcohol addiction on my own. I depend on Your strength to break every chain of addiction in my life. (Philippians 4:13)
- In the name of Jesus, I rebuke and cast out the spirit of addiction that binds me to alcohol. I declare my freedom by the power of the Holy Spirit. (Isaiah 10:27)
- Father, I plead the blood of Jesus over my body, mind, and spirit. Let Your blood cleanse me from every craving for alcohol and its destructive effects. (Revelation 12:11)
- I declare that I am no longer a slave to alcohol addiction. Whom the Son sets free is free indeed, and I walk in the liberty of Christ. (John 8:36)
- In the name of Jesus, I break every generational curse and pattern of alcohol addiction in my family. I declare that it will not pass to me or future generations. (Exodus 20:5-6)

- Lord, renew my mind and transform my thoughts. Replace every desire for alcohol with a desire for Your Word and presence. (Romans 12:2)
- Father, heal every emotional wound or trauma that has caused me to seek comfort in alcohol. Let Your peace and love fill every void in my heart. (Psalm 147:3)
- I declare that my body is the temple of the Holy Spirit. I will no longer defile it with alcohol, but I dedicate it to You, Lord. (1 Corinthians 6:19-20)
- Lord, strengthen me to resist every temptation to drink. When I am weak, remind me of Your promises and give me the grace to stand firm. (1 Corinthians 10:13)
- In Jesus' name, I renounce every lie of the enemy that alcohol can bring peace, comfort, or joy. I declare that only You, Lord, can satisfy my soul. (John 4:14)
- Father, heal my body from the damage caused by alcohol abuse. Restore my organs, my brain, and my overall health in Jesus' name. (Jeremiah 30:17)
- I rebuke the spirit of bondage that keeps me tied to alcohol addiction. I declare that I am free and victorious in Jesus Christ. (Romans 8:15)
- Lord, surround me with godly people who will encourage me, pray for me, and hold me accountable in my journey to freedom. (Proverbs 27:17)
- I declare that I have victory over alcohol addiction. I am more than a conqueror through Christ who loves me. (Romans 8:37)
- Father, help me to find contentment and joy in You alone. Replace every unhealthy desire with a hunger for Your presence. (Psalm 16:11)

- In the name of Jesus, I break every stronghold of shame and guilt caused by alcohol addiction. I receive Your forgiveness and walk in newness of life. (2 Corinthians 5:17)
- Lord, remind me daily that my identity is in Christ, not in addiction or failure. I am a child of God, redeemed and restored by Your grace. (Ephesians 1:7)
- I cancel every plan of the enemy to use alcohol addiction to destroy my life, relationships, and purpose. I declare that no weapon formed against me shall prosper. (Isaiah 54:17)
- Father, I thank You for setting me free from alcohol addiction. I praise You for restoring my peace, health, and purpose in Jesus' name. (Psalm 103:1-5)

Prayer Points Against Blood Diseases

- Heavenly Father, I thank You for being Jehovah Rapha, the Lord who heals. I praise You for Your power to heal and restore my blood and entire body. (Exodus 15:26)
- Lord, I acknowledge that You are the Creator of my body. I trust in Your power to heal every blood-related disease and restore my health completely. (Psalm 139:13-14)
- Father, I plead the blood of Jesus over my body. Let the blood of Jesus cleanse my blood and remove every sickness, impurity, and disease. (Revelation 12:11)
- By the stripes of Jesus, I declare healing over my blood. I receive complete restoration and wholeness through Christ's sacrifice. (Isaiah 53:5)

- In the name of Jesus, I rebuke and cast out the spirit of infirmity attacking my blood. I command every affliction to leave my body now. (Luke 13:11-13)
- I declare that no disease, disorder, or infection in my blood has power over me. I am healed and victorious in Jesus' name. (Romans 8:37)
- Lord, purify my blood from every toxin, virus, or abnormality. Restore the function and health of every cell in my blood. (Leviticus 17:11)
- In Jesus' name, I break every generational curse or hereditary disease affecting my blood. I declare that I am free from these patterns by the power of Christ. (Galatians 3:13)
- Father, I command my blood to function perfectly as You designed it. Let every red blood cell, white blood cell, and platelet operate in divine order. (Ezekiel 37:5)
- Lord, I cancel every negative medical report concerning my blood. I believe Your report that declares healing and life for me. (Isaiah 53:1)
- I declare that Your Word is life to my body and health to my blood. I meditate on Your promises of healing and restoration. (Proverbs 4:20-22)
- In Jesus' name, I destroy every root cause of blood diseases, whether physical, spiritual, or emotional. I declare total healing. (Matthew 15:13)
- Lord, strengthen my immune system and every organ that works with my blood. Let my body be energized and protected by Your power. (Psalm 18:32)

- Father, reverse any damage caused by blood diseases. Restore my health and give me a new lease on life. (Jeremiah 30:17)
- Lord, I pray for divine immunity and protection against any future attack of blood diseases. Cover me with the shield of faith. (Ephesians 6:16)
- In the name of Jesus, I cancel every plan and attack of the enemy against my blood and health. I declare that no weapon formed against me shall prosper. (Isaiah 54:17)
- Father, I receive Your divine health and wholeness. I declare that I will live in strength and vitality all the days of my life. (3 John 1:2)
- Lord, grant me the wisdom to care for my body and make choices that promote my health. Guide me in the right paths. (James 1:5)
- I rebuke the spirit of fear concerning my health. I trust in Your promises, Lord, and walk in faith and peace. (2 Timothy 1:7)
- Heavenly Father, I thank You for hearing my prayers and for healing my blood. I give You all the glory for restoring my health and strength. (Psalm 103:1-3)

Prayer Points Against Autoimmune Diseases

- Heavenly Father, I thank You for being the God who heals all diseases. I praise You for Your love, faithfulness, and the victory You have already given me through Jesus Christ. (Exodus 15:26)
- Lord, I acknowledge that You are the Creator of my body. You formed me perfectly, and I trust You to

restore every part of me to Your divine design. (Psalm 139:14)

- By the stripes of Jesus Christ, I declare healing over my body. I proclaim total restoration from every autoimmune condition in Jesus' name. (Isaiah 53:5)
- In the name of Jesus, I rebuke and cast out the spirit of infirmity that causes autoimmune diseases. I command it to leave my body now and forever. (Luke 13:11-13)
- Father, I plead the blood of Jesus over my immune system and every organ affected by autoimmune diseases. Let Your blood cleanse and heal every abnormality. (Revelation 12:11)
- Lord, I command my immune system to function as You designed it, recognizing and protecting my body instead of attacking it. (Ezekiel 37:5)
- In the name of Jesus, I destroy the root cause of autoimmune diseases in my body, whether physical, spiritual, or emotional. I declare freedom and healing. (Matthew 15:13)
- I break every generational curse or inherited condition of autoimmune diseases in my bloodline. I declare that I am free through the blood of Jesus. (Galatians 3:13)
- Father, restore every part of my body that has been damaged by autoimmune diseases. Let every tissue, organ, and cell function perfectly again. (Jeremiah 30:17)
- In the name of Jesus, I cancel every plan of the enemy to use autoimmune diseases to steal, kill, or destroy my health and purpose. (John 10:10)

- I declare that my body is the temple of the Holy Spirit, and I will live in divine health and wholeness. No disease will prosper in me. (1 Corinthians 6:19-20)
- Lord, renew my strength and vitality daily. Let my body, mind, and spirit be refreshed and energized by Your presence. (Isaiah 40:31)
- I rebuke the spirit of fear, doubt, and anxiety concerning my health. I place my trust in Your Word, Lord, and walk in peace. (2 Timothy 1:7)
- Father, grant me wisdom to make decisions that promote healing and health. Guide me in the right treatments, habits, and lifestyle changes. (James 1:5)
- I declare victory over autoimmune diseases. They have no power over me, for I am more than a conqueror through Christ who strengthens me. (Romans 8:37)
- Lord, heal every emotional wound or trauma that may be contributing to this condition. Fill my heart with Your peace and joy. (Psalm 147:3)
- Father, cover me with Your wings of protection and shield me from every spiritual attack against my health. Let Your presence surround me. (Psalm 91:4)
- I speak life into every cell, tissue, and organ in my body. I declare that my body will function in the perfection God created it to function. (Proverbs 18:21)
- Lord, turn this battle into a testimony of Your power and grace. Let my healing glorify Your name and encourage others. (Psalm 118:17)
- Heavenly Father, I thank You for hearing my prayers and for the healing You have begun in me. I trust You

for complete deliverance and restoration. (Psalm 103:1-3)

Prayer Points for Breakthroughs

- Father, in the name of Jesus, I ask for divine favor and open doors in my life! Let every closed opportunity be opened now! (Revelation 3:8)

- Lord, let Your hand of favor rest upon me, making ways where there seem to be no ways! (Isaiah 43:19)

- Every power delaying my breakthrough, be destroyed by fire in Jesus' name! (Daniel 10:12-13)

- I command every spiritual roadblock stopping my progress to be removed now by the power of God! (Zechariah 4:7)

- Father, let the floodgates of heaven open and release financial blessings into my life! (Malachi 3:10)

- Every spirit of lack, debt, and financial hardship, be broken in Jesus' name! (Deuteronomy 8:18)

- Lord, grant me divine wisdom, knowledge, and understanding to excel in my work! (Proverbs 22:29)

- Every demonic hindrance blocking my business or promotion, be destroyed now in Jesus' name! (Psalm 90:17)

- Lord, align my life with my kingdom spouse and remove every delay in my marital destiny! (Proverbs 18:22)

- Every demonic interference in my marriage or relationships, be broken in Jesus' name! (Matthew 19:6)

- By the stripes of Jesus, I declare my healing and deliverance from every sickness and affliction! (Isaiah 53:5)

- Every yoke of infirmity, be broken and cast out of my life now in Jesus' name! (Jeremiah 30:17)

- Lord, fill me with Your Spirit and give me the grace to walk in righteousness! (Matthew 6:33)

- I command the heavens to open over my life, and I receive divine encounters and fresh anointing! (Joel 2:28)

- Every evil plan of the enemy against my breakthrough, be destroyed by fire in Jesus' name! (Isaiah 54:17)

- Lord, arise and fight my battles, giving me victory on every side! (Exodus 14:14)

- I break every delay and stagnation, and I receive divine speed to accomplish my purpose! (Amos 9:13)

- Father, restore everything I have lost, and let my breakthrough come speedily! (Joel 2:25)

- Lord, I thank You because my breakthrough is here, and I receive it by faith! (1 Thessalonians 5:18)

- I rejoice in the victory You have given me, and I declare that testimonies will follow! (Psalm 126:1-2)

Prayer Points Against the Spirit of Rejection

- Heavenly Father, I thank You for Your unconditional love. I praise You for accepting me into Your family and calling me Your child. (John 1:12)
- Lord, I declare that my identity is in You. I am fearfully and wonderfully made, and I am chosen by You for a divine purpose. (Psalm 139:14, Ephesians 1:4)
- In the name of Jesus, I break the power of the spirit of rejection over my life. I renounce every lie that tells me I am unloved, unworthy, or unwanted. (2 Timothy 1:7)
- Father, heal every emotional wound caused by rejection. Restore my heart and fill every void with Your peace and love. (Psalm 147:3)
- Lord, I renounce every negative word spoken over me that caused rejection. I cancel their power in the name of Jesus. Let only Your Word define me. (Isaiah 54:17)
- I plead the blood of Jesus over my mind, heart, and soul. Let Your blood cleanse me from the effects of rejection and restore my confidence in You. (Revelation 12:11)
- In Jesus' name, I break every generational curse or pattern of rejection in my family. I declare that it will not continue in my life or my descendants. (Galatians 3:13)
- Lord, I forgive anyone who has rejected or hurt me. I release them into Your hands and choose to walk in forgiveness and love. (Matthew 6:14-15)

- I declare that I am highly favored by God. His favor surrounds me as a shield, and His approval is all I need. (Psalm 5:12)
- I cancel every lie of the enemy that tells me I am not good enough, loved, or valued. I declare that I am accepted in the Beloved. (Ephesians 1:6)
- Father, restore every relationship that has been broken by rejection, where it aligns with Your will. Let Your love bring healing and reconciliation. (Colossians 3:13)
- Lord, help me to see myself through Your eyes. Remind me that I am Your masterpiece, created for good works in Christ. (Ephesians 2:10)
- I rebuke the fear of rejection in Jesus' name. I will no longer live in fear of people's opinions or judgments. I walk boldly in my identity in Christ. (Proverbs 29:25)
- Father, fill me with Your perfect love that casts out all fear. Let Your love anchor me and remind me that I am never alone. (1 John 4:18)
- In Jesus' name, I break the stronghold of loneliness and isolation caused by rejection. I declare that I am never alone because You are with me. (Deuteronomy 31:6)
- I declare that I am loved, chosen, and accepted by God. I speak life over my destiny and reject every negative thought or label. (Proverbs 18:21)
- Lord, let Your peace guard my heart and mind. Replace every anxious thought with the assurance of Your love and purpose for me. (Philippians 4:6-7)
- I cancel every demonic assignment of rejection against my life. I declare that it will not prosper, for I am covered by the blood of Jesus. (Isaiah 54:17)

- Father, restore my joy and confidence in You. Let me walk in the fullness of life that You have promised. (John 10:10)
- Lord, I thank You for delivering me from the spirit of rejection. I rejoice in Your love and acceptance, knowing that I am forever secure in You. (Romans 8:38-39)

Prayer Points for Inner Healing

- Heavenly Father, I thank You for being my healer and restorer. Thank You for Your love that binds up the wounds of the broken-hearted. (Psalm 147:3)
- Lord, I surrender my heart to You. I invite You to search and heal every part of me that is hurting or broken. (Psalm 139:23-24)
- Father, I acknowledge that You alone have the power to restore my soul. Bring peace to my troubled heart and replace my pain with joy. (Psalm 23:3)
- Lord, I ask You to heal the wounds of my past. Uproot every seed of bitterness, anger, and hurt that has taken root in my heart. (Isaiah 43:18-19)
- Father, I release forgiveness to those who have hurt me. I let go of resentment and choose to forgive as You have forgiven me. (Matthew 6:14-15)
- In Jesus' name, I break the spirit of rejection over my life. I declare that I am loved, accepted, and chosen by God. (Ephesians 1:4-6)
- I renounce every negative thought, lie, or belief that has kept me bound in pain. I declare that I have the mind of

Christ and will think on what is true, noble, and pure. (Philippians 4:8)

- Lord, bring emotional wholeness into my life. Restore my ability to love, trust, and feel joy again. Heal my heart completely. (Jeremiah 30:17).
- Father, I pray for healing from every traumatic experience I've endured. Erase the pain and bring peace to the memories that haunt me. (2 Corinthians 5:17)
- In the name of Jesus, I break every unhealthy soul tie and emotional bond that has brought pain or hindered my healing. I declare freedom over my soul. (1 Corinthians 6:19-20)
- Lord, grant me peace of mind. Silence the voices of fear, doubt, and anxiety in my life, and let Your peace guard my heart and mind. (Philippians 4:6-7)
- I declare victory over bitterness and unforgiveness. I will not let them have power over my life, for I am free in Christ. (Ephesians 4:31-32)
- Father, fill me with Your perfect love that casts out all fear, insecurity, and pain. Let Your love overflow in my heart. (1 John 4:18)
- In Jesus' name, I break every generational cycle of hurt, pain, and emotional trauma. I declare that it will not continue in my life or my family. (Galatians 3:13)
- Lord, I cancel every hurtful word or curse spoken over me that has caused emotional pain. I replace them with Your Word, which brings life and healing. (Proverbs 18:21)

- Father, renew a right spirit within me. Remove anything that hinders my growth and fill me with Your Spirit of peace and joy. (Psalm 51:10)
- Lord, replace my mourning with joy and my heaviness with a garment of praise. I declare that I will rejoice in Your goodness. (Isaiah 61:3)
- Father, heal my ability to build healthy relationships. Help me to trust again and surround me with people who reflect Your love and grace. (Ecclesiastes 4:9-10)
- I declare freedom from the fear of being hurt again. I place my trust in You, Lord, knowing that You will protect my heart. (2 Timothy 1:7)
- Heavenly Father, I thank You for hearing my prayers and for the healing You have begun in me. I trust You to restore me fully and use me for Your glory. (Psalm 103:1-3)

Prayer Points Against the Spirit of Anger

- Heavenly Father, I thank You for Your peace that surpasses all understanding. Thank You for calming the storms in my heart and mind. (Philippians 4:7)
- Lord, I acknowledge that You are in control of my emotions. I surrender my anger to You and ask for Your help to manage it. (Ephesians 4:26-27)
- Father, I repent for any time I have allowed anger to control my actions, thoughts, or words. Forgive me and cleanse me with the blood of Jesus. (1 John 1:9)

- In the name of Jesus, I break the stronghold of anger over my life. I reject every spirit that fuels rage, bitterness, and resentment. (2 Corinthians 10:4-5)
- Lord, let Your love fill my heart and overflow in my words and actions. Replace anger with patience, kindness, and understanding. (1 Corinthians 13:4-5)
- I bind the spirit of anger and its influences over my life in Jesus' name. I command it to leave me now and never return. (Matthew 18:18)
- Father, help me to cultivate a gentle and quiet spirit. Let my responses reflect Your grace and not my emotions. (1 Peter 3:4)
- Lord, I renounce every thought and trigger that stirs up anger within me. Help me to think on what is true, noble, and praiseworthy. (Philippians 4:8)
- In Jesus' name, I break every generational curse or pattern of anger in my family. It will not continue in my life or my descendants. (Exodus 20:5-6)
- Father, give me wisdom to control my tongue and actions when I feel anger rising. Let my words bring life and healing, not destruction. (Proverbs 15:1)
- Lord, replace every angry thought and emotion with Your perfect peace. Calm my heart and remind me that You are my defender. (Colossians 3:15)
- Father, I choose to forgive those who have hurt or offended me. I will not let anger take root in my heart through unforgiveness. (Matthew 6:14-15)
- Lord, fill me with the fruit of the Spirit, especially self-control. Help me to respond with wisdom and not react out of anger. (Galatians 5:22-23)

- I cast every frustration, disappointment, and offense at Your feet, Lord. I refuse to carry burdens that lead to anger. (1 Peter 5:7)
- In Jesus' name, I declare victory over the spirit of anger. It has no power over my mind, emotions, or actions. (Romans 8:37)
- Father, heal any emotional wounds or hurts that fuel my anger. Restore my heart and fill it with Your peace and joy. (Psalm 34:18)
- I break the spirit of offense in my life. I choose to overlook offenses and walk in love and humility. (Proverbs 19:11)
- Lord, guide me in every situation where anger might arise. Help me to see things through Your perspective and respond with grace. (Proverbs 3:5-6)
- Father, develop patience within me. Teach me to be slow to anger and quick to listen and understand. (James 1:19-20)
- Lord, I thank You for delivering me from the spirit of anger. I praise You for the peace and self-control You have given me through Christ. (Psalm 107:2)

Prayer Points Against the Spirit of Unforgiveness

- Heavenly Father, I thank You for forgiving my sins through the blood of Jesus. Thank You for Your grace and mercy that make me whole. (Ephesians 1:7)
- Lord, I acknowledge that harboring unforgiveness is against Your will. I repent of any resentment, bitterness, or anger I have held onto. (1 John 1:9)

- Father, help me to forgive those who have hurt, offended, or betrayed me. Teach me to release them into Your hands, just as You have forgiven me. (Matthew 6:14-15)
- In the name of Jesus, I break the stronghold of unforgiveness in my life. I command every spirit of bitterness and resentment to leave me now. (2 Corinthians 10:4-5)
- Lord, heal every emotional wound that unforgiveness has caused. Bring restoration to my heart and fill me with Your peace. (Psalm 147:3)
- Father, replace every trace of unforgiveness in my heart with Your unconditional love. Teach me to love as You love. (1 Corinthians 13:4-7)
- I renounce every desire for revenge or retaliation. I choose to let go of vengeance, trusting that You will bring justice in Your time. (Romans 12:19)
- Lord, I pray for those who have wronged me. Bless them and work in their hearts, just as You are working in mine. (Matthew 5:44)
- In the name of Jesus, I break every generational pattern of unforgiveness in my family. It will no longer have power over my life or my descendants. (Galatians 3:13)
- I plead the blood of Jesus over my mind and heart. Let it cleanse me from every trace of anger, resentment, and unforgiveness. (Hebrews 9:14)
- I declare that I am free from the bondage of unforgiveness. My heart is open to love, peace, and joy in the Holy Spirit. (John 8:36)

- In Jesus' name, I cast off the spirit of bitterness. I declare that it will no longer take root in my life. (Ephesians 4:31)
- Lord, create in me a heart that is quick to forgive and slow to take offense. Let me reflect Your character in all my relationships. (Colossians 3:13)
- Father, I ask You to heal the painful memories that keep unforgiveness alive. Replace them with Your peace and truth. (Isaiah 43:18-19)
- I declare that unforgiveness has no hold over me. I am victorious in Christ and will walk in freedom and love. (Romans 8:37)
- Lord, fill me with the fruit of the Spirit—especially love, patience, and kindness—so that unforgiveness will have no room in my heart. (Galatians 5:22-23)
- Father, bring peace and reconciliation to every broken relationship caused by unforgiveness. Restore what the enemy has tried to destroy. (Romans 12:18)
- I declare that forgiveness will be my lifestyle. I will not let anger or resentment take root in my heart. (Ephesians 4:26-27)
- In Jesus' name, I break every unhealthy soul tie connected to unforgiveness. I release myself from every emotional bondage. (1 Corinthians 6:19-20)
- Lord, I thank You for delivering me from the spirit of unforgiveness. I praise You for the peace and joy that now fill my heart. (Psalm 103:1-3)

Prayer Points Against the Spirit of Rebellion and Disobedience

- Heavenly Father, I thank You for being the ultimate authority in my life. I honor You as my Lord and King, and I submit to Your will. (1 Chronicles 29:11-12)
- Lord, I repent for any rebellion or disobedience in my life. Forgive me for rejecting Your instructions and turning away from Your path. (1 John 1:9)
- In the name of Jesus, I break the power of rebellion and disobedience over my life. I declare that it has no authority over me. (1 Samuel 15:23)
- Father, I surrender my will to You. Help me to align my thoughts, desires, and actions with Your perfect will. (Luke 22:42)
- I bind the spirit of rebellion operating in my life, my family, or my environment. I cast it out in the name of Jesus. (Matthew 18:18)
- Lord, create in me a heart that is eager to obey You. Help me to delight in Your commands and follow them with joy. (Psalm 119:33-34)
- In Jesus' name, I break every generational curse or pattern of rebellion and disobedience in my bloodline. I declare freedom for myself and my family. (Galatians 3:13)
- Father, grant me a spirit of humility that resists pride, arrogance, and rebellion. Teach me to walk humbly before You. (Micah 6:8)
- I declare that I submit myself fully to God. I resist the devil and his temptations to rebel, and he must flee from me. (James 4:7)

- Lord, I cast down every rebellious thought and imagination that exalts itself against Your knowledge. I bring every thought into obedience to Christ. (2 Corinthians 10:5)
- Father, fill me with the fear of the Lord, which is the beginning of wisdom. Help me to honor and respect Your authority in every area of my life. (Proverbs 9:10)
- Lord, I reject any influence or peer pressure that encourages rebellion or disobedience. Help me to stand firm in righteousness. (Exodus 23:2)
- I declare that I will not be controlled by the desires of my flesh that lead to rebellion. I choose to walk by the Spirit. (Galatians 5:16)
- Father, help me to honor and obey the spiritual authorities You have placed in my life. Teach me to submit with humility and respect. (Hebrews 13:17)
- In the name of Jesus, I break the spirit of disobedience at work in my life or family. I declare that we will walk in obedience to God's Word. (Ephesians 2:2)
- Lord, give me a teachable spirit that accepts correction and discipline. Help me to grow in wisdom and maturity. (Proverbs 12:1)
- I declare that I am victorious over the spirit of rebellion. I walk in obedience, submission, and alignment with God's will. (Romans 8:37)
- Father, replace any rebellion in my heart with righteousness, peace, and joy in the Holy Spirit. (Romans 14:17)

- Lord, strengthen me to resist every temptation to disobey Your Word. Help me to overcome through the power of the Holy Spirit. (1 Corinthians 10:13)
- Heavenly Father, I thank You for delivering me from the spirit of rebellion and disobedience. I praise You for giving me a heart that longs to obey and honor You. (Psalm 103:1-3)

Prayer Points Against Fear

- Father, I thank You because You are always with me. I am grateful that I do not have to face fear alone. (Isaiah 41:10)
- Lord, I declare that You have not given me a spirit of fear but of power, love, and a sound mind. I receive Your peace today. (2 Timothy 1:7)
- In the name of Jesus, I bind the spirit of fear operating in my life. I command it to leave me now and never return. (Matthew 18:18)
- Father, let Your perfect love fill my heart and cast out every form of fear. I receive Your assurance and security. (1 John 4:18)
- Lord, let Your peace, which surpasses all understanding, guard my heart and mind against fear and anxiety. (Philippians 4:6-7)
- I cast down every fearful thought and imagination that exalts itself against the knowledge of God. I bring my thoughts into obedience to Christ. (2 Corinthians 10:5)

- In Jesus' name, I declare that I am more than a conqueror through Christ who loves me. Fear has no hold over my life. (Romans 8:37)
- Lord, I trust in You as my refuge and fortress. You are my God, and in You, I will not be afraid. (Psalm 91:2)
- I declare that no weapon formed against me shall prosper, and every tongue that rises against me in judgment is condemned. (Isaiah 54:17)
- Father, fill me with boldness and courage to face every situation with faith. Strengthen me to walk in victory over fear. (Joshua 1:9)
- Lord, I reject the fear of the unknown and place my trust in Your plans for my life, which are good and full of hope. (Jeremiah 29:11)
- I declare that even when I walk through the darkest valley, I will fear no evil, for You are with me, Lord. (Psalm 23:4)
- In the name of Jesus, I break every spirit of intimidation and timidity. I will stand firm and confident in the Lord. (Ephesians 6:10-11)
- Father, I trust in Your faithfulness. You have never failed me, and I know You will continue to deliver me from all fear. (Deuteronomy 31:6)
- Lord, in my weakness, Your strength is made perfect. I rely on You to overcome every fear in my life. (2 Corinthians 12:9)
- I declare that I am free from the bondage of fear. I will not live in anxiety or dread but in the liberty of Christ. (Romans 8:15)

- In the name of Jesus, I break every generational curse of fear in my family line. It will not continue in my life or my descendants. (Galatians 3:13)
- Holy Spirit, comfort me in moments of fear and remind me of God's promises. Fill me with peace and assurance. (John 14:26-27)
- Lord, increase my faith to trust You completely in every situation. Let faith replace fear in my life. (Hebrews 11:6)
- Father, I thank You for delivering me from all fear. I praise You for giving me peace, boldness, and confidence in You.
- Heavenly Father, I thank You for giving me the wisdom to live a life that honors You. Thank You for teaching me how to speak words of life and avoid gossip. (James 1:5)
- Lord, I repent of any time I have spoken negatively about others or participated in gossip. Cleanse me from this sin, and help me to guard my tongue. (1 John 1:9)
- In the name of Jesus, I break the power of the spirit of gossip over my life. I declare that my tongue will not be used to spread lies, rumors, or slander. (Proverbs 16:28)
- Lord, set a guard over my mouth and keep watch over the door of my lips. Help me to speak only what is edifying and true. (Psalm 141:3)
- Father, I declare that my words will bring life and healing, not destruction or division. Let my speech always reflect Your love. (Proverbs 18:21)

- I renounce every form of negative and idle conversation that leads to gossip. I will not entertain or spread harmful words. (Matthew 12:36)
- Lord, purify my heart and thoughts so that no corrupt or malicious words come out of my mouth. Let my words reflect the purity of my heart. (Matthew 15:18-19)
- Father, help me resist the temptation to gossip when I hear others speaking negatively about someone. Give me the courage to redirect conversations to what is positive and righteous. (James 4:7)
- I declare that I will show kindness and compassion in my words, choosing to build others up instead of tearing them down. (Ephesians 4:29)
- In Jesus' name, I break any influence of gossipers in my life. Surround me with people who speak truth, wisdom, and love. (Proverbs 13:20)
- Lord, give me wisdom in my relationships to recognize and avoid situations where gossip may arise. Help me to be a peacemaker instead of a participant in division. (Proverbs 11:13)
- Father, teach me to speak the truth in love and to use my words for encouragement, correction, and building others up. (Ephesians 4:15)
- Lord, deliver me from the need to gossip for attention, approval, or acceptance. Let my identity be rooted in Christ alone. (Galatians 1:10)
- Holy Spirit, give me discernment to recognize gossip and the courage to avoid it. Help me to walk in wisdom and integrity. (Philippians 1:9-10)

- In Jesus' name, I break every generational pattern of gossip or slander in my family. I declare that my family and I will speak words of life and unity. (Galatians 3:13)
- Lord, fill my heart with Your Word so that what overflows from my mouth will be truth, wisdom, and encouragement. (Colossians 3:16)
- Father, place godly people in my life who will hold me accountable and encourage me to use my words wisely. (Proverbs 27:17)
- I declare that I am free from the spirit of gossip. My words will honor God, bring peace, and build others up. (Romans 14:19)
- Lord, heal any wounds caused by gossip, whether spoken by me or about me. Bring restoration and peace to those relationships. (Psalm 147:3)
- Father, I thank You for delivering me from the temptation and habit of gossip. I praise You for transforming my speech to glorify You. (Psalm 19:14)

Prayer Points Against Things and Objects Used as a Point of Contact Against You

- Father, in the name of Jesus, I nullify every evil power attached to any object used as a point of contact against me! (Isaiah 54:17)
- I command every demonic object, charm, or cursed item used against me to lose its power now in Jesus' name! (Deuteronomy 7:25-26)

- Every item stolen from me and used for witchcraft, I declare it powerless in Jesus' name! (Job 5:12)

- Any hair, clothing, picture, gift, or personal belonging of mine used to work evil against me, I withdraw my essence from it by the blood of Jesus! (Leviticus 19:31)

- Every spoken word, curse, or incantation made over any object representing me, I cancel it by the power of God! (Numbers 23:23)

- I break every spell, hex, or enchantment that has been placed on any object linked to my life! (Isaiah 8:10)

- Father, release Your consuming fire to burn and destroy any object that has been dedicated against me! (Hebrews 12:29)

- Any demonic altar where my belongings were placed, catch fire now in Jesus' name! (1 Kings 18:38)

- I sever every spiritual connection between me and any cursed object or demonic point of contact! (2 Corinthians 6:14-15)

- I reject and renounce any item given to me by the enemy to establish an evil covenant—I disconnect myself by the blood of Jesus! (Colossians 2:14)

- Lord, I anoint and sanctify all my belongings with the blood of Jesus—no evil shall be transferred through them! (Exodus 12:13)

- Any object in my possession unknowingly carrying demonic energy, be exposed and removed in Jesus' name! (Psalm 91:10)

- I take back my destiny from any satanic hands that have tried to use objects against me! (Luke 10:19)
- I declare that no evil weapon, whether physical or spiritual, shall have power over my life! (Isaiah 54:17)

Prayer Points for Discernment

- Heavenly Father, I thank You for being the source of all wisdom and understanding. I praise You for making Your wisdom available to me. (James 1:5)
- Lord, fill me with the spirit of discernment so that I can distinguish between good and evil, truth and deception, light and darkness. (Hebrews 5:14)
- Holy Spirit, guide me in every decision I make. Help me to hear Your voice clearly and follow Your leading. (John 16:13)
- Father, grant me wisdom and discernment in my daily choices. Help me to see situations through Your perspective and respond accordingly. (Proverbs 3:5-6)
- In the name of Jesus, I rebuke and break the spirit of confusion. I declare that I have a sound mind and clarity in every situation. (2 Timothy 1:7)
- Lord, give me discernment in my relationships. Help me to recognize those sent by You and avoid relationships that may harm my walk with You. (Proverbs 12:26)
- Father, I declare that my ears are open to Your voice, and my heart is sensitive to Your guidance. Help me to quickly discern Your will in every matter. (Isaiah 30:21)

- Lord, protect me from deception in every form. Expose every lie of the enemy and help me to stand firmly in Your truth. (Matthew 24:4)
- Father, reveal the hidden motives of situations and people around me. Help me to discern intentions clearly and act with wisdom. (Jeremiah 17:9-10)
- I declare that I have the mind of Christ. My thoughts are aligned with God's truth, and I discern spiritual matters with clarity. (1 Corinthians 2:16)
- Lord, give me patience and understanding as I seek Your wisdom. Teach me to wait on You and trust in Your timing. (Psalm 27:14)
- Father, grant me discernment in my ministry and service to You. Help me to know how to lead, guide, and make decisions that glorify You. (Ephesians 1:17-18)
- Lord, help me to discern the meaning and source of every dream and vision. Let me understand which ones are from You and reject those that are not. (Acts 2:17)
- Father, give me the boldness to act on the discernment You give me. Help me to stand firm in truth even when it's difficult. (Joshua 1:9)
- In the name of Jesus, I declare that I will not be ignorant of the enemy's schemes. I will discern and overcome every strategy of darkness. (2 Corinthians 2:11)
- Lord, guide me in my financial decisions. Help me to discern opportunities and avoid traps that could lead to loss. (Proverbs 21:5)
- Father, grant me discernment in spiritual warfare. Help me to identify and overcome the plans of the enemy with wisdom and strategy. (Ephesians 6:12-13)

- Holy Spirit, give me the ability to discern and understand the deep truths of Scripture. Open my eyes to see what You are saying through Your Word. (Psalm 119:18)
- Lord, when I face difficult decisions, help me to discern the best path to take. Give me peace as I walk in Your will. (Isaiah 48:17)
- Father, I thank You for always leading me in the way I should go. I trust that as I seek discernment, You will never let me walk in darkness. (Psalm 32:8)

Prayer Points for Restoration of Zeal for the Lord

- Heavenly Father, I thank You for Your unchanging love and faithfulness toward me, even in times when my zeal for You has wavered. (Lamentations 3:22-23)
- Lord, I repent for allowing spiritual laziness, distractions, or worldly desires to quench my passion for You. Forgive me and renew my heart. (Revelation 2:4-5)
- Father, let the fire of the Holy Spirit ignite in me again. Restore my hunger and thirst for Your presence and Your Word. (Matthew 5:6)
- Lord, renew my mind and transform my thoughts so that I focus on the things of the Spirit and not of the flesh. (Romans 12:2)
- Father, give me a heart that seeks to obey You fully. Help me to walk in Your ways and delight in doing Your will. (Psalm 40:8)

- In the name of Jesus, I break the spirit of lukewarmness and declare that I will be on fire for You all the days of my life. (Revelation 3:15-16)
- Lord, restore my desire to study and meditate on Your Word daily. Let it become my source of strength, joy, and direction. (Psalm 119:105)
- Father, I declare that I will serve You with boldness and confidence. Let my passion for You lead me to share the Gospel with others. (2 Timothy 1:7)
- Lord, rekindle my prayer life. Let me seek You consistently and fervently, knowing that prayer is the key to intimacy with You. (1 Thessalonians 5:17)
- In Jesus' name, I reject every distraction, laziness, or hindrance that keeps me from pursuing You wholeheartedly. (Hebrews 12:1-2)
- Father, restore my passion for worship. Let me worship You in spirit and in truth, with a heart full of gratitude and reverence. (John 4:24)
- Lord, give me a renewed burden for the lost. Fill my heart with compassion and zeal to bring others into Your kingdom. (Matthew 9:37-38)
- I declare victory over every form of spiritual fatigue or weariness. I receive strength and refreshing from the Lord. (Isaiah 40:31)
- Father, restore the joy of my salvation and let my service to You be done with gladness and a willing heart. (Psalm 51:12)
- Lord, let me encounter You in a fresh and powerful way. Revive my spirit and draw me closer to You. (James 4:8)

- Father, restore in me a holy reverence and awe for You. Let the fear of the Lord guide my actions and decisions. (Proverbs 9:10)
- In the name of Jesus, I break every spirit of complacency and declare that my worship and service to God will be passionate and wholehearted. (Colossians 3:23)
- Lord, give me an unquenchable hunger for Your presence. Let me desire You more than anything else in this world. (Psalm 42:1-2)
- Holy Spirit, help me to stay committed to God and to keep my spiritual zeal alive. Teach me and guide me in all truth. (John 14:26)
- Father, I thank You for restoring my zeal for You. I praise You for reigniting the fire in my spirit and for Your steadfast love. (Psalm 103:1-5)

Prayer Points for Marriage Reconciliation

- Heavenly Father, I thank You for the covenant of marriage and for bringing us together as one. I honor You for this sacred union. (Genesis 2:24)
- Lord, we invite Your presence into our marriage. Be the foundation of our relationship and guide us back to unity. (Ecclesiastes 4:12)
- Father, I repent of any actions, words, or attitudes that have hurt my spouse or caused division. Forgive me, and teach me to love with humility. (1 John 1:9)

- In the name of Jesus, I rebuke every spirit of division, strife, and separation in my marriage. I declare that unity and love will prevail. (Mark 10:9)
- Lord, soften our hearts toward one another. Help us to release all bitterness, anger, and unforgiveness, and to walk in love and compassion. (Ephesians 4:31-32)
- Father, restore the love, passion, and commitment in our marriage. Rekindle the spark that brought us together. (Song of Solomon 2:16)
- Lord, help us to communicate with understanding, respect, and kindness. Let every word we speak bring healing and restoration. (Proverbs 15:1)
- In the name of Jesus, I break every ungodly influence or interference from third parties in our marriage. Shield us from anything or anyone trying to divide us. (Matthew 19:6)
- Lord, give us patience and understanding for each other's weaknesses. Help us to grow together in love and grace. (Colossians 3:13-14)
- I declare that forgiveness flows freely in our marriage. We will not hold onto past hurts but will extend grace to one another. (Matthew 6:14-15)
- Father, heal any wounds or scars in our hearts caused by words, actions, or past experiences. Let Your healing power flow through us. (Psalm 147:3)
- Lord, deliver us from pride and selfishness. Teach us to walk in humility and to consider each other's needs above our own. (Philippians 2:3-4)

- Father, give us a fresh start in our marriage. Help us to rebuild trust, love, and commitment under Your guidance. (Isaiah 43:19)
- Lord, grant us wisdom in every decision we make as a couple. Help us to align our plans with Your will. (James 1:5)
- In Jesus' name, I declare that our marriage is victorious through Christ. No weapon formed against us shall prosper. (Isaiah 54:17)
- Father, bless our marriage with peace, joy, and prosperity. Let Your favor rest upon us as we walk in unity. (Psalm 133:1)
- Holy Spirit, guide us in our journey as husband and wife. Teach us how to love, honor, and cherish one another. (John 14:26)
- I declare that our marriage is a covenant made before God, and it will stand firm through every trial and challenge. (Malachi 2:14)
- Lord, give us the strength to persevere through difficulties. Help us to remain faithful and committed to each other. (Galatians 6:9)
- Father, I thank You in advance for restoring and reconciling our marriage. I believe in Your power to make all things new. (2 Corinthians 5:18)

Prayer Points Against Spiritual Attacks on Marriage

- Heavenly Father, I thank You for the gift of marriage. I honor You for bringing us together in a holy covenant. (Genesis 2:24)

- Lord, I cover my marriage with the blood of Jesus. Let no weapon formed against us prosper. (Isaiah 54:17)
- In the name of Jesus, I come against every spirit of division, strife, and contention seeking to destroy my marriage. (Mark 10:9)
- Father, shield our marriage from any ungodly third-party influences, whether they be people, spirits, or situations trying to sow discord. (Proverbs 4:23)
- Lord, I rebuke every spirit of confusion, miscommunication, and misunderstanding in our marriage. Let peace and clarity reign. (1 Corinthians 14:33)
- Father, I declare that we are one in Christ. No force of darkness will separate what You have joined together. (Matthew 19:6)
- In Jesus' name, I break every generational curse affecting our marriage. We are redeemed by the blood of Jesus and free from ancestral bondage. (Galatians 3:13)
- Lord, protect our hearts and minds from temptation. Remove any spirit of infidelity, lust, or betrayal that seeks to harm our union. (1 Corinthians 10:13)
- Father, I declare that no financial struggles or attacks will cause strain in our marriage. Bless the work of our hands and provide for our needs. (Philippians 4:19)
- In the name of Jesus, I destroy every evil altar raised against our marriage. Let every curse and evil word spoken against us be nullified. (Numbers 23:23)
- Lord, restore emotional intimacy and trust in our marriage. Help us to connect deeply and love each other as You love us. (Ephesians 5:25)

- Father, I break every spirit of anger, bitterness, and unforgiveness in our marriage. Replace it with love, patience, and understanding. (Ephesians 4:31-32)
- I declare that we are victorious over every spiritual attack against our marriage. We are more than conquerors through Christ. (Romans 8:37)
- Lord, give us strength to stand together during difficult times. Let our faith in You and love for each other be unshaken. (Ecclesiastes 4:9-12)
- Father, build a hedge of protection around our marriage. Let no harm, spiritual or physical, come near us. (Job 1:10)
- In Jesus' name, I bind and render powerless every monitoring spirit watching over our marriage to bring harm or division. (Psalm 91:11-12)
- Lord, let Your purpose for our marriage prevail. Help us to glorify You through our union and fulfil the plans You have for us. (Jeremiah 29:11)
- Father, teach us to forgive quickly and reconcile with humility. Let no root of bitterness take hold in our hearts. (Colossians 3:13)
- Lord, help us to be spiritually vigilant and to recognize any schemes of the enemy against our marriage. (1 Peter 5:8)
- Father, I thank You for intervening in every area of our marriage under attack. I trust You to bring healing, peace, and restoration. (Psalm 34:17-19)

Prayer Points Against Spiritual Attacks on Husband/Wife

- Father, I thank You for my spouse and for Your divine covering over their life. I praise You for keeping them safe and shielding them from harm. (Psalm 91:1-2)
- Lord, I cover my spouse with the blood of Jesus. Let no evil come near them, and let every plan of the enemy be destroyed. (Revelation 12:11)
- Father, grant my spouse the spirit of discernment to recognize and reject every trap, deception, and strategy of the enemy. (1 Corinthians 2:14)
- In the name of Jesus, I bind and cast out every spirit of spiritual blindness, confusion, and manipulation sent to attack my spouse. (2 Corinthians 4:4)
- Lord, I pray that every open door of sin, weakness, or ignorance that the enemy could use to attack my spouse will be shut permanently by the power of the Holy Spirit. (Ephesians 4:27)
- Father, I declare Your divine protection over my spouse. Let Your angels encamp around them and guard their going out and coming in. (Psalm 34:7)
- Lord, empower my spouse to overcome every temptation and attack of the enemy. Help them to stand firm in their faith. (1 Corinthians 10:13)
- In Jesus' name, I break every generational curse, stronghold, or bondage affecting my spouse. They are free by the blood of Jesus. (Galatians 3:13)
- Lord, clothe my spouse with the full armor of God so they can stand against the wiles of the devil and remain victorious. (Ephesians 6:11-13)

- Father, make my spouse spiritually alert and vigilant. Let them recognize any subtle attack or scheme of the enemy and reject it immediately. (1 Peter 5:8)
- Lord, give my spouse wisdom and understanding in all their decisions and actions. Let them follow Your guidance and not be swayed by the enemy. (Proverbs 3:5-6)
- In Jesus' name, I dismantle every evil altar or curse raised against my spouse's life, destiny, or purpose. (Numbers 23:23)
- Father, surround my spouse with a hedge of divine protection. Let no evil force penetrate or harm them. (Job 1:10)
- Lord, I pray for peace in my spouse's mind and emotions. Protect them from stress, anxiety, and any mental attack. (Philippians 4:7)
- In Jesus' name, I cancel every negative influence, relationship, or connection that the enemy is using to attack my spouse. (Psalm 1:1-2)
- Father, ignite in my spouse a deeper hunger for Your Word and presence. Let Your Word be their guide and strength. (Psalm 119:105)
- Lord, I declare that my spouse is victorious over every plan and scheme of the enemy. No weapon formed against them will prosper. (Isaiah 54:17)
- Father, cover my spouse with Your wings. Let Your presence shield them from every attack, both seen and unseen. (Psalm 91:4)

- In the name of Jesus, I rebuke the spirit of fear in my spouse's life. They will walk in boldness, faith, and courage. (2 Timothy 1:7)
- Lord, I thank You for delivering my spouse from every spiritual attack. I praise You for the victory and protection You have secured for them. (Colossians 1:13)

Prayer Points Against the Spirit of Pride

- Heavenly Father, I thank You for the example of humility shown through Jesus Christ. Thank You for teaching us to walk in love and submission to Your will. (Philippians 2:5-8)
- Lord, I repent of every prideful thought, word, or action. Forgive me for any way I have exalted myself above others or resisted Your correction. (Proverbs 16:18)
- Father, I surrender my heart, mind, and will to You. Take away any spirit of pride within me and replace it with a humble and contrite spirit. (James 4:10)
- In the name of Jesus, I break every stronghold of pride and arrogance operating in my life. I declare that pride will not have dominion over me. (2 Corinthians 10:4-5)
- Lord, give me a heart that is humble and teachable. Help me to depend fully on You in all things and not on my own understanding. (Proverbs 3:5-6)
- In the name of Jesus, I rebuke every spirit of self-exaltation and self-righteousness. I choose to walk in humility before God and man. (Luke 14:11)

- Father, teach me to serve others with humility, as Jesus did. Help me to value others above myself and to seek their good. (Philippians 2:3-4)
- Lord, I declare that You are the Lord of my life. Pride will not rule over me; instead, I will submit to Your authority in every area. (Colossians 3:12)
- Father, renew my mind so that I see myself and others through Your eyes. Help me to think soberly and not to have an inflated view of myself. (Romans 12:3)
- In Jesus' name, I renounce every spirit of pride that comes through comparing myself to others. I embrace my identity and purpose in Christ. (2 Corinthians 10:12)
- Lord, surround me with godly counsel and accountability. Let others speak truth into my life to keep me humble and aligned with Your Word. (Proverbs 11:14)
- Father, I reject the pride that comes from worldly achievements or possessions. I will boast only in You, my Lord and Savior. (Jeremiah 9:23-24)
- Lord, soften my heart so that I am sensitive to Your correction and guidance. Let pride not harden me against Your voice. (Hebrews 3:15)
- Father, I submit to Your authority in every area of my life. Help me to walk in obedience and humility, trusting in Your plans. (James 4:7)
- In the name of Jesus, I silence every voice of boastfulness and arrogance in my life. I will only glorify and boast in You, Lord. (1 Corinthians 1:31)

- Lord, give me a broken and contrite spirit that pleases You. Let me always come before You with humility and reverence. (Psalm 51:17)
- I declare that I am free from the spirit of pride. I walk in the humility and grace of God, empowered by the Holy Spirit. (2 Timothy 1:7)
- Father, give me the wisdom to act justly, love mercy, and walk humbly with You. Let my life reflect Your glory and grace. (Micah 6:8)
- In Jesus' name, I bind every spirit of rebellion and self-centeredness. I align myself with God's Word and His will for my life. (1 Samuel 15:23)
- Lord, I thank You for Your grace that helps me overcome pride. I am grateful that You resist the proud but give grace to the humble. (1 Peter 5:5)

Prayer Points to Activate the Fruits of the Spirit in Your Life

- Father, I thank You for the gift of the Holy Spirit who lives in me and empowers me to walk in Your will. (John 14:26)
- Lord, I surrender my heart, mind, and life to the Holy Spirit. Let Him take full control so that I may bear good fruit. (Galatians 5:16-17)
- Father, fill my heart with Your unconditional love. Teach me to love You, myself, and others as You love. Let love guide all my actions. (1 Corinthians 13:4-7)

- Lord, let Your joy overflow in my life regardless of circumstances. Help me to find strength in Your presence and promises. (Nehemiah 8:10)
- Father, I ask for peace that surpasses all understanding. Calm every storm in my life and help me to trust You completely. (Philippians 4:7)
- Lord, teach me to wait on You and to remain calm in difficult situations. Let patience grow in my heart as I trust in Your timing. (James 1:4)
- Father, fill me with the spirit of kindness so I may reflect Your love to those around me. Help me to extend grace and compassion to others. (Ephesians 4:32)
- Lord, develop goodness in me so I may walk in integrity and always seek to do what pleases You. (Romans 12:21)
- Father, help me to remain faithful to You, Your Word, and the assignments You've given me. Let me be trustworthy and steadfast in all things. (Matthew 25:21)
- Lord, give me a gentle spirit that reflects Your meekness and humility. Help me to respond to others with tenderness and care. (Philippians 4:5)
- Father, help me to exercise self-control in my thoughts, words, and actions. Strengthen me to resist temptation and live a disciplined life. (2 Timothy 1:7)
- Lord, I declare that my life will bear much fruit, bringing glory to Your name. Let every fruit of the Spirit manifest fully in me. (John 15:8)
- In the name of Jesus, I break every hindrance to the manifestation of the fruits of the Spirit in my life. Let nothing block my growth in You. (Hebrews 12:1)

- Father, transform me daily by the renewing of my mind so that my life reflects Your character and Spirit. (Romans 12:2)
- Lord, give me a humble heart that is willing to learn, grow, and submit to Your will. Help me to live as a vessel of honor for You. (Micah 6:8)
- Father, help me to remain consistent in bearing the fruits of the Spirit, whether in times of joy or difficulty. (Psalm 1:3)
- Holy Spirit, guide me in all my decisions and actions so that my life produces fruit that pleases the Father. (John 16:13)
- Lord, draw me closer to You so that I may grow deeper in intimacy with You. Let my relationship with You bring forth abundant spiritual fruit. (James 4:8)
- In the name of Jesus, I declare that the desires of the flesh are crucified, and I now walk in the Spirit, bearing His fruits. (Galatians 5:24-25)
- Father, I thank You for the good work You are doing in my life. I praise You for the fruits of the Spirit that will manifest abundantly for Your glory. (Philippians 1:6)

Prayer Points Against Spiritual Attacks on Finances, Opportunities, Promotions, and Breakthroughs

- Father, I thank You for being my provider and sustainer. I acknowledge that every good and perfect gift comes from You. (James 1:17)
- Lord, I repent for any way I have mishandled the resources, opportunities, and blessings You have given

me. Forgive me and restore me by Your mercy. (Proverbs 3:9-10)
- In the name of Jesus, I break every chain of financial bondage and lack in my life. I declare that poverty has no power over me. (Deuteronomy 28:12-13)
- Lord, by the fire of the Holy Spirit, I destroy every evil altar speaking against my finances, opportunities, and breakthroughs. (Judges 6:25-26)
- Father, open every door of opportunity that has been shut by the enemy. Let no demonic force block my access to divine blessings. (Revelation 3:8)
- Lord, restore everything the enemy has stolen from my finances, opportunities, and promotions. I declare total restoration in Jesus' name. (Joel 2:25)
- Father, rebuke the devourer for my sake. I decree that my finances are protected and fruitful in the name of Jesus. (Malachi 3:11)
- In the name of Jesus, I break every generational curse of financial stagnation, failure, and lack operating in my life and family. (Galatians 3:13)
- Lord, let Your favor go before me and open doors of promotion, opportunities, and breakthroughs. Let me find favor in the sight of God and man. (Psalm 5:12)
- I bind every spirit of delay, denial, and hindrance working against my opportunities and breakthroughs. I command them to release their hold in Jesus' name. (Daniel 10:13)
- Father, I declare that I will walk in abundance and not lack. I proclaim that You are my shepherd, and I will not want. (Psalm 23:1)

- Lord, grant me wisdom and understanding to manage my finances and opportunities according to Your will. (Proverbs 4:7)
- In Jesus' name, I break every evil covenant and agreement that is working against my financial prosperity and breakthroughs. (Isaiah 28:18)
- Lord, I declare that promotion comes from You. I reject every manipulation of the enemy against my career and advancement. (Psalm 75:6-7)
- Father, I command financial breakthroughs to locate me now. I decree that I will be a lender and not a borrower. (Deuteronomy 28:12)
- Lord, I refuse to operate in fear concerning my finances and future. I trust in Your provision and power to bless me. (2 Timothy 1:7)
- Father, connect me to the right people and resources that will lead to my financial and professional breakthroughs. (Proverbs 18:16)
- Lord, release Your angels to fight every spiritual battle against my finances, opportunities, and promotions. Let every obstacle be removed. (Psalm 91:11)
- I declare victory over every spiritual opposition and attack against my financial stability, promotions, and opportunities in Jesus' name. (Isaiah 54:17)
- Father, I thank You for the breakthroughs, promotions, and financial blessings that are coming into my life. I give You all the glory and praise. (1 Thessalonians 5:18)

Prayer Points to Gain Wisdom

- Father, I thank You for being the giver of wisdom and understanding. I praise You for Your infinite knowledge and guidance. (James 1:5)
- Lord, I ask for wisdom in every area of my life. Let Your wisdom guide my decisions and lead me in the path of righteousness. (Proverbs 2:6)
- Father, teach me to walk in the fear of the Lord, which is the beginning of wisdom. Help me to revere and honor You in all that I do. (Proverbs 9:10)
- Holy Spirit, I invite You to fill me with the spirit of wisdom and revelation so that I may know You more deeply. (Ephesians 1:17)
- Lord, give me discernment to know what is right and pleasing in Your sight. Help me to distinguish between good and evil in all circumstances. (Hebrews 5:14)
- Father, grant me wisdom to make the right decisions daily in my family, work, ministry, and relationships. (Proverbs 3:5-6)
- Lord, teach me to speak with wisdom and grace. Let my words build up and encourage others, reflecting Your truth. (Colossians 4:6)
- Father, grant me a humble and teachable heart that is open to correction and learning from You and others. (Proverbs 1:5)
- Lord, equip me with the wisdom needed to lead in my home, workplace, and ministry with integrity and excellence. (James 3:17)

- Father, give me the wisdom to manage my finances according to Your will. Teach me to be a faithful steward of all You've entrusted to me. (Proverbs 21:20)
- Lord, give me wisdom to build healthy and godly relationships. Teach me to be patient, understanding, and loving toward others. (Proverbs 17:27)
- Father, let Your Word be my ultimate guide and fulfilment. Teach me to meditate on it daily for wisdom and direction. (Psalm 119:105)
- Lord, grant me the wisdom to understand and fulfil the purpose You have for my life. Let my decisions align with Your will. (Jeremiah 29:11)
- In the name of Jesus, I renounce every spirit of foolishness, ignorance, and error. I declare that I walk in the wisdom of God. (Proverbs 14:16)
- Lord, give me wisdom to overcome every challenge and obstacle in my life. Teach me to rely on Your strength and guidance. (James 1:2-4)
- Father, let all the wisdom You give me bring glory to Your name. Help me to use it to serve others and advance Your kingdom. (1 Corinthians 1:31)
- Lord, give me wisdom to recognize and flee from temptation. Strengthen me to make decisions that honor You. (1 Corinthians 10:13)
- Father, grant me wisdom to raise my children in Your ways, teaching them to love and serve You wholeheartedly. (Proverbs 22:6)
- Lord, in moments of uncertainty, grant me clarity and wisdom. Teach me to trust in Your plan and timing. (Isaiah 30:21)

- Father, I thank You in advance for the wisdom You have imparted to me. I praise You for Your guidance and faithfulness. (1 Thessalonians 5:18)

Prayer Points for Wisdom, Knowledge, and Understanding to Create Generational Wealth

- Father, I thank You for being my source and provider. I praise You for giving me the ability to create wealth and for Your promise of abundance. (Deuteronomy 8:18)
- Lord, grant me divine wisdom to create wealth according to Your will. Teach me how to manage resources and make decisions that glorify You. (Proverbs 24:3-4)
- Father, fill me with knowledge and insight into business ideas, investments, and opportunities that will bring generational blessings. (Proverbs 18:15)
- Lord, give me deep understanding and discernment to navigate financial matters wisely. Teach me strategies to build and sustain wealth. (Proverbs 4:7)
- In the name of Jesus, I break every spirit of poverty, financial stagnation, and lack operating in my life and family. (Galatians 3:13)
- Father, rebuke every devourer seeking to destroy my finances and investments. Protect all that I build for Your glory. (Malachi 3:11)
- Lord, I declare that the wealth You give me will be a blessing to my children and future generations. Help me to leave a godly legacy. (Proverbs 13:22)

- Father, release creative ideas and innovative solutions that will set me apart in my work, business, or ministry. (Exodus 35:31-32)
- Lord, let Your favor surround me as I pursue wealth-creating opportunities. Grant me open doors and divine connections. (Psalm 5:12)
- Father, help me to remain generous and faithful in giving, knowing that You bless cheerful givers. (2 Corinthians 9:6-7)
- Lord, give me wisdom to identify the right investments and business opportunities that will yield lasting wealth. (Ecclesiastes 11:2)
- Father, protect the wealth You entrust to me from destruction, loss, or misuse. Let it be used only for purposes that honor You. (Isaiah 54:17)
- Lord, guide me to avoid financial pitfalls, scams, and poor decisions. Let Your Spirit direct my steps in all financial matters. (Proverbs 3:5-6)
- Father, grant me the discipline to save, invest, and manage my resources wisely. Teach me to prioritize according to Your principles. (Proverbs 21:20)
- Lord, I declare that You will multiply the work of my hands and the resources entrusted to me for generational impact. (Matthew 25:21)
- Father, break every yoke of debt and financial oppression in my life. I declare freedom to prosper and to bless others. (Proverbs 22:7)
- Lord, anoint me with the ability to create wealth that is rooted in Your kingdom principles and free from worldly corruption. (Isaiah 45:3)

- Father, teach my family and me to work in unity to build and sustain wealth. Let us always seek Your wisdom in financial matters. (Amos 3:3)
- Lord, teach me to pass on not only wealth but also wisdom, faith, and godly values to the next generation. (Psalm 78:4)
- Father, I thank You for the wealth, wisdom, and opportunities You are bringing into my life. I praise You for making me a vessel of generational blessings. (Philippians 4:19)

Prayer Points to Break Long-Standing Curses, Evil Covenants, and Traditions in the Church

- Father, I thank You for the victory we have in Christ Jesus, who has redeemed us from every curse and evil covenant through His shed blood. (Galatians 3:13)
- Lord, we repent on behalf of the church for any way we have knowingly or unknowingly engaged in ungodly practices, traditions, or covenants. Forgive us and cleanse us by Your mercy. (2 Chronicles 7:14)
- In the name of Jesus, we renounce every evil covenant, oath, or agreement that the church has entered into, knowingly or unknowingly. We declare them null and void by the blood of Jesus. (Isaiah 28:18)
- Lord, by the power of the cross, we break every long-standing curse affecting the church's leadership, members, and mission. We declare that no curse shall prosper against us. (Numbers 23:23)

- Father, we destroy every evil altar that has been erected within or against the church, knowingly or unknowingly. Let Your holy fire consume them now in Jesus' name. (Judges 6:25-26)
- Lord, expose and uproot every tradition, practice, or ritual within the church that does not align with Your Word. Let Your truth prevail. (Matthew 15:3)
- Father, give the church wisdom and discernment to recognize any hidden curses or covenants that have infiltrated our worship, teachings, or leadership. (Jeremiah 33:3)
- Lord, sanctify the church by Your Word and Spirit. Purify our worship, our leaders, and our congregation so we may serve You in spirit and truth. (John 17:17)
- In Jesus' name, we break every generational pattern or cycle of failure, division, or stagnation that has hindered the church's growth and mission. (Lamentations 5:7)
- Lord, we declare that the church will fulfil its divine purpose. We reclaim the destiny of the church for Your glory and the advancement of Your kingdom. (Ephesians 3:10)
- Father, we plead the blood of Jesus over the foundation and land of the church. Purify it from any defilement caused by ungodly acts or covenants. (Leviticus 26:40-42)
- In Jesus' name, we bind and cast out every spirit of religion, legalism, and control that has hindered the flow of the Holy Spirit in the church. (2 Corinthians 3:17)
- Father, we destroy every work of witchcraft, sorcery, or occult practices that have infiltrated the church. We

declare Your light will expose and expel every hidden darkness. (Acts 19:19)

- Lord, restore pure and holy worship in the church. Let every form of idolatry, man-centered practices, and false teachings be removed. (John 4:24)
- Father, anoint the leaders of the church with wisdom, humility, and the fear of the Lord. Equip them to lead Your people into truth and righteousness. (1 Timothy 3:1-5)
- Lord, break every curse of division and disunity in the church. Let the body of Christ come together in love and purpose for Your glory. (Psalm 133:1)
- In the name of Jesus, we declare that the church is free from every bondage, manipulation, and oppression of the enemy. (Isaiah 61:1)
- Lord, send a revival to the church. Let Your Spirit move mightily, breaking every stronghold and renewing our passion for You. (Habakkuk 3:2)
- Father, we plead the blood of Jesus over the entire church—its people, leadership, ministries, and mission. Let Your blood speak better things for us. (Hebrews 12:2)
- Father, we thank You for delivering the church from every curse, covenant, and ungodly tradition. We declare that Your name will be glorified in the church forever. (Psalm 107:1-2)

Prayer Points Against Delay and Retrogression

- Father, I thank You because Your plans for me are good, to prosper me and give me a future filled with hope. (Jeremiah 29:11)
- In the name of Jesus, I break every chain of delay hindering my progress, breakthroughs, and promotions. (Daniel 10:12-13)
- I decree and declare that every force of backwardness and stagnation working against my life is destroyed by fire. (Deuteronomy 1:6-7)
- Father, let every altar speaking delay over my life, family, business, or ministry be shattered by the power of the Holy Ghost. (Judges 6:25-26)
- Lord, grant me divine speed to recover lost time, opportunities, and blessings. Let my destiny move forward without hindrance. (Amos 9:13)
- I command every power delaying my destiny to be destroyed. My life and progress will not be manipulated. (Isaiah 54:17)
- I break every inherited curse of delay and stagnation in my bloodline. I step into the blessings and favor of God. (Galatians 3:13)
- Father, every spirit of financial stagnation that has blocked my prosperity, I command it to be removed in Jesus' name. (Deuteronomy 8:18)
- Lord, every force delaying my marriage or marital breakthrough, be destroyed by fire. Let my divine spouse be released. (Genesis 2:18)

- I reject demotion, limitation, and professional stagnation. I move forward into the next level of my calling and purpose. (Psalm 75:6-7)
- I come against every spirit of procrastination and distraction causing delays in my assignments and destiny fulfilment (Ecclesiastes 11:4)
- Lord, disconnect me from any person, environment, or association that causes delay or retrogression in my life. (2 Corinthians 6:14)
- I cancel the pattern of getting close to breakthrough but never achieving it. I break this cycle in Jesus' name. (Psalm 102:13)
- Every demonic cycle of repeated failure in my life is broken. I step into consistent progress and success. (Isaiah 43:19)
- Father, restore the years the enemy has stolen. Let everything, I have lost be restored sevenfold. (Joel 2:25-26)
- Lord, let doors of opportunity, promotion, and breakthroughs open for me by Your supernatural favor. (Revelation 3:8)
- I release the anointing for divine speed upon my life. Let me accomplish in months what should take years. (1 Kings 18:46)
- I command every spiritual barrier, hindrance, and blockage against my progress to be removed by fire. (Isaiah 57:14)
- I declare that from today, I shall move forward. No more stagnation, no more delays, no more backwardness. (Exodus 14:15)

- Father, I thank You because my prayers are answered, and I will see tangible progress in every area of my life. (Mark 11:24)

Prayer Points Against Demonic Altars and Covenants from Old Residences, Schools, Workplaces, or Places of Worship

- Father, I thank You because You have given me victory over every demonic altar and covenant through the blood of Jesus Christ. (Colossians 2:14-15)
- In the name of Jesus, I sever every ungodly spiritual tie between me and any former place of residence, education, workplace, or worship that has held me captive. (2 Corinthians 6:14-17)
- I renounce and break every covenant I knowingly or unknowingly entered into through past associations, dedications, or rituals in my old residence, school, workplace, or place of worship. (Galatians 3:13)
- Father, let Your consuming fire destroy every demonic altar erected against my destiny from my past locations. (Judges 6:25-26)
- Lord, cleanse my foundation from every ancestral or environmental pollution that came from where I used to live, study, work, or worship. (Psalm 11:3)
- I cancel every negative word, incantation, or prayer spoken over my life in past places of residence, school, or worship, in Jesus' name. (Isaiah 54:17)
- I reject and revoke any evil dedication or spiritual initiation done on my behalf while I was in those locations, in Jesus' name. (1 Corinthians 10:21)

- I break every soul tie with ungodly people, teachers, coworkers, or religious leaders and associates that connected me to demonic influences. (1 Corinthians 15:33)
- I close every demonic gateway that was opened to my life through past involvement with ungodly practices in those locations. (Ephesians 4:27)
- I nullify every sacrifice, ritual, or blood offering made to keep me bound to demonic influences from my past environments. (Leviticus 17:7)
- In the name of Jesus, I command every monitoring spirit assigned to follow me from my past to be destroyed by fire. (Numbers 23:23)
- Every financial curse attached to my past residence, school, or place of worship, I break it now in Jesus' name. (Deuteronomy 8:18)
- I reject every familiar spirit trying to manipulate my present and future through past connections. (Leviticus 19:31)
- Father, separate me completely from every evil influence and oppression that came from my past locations. (2 Corinthians 6:17)
- I recover every blessing, opportunity, and breakthrough that was stolen from me through past demonic affiliations. (Joel 2:25)
- I refuse to be tied to my past. I move forward in destiny, purpose, and blessings in Jesus' name. (Philippians 3:13-14)

- Every evil seed planted in my life from past places of residence, school, or worship, be uprooted by fire now. (Matthew 15:13)
- I cover myself, my home, and my future with the blood of Jesus. No past demonic influence will find access into my life again. (Revelation 12:11)
- I decree and declare that I am free from every past demonic altar and covenant. I walk in victory, blessings, and divine favor. (John 8:36)
- Father, I thank You for setting me free from every chain of my past. I walk in newness and divine protection. (Psalm 107:1-2)

Prayer Points Against Witchcraft, Demonic Altars, and Evil Covenants Set Up in the Workplace

- Father, I thank You because You are my shield and protector. No weapon formed against me in my workplace shall prosper. (Isaiah 54:17)
- I cover my workplace with the blood of Jesus. Let every satanic presence be uprooted and destroyed. (Revelation 12:11)
- In the name of Jesus, I break and nullify every demonic covenant, agreement, or ritual established in my workplace. (Colossians 2:14-15)
- Lord, let Your fire consume every witchcraft altar raised in my workplace to manipulate or oppress me. (Judges 6:25-26)

- I close every spiritual gateway that allows witchcraft and demonic activities to operate in my workplace. (Ephesians 4:27)
- I cancel every word curse, incantation, and negative declaration spoken against me by colleagues, superiors, or clients. (Proverbs 26:2)
- I bind and paralyze every monitoring spirit assigned to track my progress or cause delays in my career. (Numbers 23:23)
- I nullify every form of occult practice, sorcery, divination, or charm operating in my workplace. (Leviticus 19:31)
- I rebuke and cast out every Jezebelic, controlling, or manipulative spirit in my workplace. (2 Kings 9:22)
- Father, let Your consuming fire destroy every demonic plan, conspiracy, or scheme against me. (Hebrews 12:29)
- I declare that I am the light in my workplace, and no darkness shall prevail against me. (Matthew 5:14-16)
- Every force resisting my promotion, progress, or breakthrough in the workplace, be dismantled now in Jesus' name. (Psalm 75:6-7)
- I break every financial curse affecting my business, salary, or workplace economy. I declare prosperity in Jesus' name. (Deuteronomy 8:18)
- I frustrate every satanic agenda of division, gossip, false accusations, and conspiracies set against me. (Psalm 35:4)

- I anoint my desk, office, and workspace with the blood of Jesus. My work shall be productive and blessed. (Deuteronomy 28:8)
- Every demonic energy, oppression, or heaviness transferred to me through coworkers, clients, or management is broken. (Isaiah 10:27)
- I blind every spiritual eye monitoring my progress, and I silence every demonic informant assigned against me. (2 Kings 6:17-18)
- I declare supernatural favor, promotion, and open doors in my career, business, and workplace. (Psalm 5:12)
- I decree and declare that no witchcraft power shall prevail over my life, career, or business in Jesus' name. (Luke 10:19)
- Father, I thank You for securing my workplace, career, and business from all forms of demonic influence. (Psalm 91:1-2)

Prayer Points Against Familiar Spirits

- Father, I thank You for delivering me from every bondage of familiar spirits and for giving me victory through Jesus Christ. (Colossians 1:13)
- In the name of Jesus, I break and renounce every connection, agreement, and covenant I or my ancestors may have had with familiar spirits. (2 Corinthians 6:14-15)
- I command every familiar spirit from my family lineage to be destroyed by fire and never operate in my life again. (Lamentations 5:7)

- I close every open door—whether through dreams, past experiences, or family ties—that has allowed familiar spirits to operate in my life. (Ephesians 4:27)
- I bind and cast out every familiar spirit assigned to monitor my life and destiny. I declare blindness upon them in Jesus' name. (Numbers 23:23)
- Every familiar spirit using witchcraft to manipulate my life, be destroyed by the fire of the Holy Ghost. (Exodus 22:18)
- I reject and cancel every form of dream manipulation and deception caused by familiar spirits. My dreams shall be divinely inspired. (Matthew 13:25)
- Every spirit of divination operating around me, I rebuke and silence you in Jesus' name. (Acts 16:16-18)
- I break every link with familiar spirits that have been operating in my household for generations. I declare my family free! (Joshua 24:15)
- I reject and destroy every demonic attachment through objects, gifts, or possessions linked to familiar spirits. (Deuteronomy 7:25-26)
- I sever every ungodly soul tie with any person, place, or experience that introduced familiar spirits into my life. (1 Corinthians 6:17)
- Every familiar spirit causing stagnation, delay, and repeated failure in my life, I cast you out now in Jesus' name. (Isaiah 43:19)
- Every evil seed, covenant, or influence planted in my life by familiar spirits, be uprooted by the blood of Jesus. (Matthew 15:13)

- I cut off all familiar spirits that may have followed me from my former residence, school, or place of worship. (Isaiah 54:17)
- I cover myself, my family, and my future with the blood of Jesus. No familiar spirit shall have power over me. (Revelation 12:11)
- I declare that I am seated with Christ in heavenly places, and no familiar spirit can operate in my life anymore. (Ephesians 2:6)
- I recover every blessing, opportunity, and breakthrough that familiar spirits have stolen from my life. (Joel 2:25)
- I receive the fire of the Holy Spirit to consume every operation of familiar spirits around me. (Acts 1:8)
- I decree and declare that I am free from every familiar spirit. I walk in victory, power, and divine authority. (John 8:36)
- Father, I thank You for delivering me completely from the influence and oppression of familiar spirits. (Psalm 107:1-2)

Prayer Points for the Release of Blessings and Favor

- Father, I thank You because You are the giver of every good and perfect gift. I acknowledge You as the source of all blessings and favor. (James 1:17)
- Lord, open the heavens over my life and pour out abundant blessings that I will not have room enough to contain. (Malachi 3:10)

- In the name of Jesus, I break every curse, limitation, or demonic blockage preventing my blessings from manifesting. (Galatians 3:13)
- I declare that the favor of God is upon me. Wherever I go, I will be favored in Jesus' name. (Psalm 5:12)
- Father, connect me with the right people who will help me fulfil my purpose and destiny. (Proverbs 18:16)
- I decree financial breakthroughs, divine provision, and supernatural wealth in my life. (Deuteronomy 8:18)
- Lord, let Your favor open doors for me in my career, business, and workplace. Let opportunities locate me. (Psalm 90:17)
- Every spirit of delay assigned to hinder my blessings, be destroyed in Jesus' name. (Daniel 10:12-13)
- I receive favor for a godly and blessed marriage. My marital destiny shall be fulfilled without hindrance. (Proverbs 18:22)
- Father, open doors that no man can shut in my life. Let divine opportunities locate me. (Revelation 3:8)
- Lord, anoint me for impact. Let my ministry and calling flourish with divine favor and increase. (Isaiah 61:1)
- I cancel every mark of rejection upon my life. I am accepted and favored wherever I go. (Ephesians 1:6)
- Father, let those in positions of power favor me and grant me access to divine opportunities. (Esther 2:17)
- Lord, accelerate my breakthroughs and let my blessings come without delay. (Amos 9:13)
- Everything that has been stolen or lost in my life, let it be restored sevenfold in Jesus' name. (Joel 2:25)

- I break every ancestral or generational curse limiting my financial breakthrough. I walk in abundance. (2 Corinthians 9:8)
- I declare that my household is blessed, and my children shall walk in divine favor. (Psalm 112:2-3)
- I receive divine health and healing. No sickness shall steal my blessings in Jesus' name. (3 John 1:2)
- I receive peace, joy, and fulfilment in every area of my life. No sorrow shall attach itself to my blessings. (Proverbs 10:22)
- Father, I thank You because my prayers have been answered, and my season of favor and blessings has begun. (Mark 11:24)

Prayer Points for the Spirit of Excellence to Operate in My Life

- Father, I thank You for creating me in Your image and giving me the ability to operate in wisdom, knowledge, and excellence. (Genesis 1:27)
- Lord, I receive the mind of Christ. Let my thoughts, decisions, and actions reflect divine wisdom and excellence. (1 Corinthians 2:16)
- Father, just as You placed the spirit of excellence upon Daniel, let it rest upon me in every area of my life. (Daniel 6:3)
- I reject every spirit of laziness, procrastination, and mediocrity. I shall operate in diligence and excellence. (Proverbs 22:29)

- Lord, grant me divine wisdom, knowledge, and understanding to excel in all that I do. (James 1:5)
- I declare that I shall stand out in my workplace, business, and career because of the spirit of excellence upon me. (Colossians 3:23-24)
- Father, let my words and actions be filled with wisdom, grace, and excellence, reflecting Your glory. (Titus 2:7-8)
- Lord, anoint me with the grace to serve You with excellence and distinction in my ministry and calling. (2 Timothy 2:15)
- I break every spirit of fear, doubt, and inferiority that hinders me from operating in excellence. (2 Timothy 1:7)
- Father, give me the strength, discipline, and endurance to pursue excellence in all that I do. (Philippians 4:13)
- Lord, grant me favor before men and position me for leadership roles where I will demonstrate excellence. (Proverbs 3:4)
- I receive divine insight and discernment to make excellent decisions that will bring glory to God. (Isaiah 11:2)
- Every generational curse or limitation that hinders excellence in my family, I break it in Jesus' name. (Galatians 3:13)
- Lord, fill me with creativity and innovative ideas that will set me apart in my industry. (Exodus 35:31-32)
- I declare financial wisdom and excellent stewardship over my resources. I shall prosper in Jesus' name. (Deuteronomy 8:18)

- Father, let me be excellent in my relationships, displaying love, integrity, and understanding. (Ephesians 4:29)
- I pray for divine acceleration and recognition of my gifts and talents to operate in excellence. (Proverbs 18:16)
- I reject every distraction that diverts me from my purpose and excellence in life. (Hebrews 12:1-2)
- Lord, align me with my divine purpose and let me fulfil it with excellence and impact. (Jeremiah 29:11)
- Father, I thank You because I am set apart for greatness. I walk in divine excellence, and my life brings You glory. (Psalm 8:5)

Prayer Points to Walk in the Spirit

- Father, I thank You for giving me the Holy Spirit as my Helper, Guide, and Teacher. (John 14:26)
- Lord, I surrender every area of my life to the Holy Spirit. Lead me in all my decisions and actions. (Romans 8:14)
- Father, make me sensitive to the promptings and voice of the Holy Spirit so I may follow Your will. (Isaiah 30:21)
- In the name of Jesus, I crucify my flesh and its desires. I refuse to be led by my emotions or sinful nature. (Galatians 5:16-17)
- Holy Spirit, fill me with Your fruit—love, joy, peace, patience, kindness, goodness, faithfulness, gentleness, and self-control. (Galatians 5:22-23)

- Lord, give me the ability to discern between the voice of the Holy Spirit and the voice of the enemy. (1 John 4:1)
- Father, fill me with wisdom and spiritual understanding so I may walk in Your perfect will. (Ephesians 1:17)
- Lord, strengthen me by Your Spirit so I may overcome temptation and walk in righteousness. (Ephesians 3:16)
- I silence every voice of distraction that tries to pull me away from walking in the Spirit. (2 Corinthians 10:5)
- Holy Spirit, draw me into deeper communion with God through prayer, worship, and meditation on the Word. (John 4:24)
- Lord, empower me to walk in boldness, proclaiming Your Word and demonstrating Your power. (Acts 1:8)
- I submit my thoughts and emotions to the Holy Spirit. I reject fear, doubt, and anxiety. (Philippians 4:7)
- Holy Spirit, help me walk in love, forgiving others just as Christ has forgiven me. (Ephesians 4:32)
- Father, ignite in me a deep hunger for Your Word, so I may grow spiritually and walk in truth. (Psalm 119:105)
- I decree that sin, darkness, and the works of the enemy have no power over me. I walk in the Spirit of holiness. (Romans 6:14)
- Lord, refine my thoughts, words, and actions so I may walk in holiness before You. (1 Peter 1:15-16)
- Holy Spirit, activate Your gifts in my life—prophecy, healing, discernment, wisdom, and more—for the glory of God. (1 Corinthians 12:7-11)
- I reject fear and doubt. I choose to walk by faith and trust in the guidance of the Holy Spirit. (2 Timothy 1:7)

- Father, let my life be a reflection of Christ, drawing others to You as I walk in the Spirit. (Matthew 5:16)
- Lord, I thank You for the victory, joy, and peace that come from walking in the Spirit every day. (Romans 8:6)

Prayer Points to Resist Temptations and Find a Way of Escape

- Father, I thank You because You are faithful and will not allow me to be tempted beyond what I can bear. (1 Corinthians 10:13)
- Lord, I submit my heart, mind, and body to You. Strengthen me to choose Your ways over the desires of the flesh. (James 4:7)
- Father, empower me by Your Spirit to resist every form of temptation that comes my way. (Matthew 26:41)
- Lord, as You have promised, provide a way of escape from every temptation I face. Help me recognize and take it. (1 Corinthians 10:13)
- I declare that sin has no dominion over me, for I walk in the righteousness of Christ. (Romans 6:14)
- Holy Spirit, help me guard my heart and mind from thoughts, desires, and influences that lead to sin. (Proverbs 4:23)
- I reject every spirit of compromise that tries to weaken my stand for holiness and righteousness. (Ephesians 5:11)

- Lord, give me spiritual discernment to recognize the enemy's schemes and avoid them. (2 Corinthians 2:11)
- I crucify the desires of the flesh and choose to walk by the Spirit in Jesus' name. (Galatians 5:16-17)
- Father, let Your Word be deeply rooted in me, so I may not sin against You. (Psalm 119:11)
- Lord, increase in me the fear of the Lord, which keeps me from evil and deception. (Proverbs 8:13)
- When I am weak, Lord, strengthen me to resist temptation and stand firm in righteousness. (2 Corinthians 12:9-10)
- Father, remove every person, place, or thing that is leading me into temptation. Let me walk in holiness. (2 Corinthians 6:17)
- I call upon the name of Jesus, my strong tower, and I am delivered from every temptation. (Proverbs 18:10)
- Lord, help me to develop a strong prayer life so that I may not fall into temptation. (Luke 22:46)
- I refuse to believe the lies of the enemy that try to deceive me into sin. I stand on God's truth. (John 8:44)
- Holy Spirit, fill me with self-control and discipline to make godly choices in every situation. (2 Timothy 1:7)
- In the name of Jesus, I break free from every cycle of sin, addiction, and temptation that has held me captive. (John 8:36)
- Lord, help me dwell in Your presence, where I find strength and escape from all temptation. (Psalm 91:1)
- Father, I thank You because through Christ, I am more than a conqueror over every temptation! (Romans 8:37)

Prayer Points for the Armor of God in My Life

- Father, I thank You for providing me with spiritual armor to stand firm against the enemy's attacks. (Ephesians 6:10-11)
- Lord, clothe me with the belt of truth. Let me walk in honesty, integrity, and Your Word so that I will not be deceived by the enemy. (John 8:32)
- Father, cover my heart with the breastplate of righteousness. Help me to live a holy and blameless life before You. (2 Corinthians 5:21)
- Lord, I put on the shoes of peace. Let me walk in Your peace, and may I bring the message of salvation to those around me. (Romans 10:15)
- I take up the shield of faith to quench every fiery dart of the enemy. Strengthen my faith so I may stand firm in trials. (Hebrews 11:6)
- Father, guard my mind with the helmet of salvation. I reject every lie and deception of the enemy and declare that my mind is renewed in Christ. (Romans 12:2)
- Lord, I wield the sword of the Spirit, which is Your Word. Let it be my weapon against every attack of the enemy. (Hebrews 4:12)
- Father, strengthen me with Your power so I may stand firm in battle and never grow weary. (Isaiah 40:31)
- In the name of Jesus, I declare that no weapon formed against me shall prosper because I am fully armed in God. (Isaiah 54:17)

- Lord, teach me to pray at all times in the Spirit, staying alert and persistent in my faith. (Ephesians 6:18)
- I reject fear, doubt, and worry. I stand in faith, knowing that I am fully covered by God's 'Armor. (2 Timothy 1:7)
- Lord, grant me spiritual discernment to recognize the enemy's schemes and overcome them by Your wisdom. (James 1:5)
- Father, help me live in righteousness and purity so that my armor remains strong and effective. (1 Peter 1:15-16)
- I cover my family with the armor of God. No attack of the enemy shall prevail against us. (Psalm 91:1-2)
- Lord, let Your armor protect me from temptation, and give me the strength to resist the devil. (James 4:7)
- I declare that I am strong in the Lord and in His mighty power. No spiritual battle shall defeat me. (Ephesians 6:10)
- Father, give me the boldness to proclaim Your Word and walk in my spiritual authority. (Luke 10:19)
- Lord, equip Your church with the full armor of God so that we may stand united against darkness. (Matthew 16:18)
- I declare that my destiny is secure in Christ. No evil force can hinder God's purpose for my life. (Jeremiah 29:11)
- Father, I thank You because I am more than a conqueror through Christ Jesus, and I walk daily in victory! (Romans 8:37)

Prayer Points to Lift a Standard Against the Enemy

- Father, I thank You because You are my refuge and strong tower. You lift a standard against every attack of the enemy. (Isaiah 59:19)
- In the name of Jesus, I declare that I am more than a conqueror, and no weapon formed against me shall prosper. (Romans 8:37, Isaiah 54:17)
- Holy Spirit, rise like a mighty flood and lift a standard against the forces of darkness in my life. (Isaiah 59:19)
- Lord, arise and scatter every enemy that seeks to destroy my destiny. Let them flee before Your power. (Psalm 68:1)
- I cancel every evil plot, conspiracy, and scheme of the enemy against my life, family, and ministry. (Job 5:12)
- I cover myself, my household, and my destiny with the blood of Jesus. Let the blood be a barrier against all demonic attacks. (Revelation 12:11)
- Father, deliver me from every trap of the enemy. Let every snare set for me be destroyed. (Psalm 91:3)
- In the name of Jesus, I break every generational curse and demonic stronghold working against my family. (Galatians 3:13)
- Lord, send Your mighty angels to fight on my behalf and frustrate every attack of the enemy. (Psalm 34:7)
- I refuse to live in fear. The Lord has given me power, love, and a sound mind. (2 Timothy 1:7)
- Father, let Your fire consume every altar of darkness raised against my life. (Hebrews 12:29)

- I command every work of the devil in my life and surroundings to be destroyed by the power of God. (1 John 3:8)
- Every power delaying my progress, be destroyed in Jesus' name. I move forward by divine acceleration. (Habakkuk 2:3)
- I receive boldness to stand against every attack of the enemy and proclaim the truth of God's Word. (Ephesians 6:19)
- I nullify every negative word spoken against my life. Only the Word of God shall stand. (Numbers 23:23)
- Father, set a hedge of fire around me and my household. No evil shall come near me. (Zechariah 2:5)
- Lord, strengthen me to stand firm in faith and not be shaken by the attacks of the enemy. (1 Corinthians 16:13)
- I decree breakthroughs in every area where the enemy has tried to block my progress. (Isaiah 45:2-3)
- Every enemy that refuses to repent, let the judgment of God be upon them, and let righteousness prevail. (Psalm 35:1-8)
- Father, I thank You because You have lifted a standard against my enemies, and I walk in total victory! (2 Corinthians 2:14)

Prayer Points to Command My Night

- Father, I cover myself, my family, and my dwelling place with the blood of Jesus—no evil shall come near me! (Exodus 12:13)

- I declare that my sleep shall be peaceful, undisturbed, and free from demonic interference! (Psalm 4:8)

- Every satanic assignment scheduled against me in the night, be canceled by the fire of God! (Isaiah 54:17)

- I reject every demonic visitation, nightmare, or spiritual attack—I am hidden under the shadow of the Almighty! (Psalm 91:1-5)

- Lord, I consecrate my dream life to You—no demonic contamination, manipulation, or initiation shall prevail! (Job 33:14-16)

- Every dream programmed by the enemy to plant fear, confusion, or delay in my life, be reversed by the blood of Jesus! (Matthew 13:25)

- Father, release Your warrior angels to stand guard over my home, my loved ones, and everything that concerns me! (Psalm 34:7)

- Let any spiritual monitoring eye watching me at night be blinded and destroyed! (2 Kings 6:18)

- Lord, speak to me in the night—reveal deep things, hidden mysteries, and divine instructions for my life! (Daniel 2:22)

- Let my spirit be sensitive to heavenly visions, prophetic dreams, and guidance from the Holy Spirit! (Joel 2:28)

- Every spirit of fear, anxiety, and oppression seeking to torment me at night, I rebuke you in Jesus' name! (2 Timothy 1:7)

- I break every satanic chain of insomnia, restlessness, or night terror—I shall have divine rest! (Proverbs 3:24)

- I take authority over the night and declare that no evil force shall rise against me! (Luke 10:19)

- My night shall be filled with God's presence, and I will wake up refreshed, renewed, and empowered for the day ahead! (Psalm 118:24)

Prayer Points for Direction and Against Confusion & Indecision

- Lord, I acknowledge You in all my ways—direct my paths and lead me into Your perfect will! (Proverbs 3:5-6)

- Father, order my steps according to Your word and let no confusion reign in my heart! (Psalm 37:23)

- I rebuke every spirit of confusion, doubt, and double-mindedness operating in my life in Jesus' name! (James 1:6-8)

- Every satanic manipulation assigned to cloud my judgment, be destroyed by fire! (1 Corinthians 14:33)

- Lord, give me divine clarity and understanding to make the right choices in my life and calling! (Proverbs 4:7)
- I receive the spirit of wisdom and revelation to discern between good and evil! (Ephesians 1:17)
- Father, let me not move ahead of You or lag behind—align my steps with Your divine timing! (Ecclesiastes 3:11)
- I refuse to be led by emotions or pressure; I choose to wait on You for direction! (Isaiah 30:21)
- I reject the spirit of fear and hesitation—by faith, I move forward in God's plan for my life! (2 Timothy 1:7)
- I declare that I have the mind of Christ, and I walk in confidence and boldness! (1 Corinthians 2:16)
- Lord, speak to me clearly and confirm Your direction in ways I will understand! (Jeremiah 33:3)
- Let every counterfeit door be shut, and let only the doors You have opened remain! (Revelation 3:7)
- I receive Your peace that surpasses all understanding to guide my heart and mind! (Philippians 4:6-7)
- Thank You, Lord, for directing my steps, removing confusion, and leading me into my destiny! (Isaiah 58:11)

Prayer Points to Nullify Self-Inflicted Curses

- Father, I humbly repent for every negative word I have spoken against myself knowingly or unknowingly. (1 John 1:9)

- Lord, forgive me for any actions, agreements, or thoughts that have brought curses upon my life. (Proverbs 18:21)

- By the blood of Jesus, I break every self-inflicted curse operating in my life! (Galatians 3:13)

- I renounce and nullify every negative declaration I have made against my destiny. (Numbers 14:28)

- Every word of failure, limitation, sickness, or poverty that I have spoken over myself, I cancel it in Jesus' name! (Isaiah 54:17)

- I declare that I am blessed, highly favored, and walking in divine purpose. (Deuteronomy 28:6)

- I replace every word of defeat with words of victory—I am more than a conqueror! (Romans 8:37)

- My life aligns with God's promises, and I will prosper in all I do. (Jeremiah 29:11)

- I renounce and break any agreement I have made with failure, fear, or oppression. (Colossians 2:14)

- By the power of the Holy Spirit, I reject every demonic influence that has entered my life through my own words. (Matthew 12:36-37)

- I declare that my mind, body, and spirit are free from every curse—I walk in liberty through Christ! (John 8:36)

- Lord, restore every lost opportunity and wasted time caused by these self-inflicted curses. (Joel 2:25)

- I cover my life, destiny, and future with the blood of Jesus—only His covenant will speak for me! (Hebrews 12:24)

- I declare that from today, my words will align with God's Word, and I will speak only life! (Proverbs 4:20-22)

- Holy Spirit, help me guard my tongue and speak blessings over myself and my destiny. (Psalm 19:14)

- Every power enforcing self-inflicted curses, your assignment is over—I am free in Jesus' name! (Isaiah 10:27)

Prayer Points Against Spiritual Attacks on Families

- Father, I thank You for being our refuge and fortress, protecting my family from every evil. (Psalm 91:1-2)

- Lord, I am grateful for Your covenant of protection and preservation over my household. (Isaiah 54:17)

- I cover my family—spirit, soul, and body—with the blood of Jesus. No weapon formed against us shall prosper. (Exodus 12:13)

- Let the blood of Jesus speak protection, deliverance, and restoration over every member of my family. (Hebrews 12:24)

- I break every generational curse and evil covenant working against my family in Jesus' name! (Galatians 3:13)

- Every ancestral or foundational bondage affecting my family's progress, be destroyed by the blood of Jesus! (Colossians 2:14)

- Every witchcraft power assigned to attack my family, be consumed by the fire of the Holy Ghost! (Exodus 22:18)

- I cancel every demonic manipulation, spell, or enchantment working against my family in Jesus' name! (Numbers 23:23)

- I bind every spirit of confusion, division, and strife seeking to destroy the unity of my family. (1 Corinthians 1:10)

- Every attack against my marriage and the marriages in my family, be nullified by the power of God! (Mark 10:9)

- I decree that my children and generations to come shall serve the Lord and fulfill their divine purpose. (Isaiah 54:13)

- Every satanic agenda against the destiny of my children is canceled by the power of God! (Jeremiah 29:11)

- I rebuke every spirit of poverty, financial stagnation, and lack targeting my family in Jesus' name! (Philippians 4:19)

- By the blood of Jesus, I declare healing and divine health over my family—sickness and disease shall not prevail! (Isaiah 53:5)

- Every monitoring spirit assigned to spy on my family, be blinded by the fire of God! (2 Kings 6:17-18)

- I break every demonic link and evil surveillance system tracking my family's progress. (Psalm 31:15)

- Lord, send Your angels to encamp around my family and fight every spiritual battle on our behalf. (Psalm 34:7)

- I declare that no plague, disaster, or evil report shall befall my family in Jesus' name! (Psalm 91:10-11)

- I declare my family victorious over every spiritual attack—we are more than conquerors in Christ! (Romans 8:37)

- Let every enemy of my family be scattered, and let peace, love, and divine favor reign in our home. (Psalm 68:1)

Prayer Points for Miracles to Take Place in Your Life

- Father, I thank You because You are the God of miracles, and nothing is impossible for You. (Luke 1:37)

- Lord, step into my situation and perform wonders that will amaze the world. (Exodus 15:11)

- Every force of darkness resisting my miracle, be destroyed in Jesus' name! (Isaiah 54:17)

- Father, let every closed door in my life be supernaturally opened now! (Revelation 3:8)

- Lord, release my miracles speedily and let delays be removed in Jesus' name! (Habakkuk 2:3)

- I declare divine provision, unexpected favor, and supernatural financial increase in my life. (Philippians 4:19)

- By the stripes of Jesus, I receive complete healing in my body, mind, and soul. (Isaiah 53:5)

- Every dead situation in my life, receive resurrection power in Jesus' name! (John 11:25)

- Lord, restore everything the enemy has stolen from me—time, health, opportunities, and relationships. (Joel 2:25)

- Father, let my family experience divine breakthroughs, healings, and testimonies. (Acts 16:31)

- Lord, let Your favor go before me and make the impossible possible in my life. (Psalm 5:12)

- I declare divine connections, supernatural restoration, and breakthrough in my marriage. (Genesis 2:18)

- Father, open doors of supernatural promotions, business breakthroughs, and divine helpers. (Deuteronomy 28:12)

- Lord, surround me with Your angels and protect me from every evil plan. (Psalm 91:11)

- Lord, let signs, wonders, and miracles follow my ministry and everything I do for Your kingdom. (Mark 16:17)

- I cancel every generational curse, spoken word, and demonic barrier hindering my miracle. (Galatians 3:13)

- Father, let Your miracle-working power rest upon me and my household. (Acts 10:38)

- What seems impossible with man is possible with You, O God. Let my testimony manifest! (Matthew 19:26)

- Lord, increase my faith to believe and receive miracles in every area of my life. (Hebrews 11:6)

- Father, I thank You because my miracles are already taking place, and I will testify soon! (Psalm 126:3)

The Courtroom of Heaven

When Prayer Needs a Legal Strategy

Have you ever found yourself praying fervently—day after day, month after month—yet nothing seems to change? The healing doesn't come. The breakthrough is delayed. The promise feels stuck in the realm of the "not yet." It's not that God isn't listening; it may be that you're using the wrong prayer strategy for the kind of resistance you're facing. In certain cases, what you're battling isn't just demonic opposition on a battlefield—it's a legal matter in the courts of heaven.

Just as earthly systems operate under legal principles, the spiritual realm is also governed by divine laws and order. The Word of God often presents Him not only as Father and King, but also as Judge (Psalm 7:11, Isaiah 33:22). This legal dimension of prayer, often overlooked, is critical when you're contending with long-standing issues that resist normal intercession or warfare tactics.

The Reality of Unanswered or Delayed Prayers

Delayed prayers are one of the most frustrating aspects of the believer's journey. We pray with faith, speak declarations, fast, sow seeds—and yet the answer seems suspended. Could it be that there's a spiritual accusation standing against you in the unseen realm? Could the enemy be legally blocking your answers because of unrepented sin, ancestral covenants, or word curses you've unknowingly empowered?

In Zechariah 3, we see Joshua the high priest standing before the angel of the Lord while Satan stands at his right hand to accuse him. Even though Joshua was chosen, he was being opposed legally because of "filthy garments"—symbolic of sin or unrighteousness. It wasn't until the Lord issued a verdict and gave him clean garments that the resistance was broken.

The Difference Between Battlefield Warfare and Courtroom Advocacy

Most spiritual warfare teachings emphasize fighting the devil in the battlefield—binding, casting out, and resisting. While this has its place, battlefield prayers deal with power, whereas courtroom prayers deal with authority and legality.

Imagine going into battle without first settling the legal right your enemy has to attack. You may win a few skirmishes, but the root of the conflict will keep resurfacing. You can shout at devils all day long, but if there's unrepented sin, a bloodline curse, or a demonic contract giving Satan legal access, he can hold back your breakthrough until that matter is settled in heaven's courts.

In the courtroom, your role shifts from a soldier to an advocate. You're not fighting; you're presenting your case before the Righteous Judge, allowing the blood of Jesus to speak on your behalf (Hebrews 12:24). The courtroom is where legal rights are revoked, verdicts are rendered, and justice is executed.

A Parable That Reveals the Strategy: Luke 18:1–8

Jesus gave a clear example of this principle in Luke 18:1–8. A widow persistently approached a judge saying, *"Grant me justice against my adversary."* Though the judge was unjust, he eventually ruled in her favor because of her persistence.

Now, if an unjust judge can deliver justice because of persistence, how much more will God, the Righteous Judge, respond to His elect who cry out to Him day and night? This parable is not about begging God but about engaging the judicial dimension of prayer—presenting your petition before the Judge to release justice and divine intervention.

Why Some Prayers Are Delayed

Many believers experience delays in answered prayers because of unresolved spiritual legalities:

- Accusations from the enemy (Revelation 12:10) that haven't been answered with repentance and the blood of Jesus.
- Unbroken covenants or generational sins still speaking against you in the realm of the spirit (Lamentations 5:7, Numbers 14:18).
- Bitterness or unforgiveness, which hinders your access to mercy (Matthew 6:14-15).
- Words spoken against your destiny, by others or even yourself (Proverbs 18:21).
- Unfulfilled divine assignments that have created spiritual imbalance.

Before commanding, warring, or even waiting—sometimes, you must petition. You must step into the courts, repent, renounce, and request a righteous verdict.

There comes a time in the believer's journey when the usual forms of prayer seem ineffective. You've declared. You've fasted. You've waged warfare and stood in faith. Yet, the issue remains. Why? Because not every battle is won on the battlefield. Some are won in the courtroom.

Heaven has a judicial system. God is not only our Father and King—He is also the Righteous Judge (Psalm 7:11; Isaiah 33:22). When long-standing problems persist—especially those rooted in bloodlines, ancestral covenants, or legal accusations—it's time to take the matter to the Courts of Heaven.

Understanding the Courtroom of Heaven

The Courtroom of Heaven is not a mystical place—it's a spiritual dimension where legal transactions are made, verdicts are rendered, and destinies are released. In this realm, the believer does not fight but instead functions as a petitioner or legal representative, appealing to the Judge of all the earth.

In this court:

- God is the **Judge** (Hebrews 12:23)
- Jesus is our **Advocate/Defense Attorney** (1 John 2:1)
- The Holy Spirit is our **Counsel/Intercessor/Witness** (John 14:26, Romans 8:26-27)
- Satan is the Accuser (Revelation 12:10)

- You are the plaintiff—a blood-bought child of God with legal access through Christ
- Angels are the court officers, recorders, and enforcers
- Books are legal records/testimonies (Psalm 139:16)
- The Word of God is the constitution.

Just as Satan appears before God to accuse (as in the case of Job and Joshua the high priest), he can use legal grounds—such as unrepented sin, word curses, or broken covenants—to delay your breakthrough.

Why the Courtroom Approach Is Needed

You use the courtroom strategy when:

- The enemy has legal access to oppose you
- You are facing generational cycles and repeated failures
- You've done all you know to do, yet nothing shifts
- There is a delay in manifestation of prophetic words
- You sense you're being resisted in the spirit realm despite prayer and fasting

This is not about begging. It's about presenting your case with the Word, the blood of Jesus, and a repentant heart.

Biblical Examples of Courtroom Encounters

1. The Persistent Widow (Luke 18:1–8)

Jesus tells a parable of a widow who persistently sought justice from an unrighteous judge. She said, "Avenge me of my adversary." Eventually, the judge ruled in her favor—not because he feared God, but because of her persistence. Jesus then says, "Will not God bring about justice for His elect?"

This reveals a legal posture in prayer—bringing your case persistently before God, the Righteous Judge, until justice is released.

2. Joshua the High Priest (Zechariah 3:1–7)

Joshua stood before the angel of the Lord while Satan stood to accuse him. Joshua wore filthy garments, symbolic of sin. The Lord rebuked Satan and issued a verdict to remove the filthy garments and clothe him in clean robes. The verdict restored Joshua's authority.

3. Job's Case (Job 1–2)

Satan appeared in the heavenly court to challenge Job's integrity. God allowed a trial to take place. Job later declared: *"Oh, that I knew where I might find Him, that I might come even to His seat!"* (Job 23:3) – "seat" here refers to God's judgment seat.

How to Engage the Courts of Heaven

Here is a simple step-by-step guide to help you engage:

1. Enter by the Blood of Jesus

Hebrews 10:19 declares we enter the Most Holy Place "by the blood of Jesus." You have legal standing because of Christ's sacrifice.

2. Approach God as Judge

Shift from battlefield prayers to legal petitions. Address Him as the Judge of all the earth, honoring His authority.

3. Repent and Renounce

Begin by repenting for any personal, ancestral, or bloodline sins that could give the enemy legal grounds. Renounce all agreements with darkness (known or unknown).

4. Silence the Accuser

Use Revelation 12:11—"they overcame him by the blood of the Lamb…"—to plead the blood against all accusations. Ask God to silence the voice of the accuser.

5. Present Your Case

Bring forth scriptures and prophetic promises. State your identity in Christ. Lay out the injustices and delays you've faced. Petition for God's judgment in your favor.

6. Ask for a Verdict

Specifically request a divine judgment, restraining order, or release of justice in the area of your need—whether healing, finances, family, or destiny.

7. Thank God and Seal It

Seal the prayer with thanksgiving and faith. Rejoice, knowing that your case has been heard in the courts of heaven.

Signs a Verdict Has Been Rendered

- Sudden breakthroughs or shifts
- Peace in your spirit
- Dreams or visions confirming the case is closed
- Manifestation of long-awaited promises
- Reversal of demonic activity or patterns

Sample prayer:

Courtroom of Heaven Petition for Protection and Favor Over My Job & Career

Righteous Judge, Lord of Heaven's Armies,

I stand before Your courtroom by the precious blood of Jesus Christ—my Advocate, my Redeemer, and my High Priest. I enter with boldness, not by my own merit, but through the finished work of the cross (Hebrews 4:16).

1. Acknowledge God as Judge and Protector

- **Psalm 5:12** – *"For You, O Lord, will bless the righteous; with favor You will surround him as with a shield."*
- **Psalm 89:14** – *"Righteousness and justice are the foundation of Your throne."*

You are the Judge who defends Your children and the Protector who guards their steps.

2. Repentance & Renunciation

Father, I repent for any way I have dishonored my work or compromised integrity—through laziness, slander, envy, pride, or cutting corners. I ask You to forgive me and cleanse my record by the blood of Jesus (1 John 1:9).

I also renounce every ungodly covenant or expectation spoken over my career:

- Soul ties or vows that bound my gifting to the enemy
- Words of rejection, failure, or lack declared over me
- Generational curses of unemployment, underemployment, or frustration

I break agreement with these covenants now, and I nullify every demonic contract that would hinder my promotion, creativity, or financial increase.

3. Present the Legal Petition

Righteous Judge, I bring these requests based on Your Word and covenant rights:

- **Psalm 75:6–7** – *"For promotion comes neither from the east nor from the west nor from the south. . . . It is God who executes judgment, putting down one and lifting up another."*
- **Proverbs 16:3** – *"Commit your work to the Lord, and your plans will be established."*
- **Deuteronomy 28:12** – *"The Lord will open to you His good treasury, the heavens, to give rain to your land in its season and to bless all the work of your hands."*

I petition that You:

1. Surround me with Your hedge of protection, blocking every plot of the enemy to steal my joy, sabotage projects, or bring false accusation.
2. Release divine favor with supervisors, clients, co-workers, and decision-makers—so that doors of promotion, opportunity, and increase are opened.

3. Activate heavenly helpers—angels assigned to advance me, network divine connections, and bring creative ideas that birth breakthroughs.
4. Shine Your light on my path, guiding every step in strategic wisdom, clarity, and excellence.

4. Request the Verdict & Enforcement

Father, issue this court order:

- Cancel every spirit of delay, rejection, confusion, and stagnation that has legal right over my career.
- Block every demonic assignment targeting my workplace, my reputation, or my finances.
- Release "favor as a shield" around me—unmerited divine influence that turns hearts and unlocks resources.
- Establish my footsteps on solid ground and upgrade my sphere of influence for Your glory.

5. Decree & Seal

"By the authority of Heaven's court, I decree:

– My work is protected from every evil device and sabotage.

– Favor surrounds me like a shield; doors are opened that no one can shut.

– I walk in divine acceleration: promotion, provision, and creative ideas flow freely.

– I fulfill my career assignment with excellence, integrity, and supernatural provision."

I seal this petition with the blood of Jesus and by the testimony of the Holy Spirit. Let it be written in the courts of Heaven. Let it be enforced on earth. In Jesus' name. Amen.

When issues linger and prayers seem unanswered, don't give up—go higher. Go to the courts of heaven, where justice is not denied, but decreed. God is faithful. He longs to release verdicts that align with your destiny. The courtroom is not a place of fear—it's a place of freedom, redemption, and divine order.

Isaiah 33:22 reminds us: *"For the Lord is our judge, the Lord is our lawgiver, the Lord is our king; he will save us."* When you engage His judicial system, you activate His saving power on a new level.

Biblical Examples of Courtroom Activity

To fully understand and embrace the Courtroom of Heaven, we must see it not as a mystical concept, but as a scriptural reality. Throughout the Bible, there are clear references to legal proceedings taking place in the spiritual realm. God often reveals Himself as Judge, and the activity around His throne resembles a heavenly courtroom—with books, verdicts, witnesses, and accusations.

Let's look at some of the most powerful examples of courtroom activity in Scripture:

Job's Trial in Heaven (Job 1–2)

The book of Job opens with a dramatic scene not on earth, but in the heavenly court:

"Now there was a day when the sons of God came to present themselves before the Lord, and Satan came also among them."
– Job 1:6

Satan enters to accuse Job, questioning his integrity and claiming that his devotion is based on God's blessings. This is a clear legal accusation, and the Lord permits a trial of Job's faith. Although Job is unaware of this courtroom activity, it directly affects his life on earth.

Key Takeaways:

- The enemy must seek permission before attacking.
- Satan's accusations are legal arguments, not just random attacks.
- Job's vindication came after his character stood the test—proving righteousness before the heavenly Judge.

This example reveals that some of the battles we face may actually be **court cases** in the spiritual realm. Understanding this allows us to respond not with fear, but with legal wisdom and spiritual authority.

Daniel's Heavenly Courtroom Vision (Daniel 7:9–10)

In one of the most vivid descriptions of a heavenly courtroom, the prophet Daniel sees the Ancient of Days taking His seat:

"I watched till thrones were put in place, and the Ancient of Days was seated...The court was seated, and the books were opened." – Daniel 7:9–10

This is not symbolic—it is a real vision of the divine judicial process. God, the Judge, is seated on His throne. Books are opened, representing destinies, records, and prophetic scrolls. Then, judgment is rendered on behalf of the saints.

Later in Daniel 7:22, we read:

"...until the Ancient of Days came, and a judgment was made in favor of the saints of the Most High, and the time came for the saints to possess the kingdom."

Key Takeaways:

- Verdicts from heaven can shift earthly power and authority.
- The saints must sometimes wait for a judgment before possession.
- Books (scrolls of destiny and records of deeds) are critical in heavenly cases.

Daniel's vision confirms that timing, inheritance, and dominion are often tied to legal proceedings in heaven. If you haven't received what God has promised, it may be time to step into the court and ask for the books to be opened on your behalf.

Zechariah and Joshua the High Priest (Zechariah 3:1–7)

In this courtroom scene, the high priest Joshua stands before the angel of the Lord. Satan is also present—accusing him. Joshua is clothed in filthy garments, symbolizing sin or disqualification.

"Then he showed me Joshua the high priest standing before the Angel of the Lord, and Satan standing at his right hand to accuse him." – Zechariah 3:1

The Lord rebukes Satan removes the filthy garments, and clothes Joshua in clean priestly robes. A verdict is rendered: Joshua is restored to serve in the temple.

Key Takeaways:

- Satan accuses God's people based on spiritual uncleanliness or sin.
- Repentance and cleansing allow for the revocation of the enemy's claims.
- God can override the accuser when we are submitted to His righteousness.

This passage is a powerful picture of intercession, restoration, and legal justice. The enemy may have a case against you, but when you enter God's courts with repentance and humility, you can receive a verdict of mercy and divine restoration.

Jesus' Teachings on Legal Proceedings in Prayer

(Luke 18:1–8 and Matthew 5:25)

Jesus didn't just model prayer—He taught legal strategy in prayer.

In Luke 18:1–8, He gives the parable of the persistent widow:

"There was in a certain city a judge who did not fear God... Now there was a widow...and she came to him, saying, 'Avenge me of my adversary.'"

The widow approaches a judge—not a soldier or a prophet—but a legal authority. Her persistence leads to a favorable verdict. Jesus uses this story to teach us that God, the Righteous Judge, will give justice to His elect who cry out day and night.

In Matthew 5:25, Jesus gives a warning that also reflects a courtroom setting:

"Settle matters quickly with your adversary who is taking you to court..."

Jesus acknowledges that there are adversaries who take people to spiritual court. Ignoring these accusations could lead to judgment. This is why early repentance and reconciliation are essential—it silences the accuser before a case is built.

Key Takeaways:

- Jesus confirmed the reality of heavenly judicial activity.
- Persistence in prayer is equivalent to legal petitioning.
- Settling issues quickly through repentance can avoid spiritual imprisonment.

Understanding Heavenly Jurisprudence

These biblical examples show that heaven operates with legal precision. The enemy doesn't attack haphazardly—he comes as a legal adversary, accusing believers before God. But the good news is this: we have a better Advocate—Jesus Christ—whose blood speaks on our behalf.

When we align ourselves with righteousness, repent, renounce ungodly covenants, and bring our petitions to the Courts of Heaven, we give God the legal right to release verdicts that overturn delay, silence the accuser, and fulfill our destiny.

Key Reasons to Enter the Courts of Heaven

There are moments in our spiritual journey when traditional prayer, fasting, or even intense warfare seem to produce little or no change. It's not because God has turned a deaf ear—rather, it may be that the issue you're dealing with requires a judicial strategy, not a combative one. In these cases, the Courtroom of Heaven becomes the most appropriate place to seek resolution, justice, and release.

Here are key reasons why believers must learn to step into the Courts of Heaven:

When You're Facing Repetitive, Long-standing Battles

Some issues in life appear to operate in cycles—financial struggles that reappear no matter what you earn, relationships that break down the same way every time, or spiritual oppression that recurs despite repeated prayer.

These persistent patterns may point to a legal issue in the spirit realm. The enemy could be using unresolved sin, ancestral covenants, or unrepented actions as legal grounds to afflict you repeatedly. When battles keep recycling, it's time to shift your strategy and bring your case before the Righteous Judge.

"Deliver me, O Lord, from my enemies; In You I take shelter."
– Psalm 143:9

Entering the courts allows you to break the pattern, revoke the enemy's legal access, and receive a fresh verdict that ends the cycle.

When Spiritual Warfare Doesn't Break the Cycle

Sometimes, you've done all you know to do:

- You've rebuked the enemy
- You've fasted and prayed
- You've spoken declarations
- You've anointed your home

...and yet, the breakthrough remains elusive. This indicates that the issue is not just about power—it's about legal authority. The battlefield strategy involves confronting the enemy in warfare, but the courtroom strategy involves presenting your case before God to nullify the legal claims of the enemy. You may be trying to bind what God wants you to bring to court. In such times, you must stop fighting and start petitioning. Only a divine judgment can settle what the battlefield cannot.

When Legal Accusations or Covenants May Be in Place

Satan is not just an enemy—he is also an accuser and adversary in legal terms (Revelation 12:10). If he is accusing you before God, and you have not repented or dealt with the root issue, he may have the legal right to hinder your prayers, destiny, or inheritance.

Common legal access points include:

- Unrepented personal sin
- Generational sins and curses (Exodus 20:5)
- Ancestral covenants or bloodline agreements
- Vows or pacts made by yourself or your ancestors
- Unforgiveness or bitterness (Matthew 6:14–15)

These spiritual contracts give the enemy permission to oppose you—even when you pray. That's why repentance and renunciation are essential in courtroom prayers. The good news is that the blood of Jesus speaks better things (Hebrews 12:24) and cancels every evil agreement when applied legally in the courts.

When Deliverance Seems Incomplete or Blocked

Many believers experience partial deliverance—some freedom but not the full manifestation. They may still battle:

- Emotional torment
- Generational patterns
- Recurring demonic attacks
- Delays in destiny fulfillment

When deliverance ministries don't fully resolve the issue, it's a sign that the legal claim of the enemy is still active. Deliverance is not just about casting out demons—it's about closing legal doors. Demons will always return to a house that hasn't been sealed legally (Luke 11:24–26). When you bring the case into the Courts of Heaven, you give God the legal right to issue final judgments that remove strongholds and restore destiny.

When Divine Verdicts and Destiny Scrolls Must Be Unlocked

Heaven holds books and scrolls that contain the details of your calling, purpose, and prophetic destiny (Psalm 139:16; Revelation 5:1–10). The enemy's goal is to block or delay what's written about you from manifesting on earth.

Sometimes, you cannot move forward in purpose until you ask the courts to unseal the scrolls of your destiny, revoke demonic interference, and request the activation of divine timing.

Daniel saw this clearly in his vision:

"The court was seated, and the books were opened." – Daniel 7:10

You are not just praying for breakthrough—you are praying for heaven's records to be accessed, your purpose to be released, and legal decrees to be issued on your behalf.

God has made provision for every case, every accusation, and every injustice. When we approach Him not only as Father and King, but also as Judge, we enter into a higher dimension of spiritual strategy.

If you're tired of praying the same way with no results, don't quit—shift. Step into the Courts of Heaven, plead your case with humility and faith, and trust that the Righteous Judge will release the verdict in your favor.

How to Enter the Courtroom of Heaven

Stepping into the Courtroom of Heaven is not mystical or complicated—it's a deliberate, reverent approach to God as the Righteous Judge, based on the finished work of Christ. Like any courtroom, there is protocol, order, and legal presentation. When we follow the spiritual pattern found in Scripture, we can gain access to divine justice and unlock destiny with authority and confidence.

Here is a step-by-step guide on how to enter and operate effectively in the Courts of Heaven:

1. Approach with Reverence and Legal Understanding

Before anything, recognize who you are approaching: God, the Righteous Judge of all the earth (Genesis 18:25). This is not the battlefield, nor is it the throne room of worship—this is a legal setting. Reverence is key. Your attitude matters.

In courtrooms, arguments and emotions don't move the judge—legal standing and evidence do. We must come with a submitted heart and a legal mindset, ready to petition based on God's Word and the blood of Jesus.

"Let us therefore come boldly unto the throne of grace, that we may obtain mercy..." – Hebrews 4:16

This boldness is not arrogance—it's access through Christ.

2. Repentance and Cleansing

(Psalm 51:1–10; Hebrews 10:22)

The first step in any courtroom proceeding is to ensure you're in right standing. Sin gives the accuser legal grounds. Before presenting any case, you must deal with your own spiritual condition.

- Ask the Holy Spirit to search your heart.
- Confess any known sins and ask for forgiveness.
- Repent on behalf of your bloodline, household, or ministry if needed.
- Ask God to cleanse you with the blood of Jesus.

"Let us draw near with a true heart in full assurance of faith, having our hearts sprinkled from an evil conscience..." – Hebrews 10:22

Clean hands and a pure heart silence the accuser and position you for justice.

3. Renounce Demonic Covenants and Generational Agreements

Next, break legal ties that may be empowering the enemy. This includes:

- Ancestral covenants
- Bloodline curses

- Occult involvement
- Soul ties
- Unholy dedications
- Inner vows

Out loud, renounce and revoke these agreements in the name of Jesus. Declare that you no longer consent to any demonic access through your bloodline or personal history.

"Our fathers sinned and are no more, but we bear their iniquities." – Lamentations 5:7

"The blood of Jesus speaks better things..." – Hebrews 12:24

Ask the courts to expunge all legal records tied to these demonic agreements through the blood.

4. Present Your Case Through the Blood of Jesus

(Hebrews 12:24)

Jesus is your Advocate and Mediator. His blood is the most powerful evidence you can present. The blood of Jesus:

- Speaks of mercy
- Cancels curses
- Silences accusations
- Overwrites all legal claims of the enemy

You are not in court to defend yourself—you are in court to present the blood of Jesus as your legal defense.

"And to Jesus the mediator of the new covenant, and to the blood of sprinkling that speaks better things..." – Hebrews 12:24

Plead the blood over your life, situation, and any accusations being used against you.

5. Bring Evidence from the Word of God

Heaven responds to its own constitution—the Word of God. Just like lawyers cite statutes in court, you must bring the Word to support your request.

Declare scriptures that:

- Promise your inheritance
- Establish your authority
- Speak against injustice
- Confirm your redemption

"Put Me in remembrance; let us contend together. State your case, that you may be acquitted." – Isaiah 43:26

When you present God's Word, you remind the court of His own laws—and He watches over His Word to perform it.

6. Declare Your Identity in Christ – Co-heirs, Sons/daughters, and Priests

You are not just a petitioner—you are a citizen of heaven, a co-heir with Christ, and a royal priesthood. The enemy counts on your ignorance. But when you declare your identity, you shift the legal authority in your favor.

"You are no longer foreigners and strangers, but fellow citizens with God's people..." – Ephesians 2:19

"You are a chosen generation, a royal priesthood..." – 1 Peter 2:9

Speak this in court:

- "I stand as a blood-washed son/daughter of the Most High."
- "I am seated in heavenly places in Christ Jesus."
- "I exercise my legal rights as an heir of the Kingdom."

This silences fear and reminds the court of your covenant position.

7. Ask for Verdicts, Judgments, or Restraining Orders to Be Issued

Now you're ready to petition the court:

- Ask for a verdict in your favor
- Request a restraining order against demonic spirits or attacks
- Appeal for a release of withheld blessings
- Ask for the scrolls of your destiny to be opened
- Petition for restoration of what was stolen or delayed

Don't be afraid to be specific. Heaven operates with clarity and purpose. You can even ask the court to issue:

- A stay of judgment
- A dismissal of accusations
- A decree of restoration
- A divine injunction against the enemy

"I will restore to you the years the locust has eaten..." – Joel 2:25

When God issues the verdict, no demon, delay, or devil can resist it. Every believer has legal access to the Courts of Heaven because of Jesus Christ. This is not about being perfect—it's about being positioned. When you follow this divine protocol with a pure heart and submitted spirit, you will see delayed answers released, destinies unlocked, and strongholds overturned. Heaven's court is open—present your case.

Structuring Your Petition in the Courts of Heaven

When you enter the Courtroom of Heaven, you are engaging in a legal transaction between Heaven and Earth. Like any courtroom, there is a divine order to how you present your case. It's not about performance—it's about following Heaven's protocols to ensure the enemy's legal rights are revoked and God's justice is released.

Below is a step-by-step structure for how to present your petition effectively in the Courts of Heaven.

1. Begin with Praise and Acknowledgment of God as Judge

Approach the Judge with reverence and honor. Acknowledge Him as holy, righteous, just, and sovereign. This sets the tone for divine protocol and positions your heart in humility.

"Enter His gates with thanksgiving, and His courts with praise..." – Psalm 100:4

"The Lord is our Judge, the Lord is our Lawgiver, the Lord is our King; He will save us." – Isaiah 33:22

Start by saying:

"Righteous Judge, I come before You today by the blood of Jesus. I acknowledge You as the Supreme Judge of Heaven and Earth. You are faithful and true, and Your judgments are perfect. I honor Your authority and submit my case before You."

2. Repent and Ask for Cleansing from Any Legal Grounds the Enemy May Be Using

Before you can petition for justice, you must clear any legal grounds the enemy is standing on. Ask the Holy Spirit to reveal anything that may need repentance—attitudes, actions, unforgiveness, secret sins, or anything inherited through your bloodline.

"If we confess our sins, He is faithful and just to forgive us…" – 1 John 1:9

"Create in me a clean heart, O God…" – Psalm 51:10

Pray:

"Lord, I repent for every sin—known and unknown—that I or my family line have committed. I ask for Your mercy. Let the blood of Jesus cleanse me of all unrighteousness and silence any accusations being made against me."

3. Renounce Any Personal or Ancestral Sins or Agreements

After repentance, renounce and revoke any covenants or agreements with darkness. These may include:

- Involvement in witchcraft, false religions, or the occult
- Bloodline vows, dedications, or pacts
- Word curses or inner vows
- Ungodly soul ties

"Have nothing to do with the fruitless deeds of darkness but rather expose them." – Ephesians 5:11

Declare:

"I renounce every agreement made with darkness by me or my ancestors. I cancel all evil dedications, covenants, and curses. I break every legal tie and command it to be nullified in the name of Jesus."

4. Present Your Case Using Scripture and Prophetic Promises

This is the heart of your petition. Lay your situation before the Judge with boldness and spiritual evidence. Present scriptures that support your case—just like a lawyer would reference laws in court. Also include prophetic words, dreams, or visions that affirm God's will for your life.

"Put Me in remembrance; let us contend together; state your case…" – Isaiah 43:26

Example:

"Your Word says no weapon formed against me shall prosper (Isaiah 54:17). You said in Jeremiah 29:11 that You have plans to prosper me and not harm me. I bring this before You as my legal right and petition for alignment with Your Word and will."

5. Plead the Blood of Jesus as Your Legal Covering

The blood of Jesus is your strongest legal defense. It overrides every accusation, cancels every sin, and speaks of redemption and mercy.

"...to Jesus the mediator of the new covenant, and to the blood of sprinkling that speaks better things..." – Hebrews 12:24

Pray:

"I plead the blood of Jesus over my life, my household, and this entire case. Let the blood speak on my behalf and silence the voice of the accuser. I stand not on my own righteousness but on the finished work of the cross."

6. Ask for Divine Judgment Against the Accuser

Once the accusations are addressed, ask God to issue a righteous judgment against the adversary. This may include the cancellation of demonic assignments, restraining orders against spiritual harassment, or legal action to recover what was stolen.

"The Lord rebuke you, Satan!" – Zechariah 3:2

"Vengeance is Mine; I will repay," says the Lord. – Romans 12:19

Declare:

"I ask, Righteous Judge, that You render judgment against every demonic spirit opposing my life, my health, my finances, and my calling. Issue a divine restraining order against the enemy and bring justice for every injustice."

7. Request Verdicts to Release Favor, Healing, Provision, etc.

Now ask the Court of Heaven for a **verdict**—a written and legal decree in the spirit to release what is due. You can request:

- Favor with man and God
- Healing in your body
- Financial restoration
- Restoration of relationships
- Fulfillment of destiny

"Ask, and it will be given to you; seek, and you will find..." – Matthew 7:7

"He will bring forth your righteousness as the light, and your justice as the noonday." – Psalm 37:6

Pray:

"I request a verdict in my favor. Let it be written and sealed in Heaven. Release the fulfillment of every promise, unlock the scrolls of my destiny, and let Your justice manifest now."

8. Listen in Prayer for God's Response

After you've presented your case, be still. Courtroom proceedings don't end with pleading—they end with a judgment. Ask the Holy Spirit to reveal the verdict, speak a confirmation, or give you instructions. You may sense peace, receive a scripture, or have a dream or vision afterward confirming your case has been heard.

"My sheep hear My voice..." – John 10:27

"Be still, and know that I am God..." – Psalm 46:10

Say:

"Holy Spirit, I wait on You. Reveal what has been decided in the courts. Let me walk in alignment with Heaven's ruling."

When you learn to structure your petition in the Courts of Heaven, you pray with legal authority and divine precision. You stop wrestling and start winning. You stop striving and start receiving.

Your case is not hopeless—you have an Advocate, and the Judge is on your side.

Prayer Posture and Language: Legal vs. Warfare

One of the most critical aspects of engaging the Courts of Heaven is understanding that not all prayers are the same. Just as there's a difference between worship, intercession, and thanksgiving, there's also a distinct difference between warfare prayers and legal petitions. Knowing when and how to shift your posture and language in prayer can be the key to unlocking stubborn situations and seeing long-awaited breakthroughs.

1. Understanding the Tone and Language of Courtroom Prayers

In the battlefield, we use commanding language—binding, loosing, resisting, and rebuking the enemy. We pray with force because we're in combat. But in the courtroom, our posture changes. We approach God as Judge, not just as Father or Warrior King. We come to present evidence, plead the blood, and make petitions—not shout at the enemy.

In legal prayer:

- You're not arguing with demons—you're addressing the Judge.
- You're not screaming to be heard—you're presenting your case in humility and order.
- You use Scripture as evidence, not emotion as persuasion.

Battlefield prayers are about power; courtroom prayers are about authority.

"The effective, fervent prayer of a righteous man avails much."
– James 5:16

In the court, you don't plead from a place of desperation—you petition from a place of covenant confidence.

2. The Role of Declarations and Legal Decrees

(Job 22:28)

Once you've received a verdict or sensed that your case has been heard, you seal it with declarations. This is not positive thinking—it's spiritual enforcement of Heaven's rulings.

"You will also declare a thing, and it will be established for you; so light will shine on your ways." – Job 22:28

A declaration is a formal statement of truth based on God's Word. A decree is a judicial order that enforces a ruling. Both are used in legal prayer to:

- Confirm what Heaven has decided
- Shut down opposing voices
- Establish God's will in your situation

You might declare:

- "I decree that every demonic accusation has been silenced by the blood of Jesus."
- "I declare a release of divine favor and restitution in my family line."

- "I enforce Heaven's verdict concerning my healing, provision, or calling."

Declarations are how you stand in agreement with the Judge's ruling and activate its manifestation on earth.

3. Difference Between Commanding Devils and Requesting Heavenly Verdicts

This is one of the most common mistakes in prayer—mixing battlefield language in the courtroom setting.

In spiritual warfare:

- You command demons to flee (Mark 16:17)
- You bind and loose with delegated authority (Matthew 18:18)
- You resist the devil (James 4:7)

But in the Courts of Heaven:

- You ask the Judge to rebuke the accuser (Zechariah 3:2)
- You petition for justice, restoration, or intervention
- You submit legal evidence (Scripture, repentance, covenant promises)

Trying to command devils during courtroom prayer is like yelling at your opponent in the middle of a court trial. It's out of order. Let the Judge issue the judgment and then enforce that ruling in the battlefield if necessary.

Use courtroom language such as:

- "I petition the court for…"

- "I present the blood of Jesus as my defense…"
- "I request a divine verdict concerning…"
- "Let a restraining order be issued against…"

This tone reflects honor, order, and legal understanding.

4. Partnering with Angels Assigned to Enforce Judgments

(Psalm 103:20)

Once a verdict has been issued in the courts, God assigns angels to carry out and enforce the judgment.

"Bless the Lord, you His angels, who excel in strength, who do His word, heeding the voice of His word." – Psalm 103:20

Heaven's angels are ministering spirits sent to assist the heirs of salvation (Hebrews 1:14). They respond not to emotion, but to the Word of God and legal decrees spoken in faith.

When you declare God's Word and enforce the verdicts of Heaven, angels are:

- Released to execute justice
- Dispatched to bring breakthrough
- Empowered to dismantle demonic structures

After your court session, you can pray:

"Father, I thank You for releasing Your angels to enforce the judgment rendered today. I commission them now in Jesus' name to carry out every aspect of the verdict according to Your will."

Warfare prayer is necessary and powerful—but when the enemy has legal ground, the most effective strategy is to take the matter to court.

Your posture in the battlefield is aggressive and authoritative.

Your posture in the courtroom is humble, legal, and reverent.

Both are valid. But knowing which to use—and when—can unlock victories that have eluded you for years.

Remember, you are not powerless. You are not without recourse. You are a legal citizen of Heaven, and through Jesus Christ, you have access to present your case and see righteous judgment prevail.

Signs That a Verdict Has Been Released

Once you have presented your case in the Courts of Heaven, it's important to remain spiritually alert and discerning. Although you may not always hear an audible response or see immediate physical changes, the spirit realm begins to respond the moment a verdict is issued in your favor. Heaven never delays justice—once legal grounds are removed and the blood of Jesus is applied, God renders righteous judgment swiftly and decisively.

Here are some of the key signs that a heavenly verdict has been released on your behalf:

1. Peace and Clarity in the Spirit

One of the first and most powerful indicators is a deep inner peace. Even if the physical circumstances haven't yet changed, you feel:

- A lifting of pressure
- A sense that something has broken
- A divine settling in your spirit
- Clarity in your thoughts and confidence in your direction

"And the peace of God, which surpasses all understanding, will guard your hearts and minds through Christ Jesus." – Philippians 4:7

This peace is not emotional—it's judicial. It often signals that the courtroom process has concluded and the Judge has ruled in your favor.

2. Sudden Breakthroughs or Divine Favor

Another powerful sign is the swift manifestation of what was once held up. You may experience:

- Instant turnaround in finances, relationships, or business
- Open doors that were previously shut
- Accelerated answers to prayers
- Reconciliation or release in areas that were blocked

What once seemed impossible begins to happen without striving, because the legal hindrance has been removed.

"So shall My word be that goes forth from My mouth; it shall not return to Me void..." – Isaiah 55:11

Breakthrough often follows a courtroom verdict—Heaven has ruled, and Earth begins to align.

3. Revelations, Dreams, or Prophetic Confirmations

After your petition, the Holy Spirit may confirm the verdict through:

- Dreams or visions
- A prophetic word
- Scriptural confirmation
- Divine impressions or insights

You may see a courtroom scene, a scroll being released, or hear phrases like "case closed," "judgment rendered," or "it is done."

These spiritual encounters are Heaven's way of communicating the result to you.

"Call to Me, and I will answer you, and show you great and mighty things…" – Jeremiah 33:3

Watch for prophetic indicators within 24–72 hours of your court session. These are signs of God's ruling being released into your reality.

4. Shift in Atmosphere Around the Issue

You may begin to notice that:

- The spiritual warfare dies down
- Conversations or people connected to the problem shift or disappear
- A supernatural calm enters the environment
- You suddenly have boldness, joy, and hope where fear and anxiety once ruled

This shift is a sign that the atmosphere has changed, and the enemy no longer has legal standing. It is often subtle but unmistakable.

"Behold, I do a new thing; now it shall spring forth…" – Isaiah 43:19

When the court rules, the atmosphere must obey. The storm ceases. The pressure lifts. The tide turns.

Closing Insight

When a verdict has been rendered in your favor, it's essential to:

- Thank God immediately
- Declare the verdict over your life regularly
- Walk in faith, knowing Heaven has ruled
- Refuse to go back into striving or fear

Don't second-guess what God has settled. What happens in the courts of Heaven is legal, lasting, and sealed by divine authority.

"I will hasten My word to perform it." – Jeremiah 1:12

Stay aligned, stay grateful, and watch the manifestation unfold.

Courtroom Pitfalls to Avoid

While the Courts of Heaven offer a powerful avenue for divine justice and breakthrough, there are spiritual pitfalls that can hinder or even block your petition from being heard or honored. Like any legal system, the protocols of Heaven must be followed with humility, integrity, and spiritual discernment. Missteps in posture, attitude, or preparation can delay the verdict or leave the accuser with continued legal grounds.

Below are the key pitfalls to avoid when approaching God's courtroom:

1. Unrepented Sin

The most common hindrance in the Courts of Heaven is unrepented sin. Sin gives the enemy legal access to accuse and resist you. Even if your petition is sincere, if known sin is left unconfessed, the enemy may block your breakthrough on technical grounds.

"If I regard iniquity in my heart, the Lord will not hear." – Psalm 66:18

"He who covers his sins will not prosper, but whoever confesses and forsakes them will have mercy." – Proverbs 28:13

Avoid entering the court with unaddressed sin. Always begin with repentance—ask the Holy Spirit to search your heart, cleanse you through the blood of Jesus, and silence the voice of the accuser.

2. Bitterness and Unforgiveness

(Matthew 6:14–15)

Unforgiveness is a major legal obstacle in the heavenly courts. When you hold onto bitterness or offense, you give the enemy a platform to claim that you are violating God's law of mercy. Forgiveness is not optional—it's a legal requirement.

"But if you do not forgive others their sins, your Father will not forgive your sins." – Matthew 6:15

When approaching the Judge, come with clean hands and a pure heart. Forgive those who wronged you, even if they never apologize. Release them to God's justice so you can receive your own.

Declare:

"Father, I choose to forgive [name/person/situation]. I release them from judgment, and I ask You to show them mercy. Let no bitterness remain in my heart that would hinder my petition."

3. Pride or a Demanding Attitude

The Courts of Heaven operate by humility, not entitlement. God is not moved by spiritual arrogance, legalistic demands, or prideful declarations. Coming to the court with an attitude of self-righteousness or entitlement can block your access to grace.

"God resists the proud but gives grace to the humble." – James 4:6

"To this one I will look: to him who is humble and contrite in spirit, and who trembles at My word." – Isaiah 66:2

The courtroom is not a place for commanding God—it's where we submit our case, appeal to His mercy, and trust in His perfect judgment. Always approach with a heart of honor and surrender, not pride or frustration.

4. Assuming Verdicts Without Petitioning

Another dangerous pitfall is assuming God will rule in your favor without presenting your case. Even if you're right, even if the enemy is unjust, Heaven requires legal petition. God operates in order—and your voice matters.

"You have not because you ask not." – James 4:2

"Ask, and it shall be given to you..." – Matthew 7:7

Don't assume that because God knows everything, He will automatically intervene. Just as earthly courts require official filing and legal arguments, the Courts of Heaven require that you:

- Present the Word as evidence
- Plead the blood of Jesus
- State your legal position as a son/daughter
- Request a specific verdict or decree

Silence in court equals delay. You must speak—by prayer, declaration, and petition—if you want the Judge to rule.

Stay Aligned, Stay Humble

Avoiding these courtroom pitfalls ensures that your prayers are strategic, heard, and honored. Always remember:

- Repent fully
- Forgive freely
- Humble yourself deeply
- Petition clearly

If you make a mistake, don't fear—repent and return. The Courts of Heaven operate not only by justice, but also by mercy. You serve a righteous Judge who desires to see your case won, your enemy silenced, and your destiny fulfilled.

Sample Courtroom of Heaven Prayer Structure

For those seeking justice, deliverance, or divine intervention when spiritual warfare hasn't brought results, this sample prayer provides a clear pattern to follow in presenting your case before the Righteous Judge in the Courts of Heaven.

Use this structure to engage Heaven's judicial system with reverence, clarity, and authority.

1. Worship & Acknowledge God as Judge

"Enter His gates with thanksgiving and His courts with praise…" – Psalm 100:4

"The Lord is our Judge, the Lord is our Lawgiver, the Lord is our King; He will save us." – Isaiah 33:22

Prayer:

Heavenly Father, Righteous Judge, I come before You today with honor, reverence, and awe. You are holy, just, and true. I acknowledge You as the Judge of all the earth. I enter Your courtroom by the blood of Jesus Christ, my Savior and Mediator. I worship You, for Your throne is founded on righteousness and justice. There is no one like You.

2. Repent – Personal and Bloodline Sin

"If we confess our sins, He is faithful and just to forgive us…" – 1 John 1:9

"Create in me a clean heart, O God…" – Psalm 51:10

Prayer:

Lord, I come with a humble heart and ask for mercy. I confess all known and unknown sins—words, thoughts, and actions that have grieved You. I repent for bitterness, pride, unforgiveness, and anything that has given the accuser legal ground. I also repent on behalf of my bloodline for generational sins—idolatry, occult practices, sexual sin, broken covenants, or any involvement with darkness. Cleanse me and my bloodline with the blood of Jesus.

3. Renounce – Break Demonic Agreements and Covenants

"Have nothing to do with the fruitless deeds of darkness but rather expose them." – Ephesians 5:11

Prayer:

Righteous Judge, I now renounce every demonic covenant made knowingly or unknowingly by me or my ancestors. I renounce all pacts, vows, dedications, blood oaths, or agreements made with idols, false gods, or the kingdom of darkness. I break every curse and cancel every assignment attached to those covenants. I revoke the enemy's legal right to afflict me in these areas and ask the Court to dismiss every accusation and charge against me.

4. Petition – Present Your Case with Scripture

"Put Me in remembrance; let us contend together. State your case..." – Isaiah 43:26

Prayer:

Father, I now bring my case before You. I present Your Word as evidence:

- You said no weapon formed against me shall prosper (Isaiah 54:17).
- You said You would restore the years the locusts have eaten (Joel 2:25).
- You said I am the head and not the tail (Deuteronomy 28:13).

I petition You today for justice concerning [name the issue: finances, health, relationships, delayed destiny, etc.]. I ask that You issue a verdict in my favor. Let what has been withheld be released. Let what was stolen be restored. Let the scroll of my destiny be unlocked and fulfilled.

5. Decree – Declare God's Verdict and Enforce It

"You will also decree a thing, and it will be established for you..." – Job 22:28

"The blood of Jesus speaks better things..." – Hebrews 12:24

Prayer:

By the authority of Your court and the blood of Jesus, I now decree:

- That every legal accusation against me is silenced.
- That divine favor is released into my life.
- That angels are dispatched to execute the court's decision.
- That every delay is broken and divine alignment begins now.

I declare: *Case closed. Verdict rendered. Justice served.*

6. Thank God – Seal It with Gratitude and Faith

"In everything give thanks; for this is the will of God..." – 1 Thessalonians 5:18

Prayer:

Thank You, Father, for hearing my petition and ruling in my favor. Thank You, Jesus, for Your blood that speaks on my behalf. Thank You, Holy Spirit, for revealing truth and guiding me through this process. I receive the verdict by faith. I walk forward in freedom, alignment, and expectation. May Your will be done in my life as it is in Heaven.

Final Tip: Wait & Listen

After praying, sit in stillness. You may receive impressions, a vision, scripture, or a sense of release. Write down anything God reveals—this may be His confirmation of the court's response.

Conclusion: Engage Heaven's Legal System When Delays Persist

There are moments in spiritual warfare where traditional prayers seem ineffective, and delays feel prolonged and unexplainable. When the enemy has gained a legal foothold—whether through ancestral covenants, unrepented sin, or demonic accusations—it's time to shift from the battlefield to the courtroom.

The Courts of Heaven offer a strategic, scriptural solution to unresolved spiritual battles. They are not a last resort, but a divine invitation for believers to access the righteous judgments of God and secure lasting breakthrough.

"For the Lord is our judge, the Lord is our lawgiver, the Lord is our king; He will save us." – Isaiah 33:22

God is not only your Father—He is also your Judge, your Lawgiver, and your King. He desires justice on your behalf, but He honors His own protocols. When you come with repentance, present your case in humility, and stand on the blood of Jesus, He will rule in your favor.

Let this truth encourage you:

- You are not helpless.
- You are not forgotten.
- You are legally authorized to appear in Heaven's court.
- Your voice, when aligned with God's Word, moves the court to action.
- God the righteous judge wants to rule in your favor.

So be bold in your petitions, consistent in your positioning, and sensitive to the leading of the Holy Spirit. Let your prayers be not just passionate—but precise, legal, and aligned with Heaven's system of justice.

When you engage Heaven's courtroom, you're not just praying for victory—you're petitioning for divine rulings that shift atmospheres, break cycles, and unlock destinies. He is ready to judge righteously. Present your case. Heaven is waiting.

About the Author

Shena Martin is a woman marked by the grace of God. An author, Gospel recording artiste, mentor and purpose coach, she is the founder of **Manna Inspirations**, a ministry dedicated to awakening purpose, cultivating spiritual growth, and releasing heaven's voice in the earth. Through her writing, music, podcasting, and mentorship, Shena has empowered countless lives to rise in their divine identity.

Born into a Christian household and shaped by deep encounters, with God from an early age, Shena carries a strong anointing for prophetic intercession, teaching, and mentorship.

She is the author of several transformative books including *Gratitude Power for Me* and *Nuggets of Deliverance*, and the host of *Nurse As Midwife*, a mentorship and coaching program equipping others to birth the vision God has placed inside them. Her debut gospel single *True Worship* is a testimony of her heart for authentic, Spirit-led worship.

Whether through a prayer, a written word, or a song, Shena seeks to reflect the grace of that has carried her. Through her journey, Shena has learned that spiritual freedom is not just a moment- it's a process and it begins with the truth of God. She is committed to helping others uncover the "nuggets" of deliverance buried in God's word and within the testimony that they share.

To learn more, visit:

☐ www.mannainspirations.com

▪ Instagram | Facebook | YouTube: *@MannaInspirations*

✉ Email: *mim.info@mannainspirations.com or mannainspirations @gmail.com*

Also by Shena Martin

Gratitude: Power For Me

In *Gratitude Power for Me*, Shena Martin invites readers into a transformative journey of thanksgiving, where gratitude becomes more than a feeling—it becomes a spiritual force. This uplifting and empowering book explores how intentional gratitude can unlock emotional healing, renew the mind, and position the believer to receive God's blessings. Through scriptural insights, personal reflections, and practical exercises, readers are encouraged to embrace gratitude as a daily practice that cultivates joy, peace, and spiritual growth.

Whether read as a devotional or used as a tool for mindset renewal, *Gratitude Power for Me* will inspire you to shift your focus, strengthen your faith, and walk in the power of a thankful heart.

www.ingramcontent.com/pod-product-compliance
Lightning Source LLC
Chambersburg PA
CBHW020937180426
43194CB00038B/218